Free Will and Values

Free Will and Values

R. KANE

State University of New York Press

Published by
State University of New York Press, Albany

Printed in the United State of America

For information, address State University of New York Press, State University Plaza,
Albany, N.Y. 12246

Library of Congress Cataloging in Publication Data

Kane, R. (Robert), 1930-
Free will and values.
(SUNY series in philosophy)
Bibliography: p
Includes index
1. Free will and determinism. 2. Values. 3. Ethical relativism. I. Title. II. Series.
BJ1461.K37 1985   123°.5   85-4100
ISBN-88706-101-x
ISBN 0-88706-102-8(pbk)

10 9 8 7 6 5 4 3 2 1

To my parents:

VIVIAN LENZI KANE

HILARY THOMAS KANE

SUNY Series in Philosophy

ROBERT C. NEVILLE, EDITOR

Contents

Preface

This book has been a dozen years in the making and in that time I have incurred many debts. The bibliography is partial payment of these debts, insofar as each author and work cited has had some influence on my thinking (even where, and sometimes especially where, disagreements are most evident). I am especially indebted to the following who have read the entire manuscript in earlier drafts—Robert Audi, Richard Bernstein, Daniel Bonevac, Charles Hartshorne, Hugh McCann, Robert Neville, Laurence Poncinie, Stephen Phillips, and Thomas Seung—and to others who have read parts or helped me with special topics—Edwin Allaire, David Armstrong, David Blumenfeld, Jean Blumenfeld, Douglas Browning, Robert Causey, Brian Cooney, Bernard Katz, Norman Martin, Aloysius Martinich, David Miller, Alexander Mourelatos, Edmund Pincoffs, Richard Rodewald, Wilfrid Sellars, Alexander Von Schönborn, Sarah Waterlow Broadie, and Michael White. Special thanks are due Thomas Seung, whose encouragement helped me through some difficult periods, to Wilfrid Sellars, who has had a formative influence on my philosophical thinking, though one could not tell it from the conclusions of this book, and to my wife Claudette, who contributed an incalculable amount to the book, not the least by her awesome determination never to lose an argument.

Research for the book was supported in part by a University Research Institute grant from The University of Texas at Austin.

A number of writings relevant to the topics of the book have appeared since the manuscript was completed and would otherwise have been discussed in it. The most relevant of these are Peter van Inwagen's *An Essay on Free Will* (Oxford, 1983) and Daniel Dennett's *Elbow Room* (MIT, Oxford, 1984).

Van Inwagen's book defends an incompatibilist view of freedom, as does this book. But the two complement each other more than they overlap. The first reason is that a third of the present book deals with questions about values and ethical relativism, which I believe are related in a unique way to the free will issue. But equally important is the fact that there are two important questions one can ask about any incompatibilist theory of freedom:

(1) What reasons can be given for thinking that freedom is incompatible with determinism?

(2) How, if at all, can an incompatiblist theory of freedom be made intelligible without appeals to obscure or mysterious forms of agency?

Van Inwagen's work, like most other recent writings on free will, is chiefly concerned with question (1). I think his treatment of question (1) is the most sophisticated and elaborate we have to date. But (also in line with most other recent writings on free will) he deals with question (2) only briefly, admitting that the incompatibilist view of agency to which his arguments lead has puzzling or mysterious features that neither he nor anyone else has been able to remove.

By contrast, my main concern in this book is with question (2). For some time I have been absorbed by the problem of how to make an incompatibilist theory of freedom intelligible in the light of modern scientific evidence without appealing to mysterious forms of agency. The failure of incompatibilists to solve this problem has left a large opening for thinkers who are unsympathetic to their view and has discouraged others who might otherwise be sympathetic. This is true of those who, like myself, share van Inwagen's intuitions and are sympathetic to his arguments, but are troubled by the failure of incompatibilists to develop a satisfying account of free agency. The task is formidable and many believe it cannot be completed. The conviction is widespread that incompatibilist conceptions of agency are essentially mysterious. I have no illusions about the finality of what I have to say on the subject. But I hope to convince some readers that progress can be made on it, and to provoke others to think about the issue in new ways.

Dennett's book, by contrast, is a defense of compatibilism which takes the novel approach of challenging the metaphors (or "intuition pumps," as he calls them) that have fueled incompatibilist intuitions. I did not see his book until mine was in the hands of editors and so do not address his specific arguments. But the kind of response I would make to Dennett and other compatibilists should be clear from chapters 3 and 9 of this book. In addition, the theory of chapters 5-8 is a response to the charges of unintelligibility and obscurity made against other incompatibilist theories. (Some of Dennett's ideas in his earlier work, *Brainstorms* (MIT, 1978), are favorably discussed in chapter 6.)

The truth is that I make significant concessions to compatibilists, more than will please many incompatibilists. I expect to get flack from both sides. Compatibilists will ask why I do not produce a knock-down conceptual argument against their view early on in the book. It is because I do not believe any such argument exists. This does not mean there is no case for incompatibilism. The case must be more roundabout, as explained in chapters 3 and 9. Incompatibilists will complain that I concede too much to the opposition. But I concede only what I think incompatibilists must concede, if their view is to be made intelligible. I have not set out to please one side at all costs, but to find the truth. There is an objectivity to philosophy which is shown by the fact that we cannot always get everything we wanted. Ideas constrain. But we can advance our understanding.

Introduction

This book is about free will and the relativity of values, two topics that seem to have little in common beyond the fact that both have been the subject of controversy for centuries. The book's thesis is that the two topics are connected in ways that afford insight into age-old debates surrounding both of them. The ancient doctrine of value relativism provides clues that are needed to resolve some of the most difficult problems about free will. This is the theme of the second of two parts of the book (chapters 5-10). In chapters 5-8, a theory about the human will and its freedom is developed, incorporating relativist themes, and drawing upon an analogy between the relativism of values and relativity in physics. Ethical, political, and theological implications of the theory are discussed in chapters 9 and 10. The whole of Part I (chapters 1-4) is devoted to defining the traditional problems about free will that the theory of Part II will try to solve. The focus of the book is, therefore, primarily on the free will issue, but issues about relativity and values emerge in Part II and play an increasingly important role as the discussion proceeds.

Before turning to the tasks of the first part, I want to add some general remarks about the two central topics of the book, value relativism and free will. Value relativism is the view that there are no objective standards by which to judge the comparative merits of competing value systems, that is, no standards supporting claims that one such system is objectively better than another.[1] Such a view is often described as "value subjectivism" when the competing value systems are those of different individuals or persons, "value relativism" when they are of different cultures or societies. But for reasons that will become clear in Part II, I prefer to use the single term "relativism" to refer to such a view in all its guises, whether applied to the value systems of different cultures, societies, groups or individuals.

Value relativism, in one or another of these forms, is an ancient view, said to have been held by some of the Sophists in Plato's time. Plato opposed it and most Western philosophers have followed him in doing so. Yet the doctrine never entirely yielded to learned authority or conventional wisdom. Revived in this century by a number of social scientists, it remains the subject of lively debate.

Opponents have often argued that value relativists, from the Sophists to some modern anthropologists, are guilty of a simple fallacy. Relativists argue from the existing diversity of, and unresolved disagreements about, values and norms in different cultures, or among different individuals, to the conclusion that there exist no objective standards by which to assess these diverse values and norms. This is a fallacious inference, to be sure, because factual differences and disagreements do not of themselves imply the absence of a single correct view about values. And the mistake is usually compounded, according to the critics, by similarly fallacious moves from "is" to "ought". When differences in judgments about what is valuable arise in different cultures or among individuals, relativists say, it should not be assumed that one is right, the other wrong. Nor should one assume that one's own judgments about the values and actions of those in other cultures have absolute validity. Once again, the critics insist that these conclusions cannot be inferred merely from the facts of cultural diversity and disagreement.[2]

Yet belief in value relativism seems to survive these facile refutations, as correct as the refutations may be on their own grounds. And it survives, I think, for a good reason. As long as philosophers and others critical of relativism continue to dispute among themselves about what the objective or absolute standards ought to be in value theory and ethics, belief in relativism will persist. For most persons who are relativists are so by default. Theirs is a leap of faith, to be sure. But it occurs because of failure to find convincing arguments for any particular objective or absolute standards of value and persisting disagreements among the learned about the nature and sources of these standards. The position of relativists in this situation is like that of physicists at the beginning of the century, who, after numerous disappointing attempts to establish the existence of an ether, decided that the more reasonable course of action was to endorse a theory of motion that did not assume the existence of an ether.

I shall be pursuing this analogy further in Part II. The aim is not to defend value relativism in an unrestricted form. It cannot be so defended. The point is rather to show that value relativism is partly true and partly false, i.e. true within certain limits, with certain qualifications, false otherwise. Postulating its qualified truth is not a prelude to moral anarchy, but a first step toward moral insight. Moreover, this step will yield an additional and surprising result. For it will suggest a way of resolving a long disputed issue about free will.

Free will is the power in human beings, and in persons or rational agents of any kind (human or divine, terrestrial or extraterrestrial), to originate or bring into existence the purposes or ends that guide their actions. It is said to be a kind of self determination, meaning by this, not the ability of the self to determine its action in accordance with its purposes (this is liberty, or freedom, of action as distinguished from freedom of the will), but the ability to determine the purposes of its actions. Those who ascribe this power to humans regard it as essential to their status as persons and moral agents, and as the source of the dignity and respect due them as persons (sometimes described by saying that human beings are to be treated as "ends in themselves" because they are capable of originating their own purposes or ends). The dispute about free will is therefore not only about the possession or non-possession of a certain power by humans. It is also about the nature of this power and its relation to moral agency, personhood and dignity. This accounts for the complexity of the dispute and for its persistence.

The theory of free will to be defended in this book may be described in terms now current as a "libertarian" or "incompatibilist" theory. That is to say, it ascribes to humans a power to determine or originate their own purposes or ends (free will) whose existence is incompatible with the truth of determinism, the view that all phenomena are necessitated or caused by antecedent circumstances. In this respect, the theory is not new. Libertarian theories of freedom of will and freedom of action are old, and they persist today, though under attack by a growing number of twentieth-century philosophers and students of the sciences of man who find them unintelligible. But, in other respects, the theory is new. It is unlike all other libertarian views of freedom proposed to date in a number of ways. One difference is the role played by the postulate of relativism just mentioned. The other differences will be described in chapter 1.

Notes

1. The notions of "value", "value system", and "relativism" presupposed by this statement are more fully discussed in chapters 5 and 7. Briefly, "value"and "value system" will be defined in terms of the notion of a valuation. A valuation is a proposition having the form "X is good or bad, right or wrong, better or worse that something else (in some respects and/or in some circumstances and/or in itself or for some purpose)". A *value* for a person is defined as a valuation that is believed true, or whose truth is presupposed by the cognitive and volitional psychological attitudes of the person. (These psychological attitudes are discussed in chapter 4, section 3 (i.e. section 4.3)). A value for a society or culture is a valuation whose truth is presupposed by the practices, customs, institutions, etc. of the society or culture. And a *value system* of a person or group is the totality of valuations whose truth is thus believed or presupposed by the person or group. For more on these notions and on "relativism" see especially sections 5.5-6, 7.10-11 and 10.1-2.

2. Such arguments are stated by Stace (37) and are discussed in Brandt (59), Hospers (61), Ladd (73), P. Taylor (54), B. Williams (72) and Harmon (72 and 75).

References to works in the Bibliography throughout the book will be in the manner of this note by the author's name followed by the last two numbers of the date of publication in parentheses.

Part I

The Free Will Issue

1.1 In the middle of the seventeenth century a celebrated debate about the freedom of the will took place between Thomas Hobbes and Bishop John Bramhall of Derry.[1] The Hobbes-Bramhall debate marks a turning point in the history of discussions of free will and provides us with a convenient point of departure. The two men discuss most of the arguments of their ancient and medieval predecessors about freedom and necessity, while at the same time anticipating new lines of argument that will become prominent in the modern era. Another reason for beginning with the Hobbes-Bramhall debate is that the libertarian view of free will I want to defend is very much like Bramhall's. I have no intention of rehabilitating the Bishop's philosophical reputation. Hobbes got the better of their debate. But, on the important issues, I think Bramhall was right.[2] Of Bramhall's view of human freedom, I am going to say what Hobbes (62) said of Bramhall's definition of determinism: "Excepting that which is not intelligible [in it], I admit [it]" (p.3).

Hobbes and Bramhall agree that freedom is a power of self determination, but they disagree about the nature of this power. For Hobbes (62), a man is self determining when he is not prevented by conditions beyond his control from determining his action in accordance with his will (i.e. intentions or desires) (p. 35). This power "to do as one wills" is what we ordinarily mean by freedom, according to Hobbes, and freedom in this sense is compatible with determinism (pp.51-2). For a man may be free to do what he intends or desires to do, while his intentions and desires are determined or necessitated by antecedent circumstances or causes. "Liberty and Necessity are Consistent: as in the water, that hath not only liberty, but a necessity of descending by the Channel; so likewise in the Actions which men voluntarily do; which because they proceed from their will, proceed from liberty; and yet, because every act of man's will, and every desire and inclination proceedeth from some cause, and that from another cause, in a continual chaine, . . . proceed from necessity" (58, pp. 71-2).

Bramhall (44) objects that the liberty Hobbes offers us is a "brutish liberty, . . . such as a bird has to fly when its wings are clipped" (p. 29). Though a man have the power to do what he wills, if the will in turn "has no power over itself, the agent is no more free than a staff in a man's hand" (p. 30). True freedom, according to Bramhall, requires not only that a self be able to determine its action in accordance with its will; it also requires, as he puts it, that the self be able to "determine itself" (p. 24), or that the will have "power" or "dominion over itself" (p. 151). Bramhall is vague about the details of his conception of self determination, but he insists that it differs from Hobbes' in at least one important respect. His conception of self determination is not compatible with the claim that the agent's will is determined by antecedent causes. At the time of choice the free agent must have the power to "rise above" past circumstances, including past influences on character and motives, in such a way that the resulting choice is not inevitable given its past (pp. 42-4).

1.2   Bramhall's response to Hobbes is instructive in several ways. His emphasis on the power *of* the will rather than merely on the power to do what one wills, shows how the free will issue received its traditional name. Bramhall understands free will as I described it in the Introduction, as the power of the self to determine or originate the intentions or purposes that guide its action. If notions of choice and decision play a significant role in his discussions, it is because of their relation to intention or purpose. To choose or decide to do something is to form the intention (or purpose) of doing it. Thus, freedom of will is often rightly interpreted by Bramhall and other traditional thinkers as freedom of choice or decision.

Second, Bramhall's response to Hobbes is a "libertarian" one as described in the Introduction. He rejects Hobbes' claim that freedom and determinism ("liberty and necessity") are compatible. Hobbes' freedom to do what one wills may be compatible with determinism. But it is a "brutish" liberty which cannot be the source of human dignity."True freedom," on the other hand, the freedom of the will, which is the source of human dignity, is not compatible with determinism.

In such remarks there is a lesson about libertarian views like Bramhall's that is sometimes overlooked. A libertarian view of freedom is usually said to be one which (i) denies that freedom and determinism are compatible and (ii) (as a consequence of ascribing an incompatibilist freedom to humans, if for no other reason) denies that determinism is true.[3] But libertarians need not, and usually do not, argue that freedom in any sense whatever is incompatible with determinism. There may be kinds of freedom, like Hobbes' freedom to do what one wills, that are compatible with determinism. What the libertarian insists upon is that these freedoms cannot be the "true freedom" which grounds human dignity. This "true freedom", however it is to be described, is not compatible with determinism.

Several traditional lines of reasoning may seem to support such a libertarian view of "true freedom" and each of them influenced Bramhall. First, it seems that, whatever else it might imply, the power of the self to determine or originate its own purposes must imply that nothing other than the self could determine or originate these purposes. This widely held conviction suggests in turn that genuinely free choices or decisions must be new beginnings, originating in the self alone, neither determined by, nor predictable in terms of, circumstances preceding them in time.[4] Some thinkers speak of the spontaneity of free decisions in this connection. Philo of Alexandria (54, p. 33) says that a man who is free is so because he possesses a "spontaneous and self determining mind". Kant (58) says in a similar vein that, since freedom "in its cosmological meaning . . . is the power or beginning a state spontaneously [it] cannot stand under another cause determining it in time" (p. 464). And Cicero (60) tells us that ancient Epicurean philosophers introduced their doctrine of the chance "swerve" of the atoms because of their "fear lest, if the atoms were always carried along by the natural and necessary force of gravity we should have no freedom whatever since the movement of the mind was controlled by the movement of the atoms" (p. 219).

Second, Bramhall argues, also in a traditional vein, that genuine self determination of purposes or ends requires that the self could have selected alternative purposes or ends, or "could have chosen otherwise" (pp. 41, 55, 174). But this power to choose otherwise, he insists, cannot be reconciled with the view that choices and decisions are determined by antecedent causes. What is determined, he says, "cannot but be, nor be otherwise", given its past (p. 32). Thus, genuinely free choices and decisions cannot be determined.

1.3   Arguments such as these for a libertarian conception of human freedom have always had great appeal. There are many who still insist today, for reasons similar to Bramhall's, that the incompatibility of freedom and determinism is a matter of simple common sense, or at least is demonstrable on the basis of common sense intuitions about human powers or abilities.[5] Yet the libertarian view of freedom has increasingly been on the defensive in this century, while the "compatibilist" view defended by Hobbes,[6] and defended after him, with increasing sophistication, by such thinkers as Jonathan Edwards (69), David Hume (55), John Stuart Mill (62), and Franz Brentano (73), has grown in stature in this century to a point where it has attained almost the position of orthodoxy in many philosophical and scientific circles.[7] When in a recent series of controversial essays, Sir Isaiah Berlin (69) affirmed the ancient thesis that free will and the practices of bestowing moral praise and blame were incompatible with determinism, he was assailed from all quarters, as if he were unnecessarily reviving an old heresy—a new Pelagius come to judgment.[8] In this case, however, defenders of orthodoxy were not churchmen defending God's omnipotence, but a new class of historians, philosophers, and students of the sciences of man who had come to believe that the more we learn about the roots of human behavior, the less room there seems to be for the older conception of an incompatibilist or indeterminist free will.

The growth of this new compatibilist, or neo-Hobbesian, orthodoxy is all the more surprising in the light of twentieth-century developments in the physical sciences, where belief in determinism has lost the secure foothold it once had. One would think that the advent of indeterministic theories in modern physics would have given new life to older libertarian theories of freedom. (Why, after all, make a point of arguing for the compatibility of freedom and determinism, if determinism is in fact false?) Yet a surprising fact about recent intellectual history is that compatibilist, and even determinist, accounts of human behavior have been growing in influence during the same period in which support for determinism has been eroding in a traditional stronghold, the physical sciences.

There are doubtless many reasons for this development. First, the indeterminacy or uncertainty postulated by modern quantum physics is significant for physical systems of very small energy, but (except in special cases) is negligible for larger systems, including those of the human scale.[9] Second, developments in sciences and fields other than physics have supported determinist and compatibilist thinking. Growth in knowledge of genetics and the biochemical influences on behavior, the advent of Freudian and other theories of unconscious motivation, studies of the physiology of the brain and central nervous system, development of techniques of behavior modification, and studies of the influence of language and culture on cognitive processes, among other trends, have contributed to the belief that more of our behavior is determined by causes beyond our control than was previously imagined.[10]

Thus, modern compatibilists can accept a certain amount of indeterminacy in nature, while regarding it as negligible for human behavior. And they can say that if some physical indeterminacy should ever have a non-negligible effect on human behavior it would interfere with, rather than enhance, freedom by diminishing the control free agents are supposed to have over their choices and actions. They can thus retain almost all of what Hobbes, Hume, and other traditional compatibilists and determinists wanted to say about the effect of past conditioning on human behavior without flying in the face of modern scientific evidence.

1.4   But the last, and perhaps most important, reason for the growing influence of compatibilist views like that of Hobbes in this century is the one that will be our main concern. It is the problem of providing a coherent alternative libertarian account of freedom. Libertarians have always had difficulty explaining what they meant by self determination without appealing to obscure and mysterious kinds of agency. And many critics now insist that, despite some apparent common sense support, libertarian accounts of freedom of agency cannot ultimately be made intelligible and thus cannot provide a legitimate alternate to compatibilist views.[11]

To understand the problem, left us return to Hobbes and Bramhall. Bramhall regards Hobbes' freedom "to do what one wills" as an empty sort of freedom, if the will in turn has "no power over itself." But Bramhall never clearly explains what he means by the will having power over itself. In fact, Hobbes insists throughout their debate that the expressions Bramhall uses to describe self determination, expressions like "the will having power over itself," or "dominion over itself," or the "self determining itself," are nothing but "confused and empty words" (62, p. 35). Moreover, Bramhall's attempts to interpret these expressions by speaking of the will as a special kind of cause (44, pp. 42, 151) or implying that the self can rise above the influence of character and motives, by a special kind of moral agency (pp. 42-4), are regarded by Hobbes as unsatisfactory. To Hobbes, these are more "confused and empty words" (62, pp. 77, 113). Bramhall sputters and fumes over these charges, but in the end he never answers them. And while subsequent libertarians have sometimes done better than Bramhall, none has succeeded in eliminating elements of obscurity from the libertarian account of self determination.

The problem libertarians face when explaining their view is one of navigating a narrow channel that passes between confusion, on the one hand, and mystery, on the other ("confusion or emptiness," as Hobbes would say). On the one hand, the confusion they must avoid is an identification of freedom with the mere absence of determination of human choices or actions by antecedent causes. If not supplemented by further appeals to special forms of causation by the self, this amounts to identifying freedom with indeterminism or chance. The absurdities of such an identification are well known. A view which says that freedom is nothing more than indeterminism or chance is unable to account for the power of control persons must exercise over their free choices or actions if they are to be held responsible for them. Chance occurrences are not controlled by anything and thus are not controlled by the agents themselves. Now it is true that libertarians are committed to indeterminism in some respect, as a consequence of their denial that freedom is compatible with determinism. The atoms must sometimes "swerve" if there is to be room in nature for "true" human freedom. But indeterminism is only a necessary condition for freedom on the libertarian view. The confusion lies in thinking that it is sufficient.

The point is relevant to earlier comments about modern physics. Ordinarily, quantum indeterminacy is negligible at the level of human behavior. But some scientists—for example, J. Eccles (70), A. H. Compton (35), and A. I. Munn (60)—have speculated in defense of libertarianism that under certain conditions undetermined subatomic occurrences in the brain might influence human choices, and hence actions, in (non-negligibly) unpredictable ways. An obvious problem with such suggestions is that by themselves they can hardly provide an adequate account of human freedom. One may argue that such uncaused occurrences in the brain would only serve to diminish the agent's freedom, rather than enhance it, by diminishing the agent's control over choices and actions. Such indeterminism in the brain would, at best, be a nuisance, and at worst, like epilepsy, a curse. Those who make suggestions about indeterminism in the brain know this. Their postulate of indeterminism is meant to satisfy only a negative condition for freedom, accounting for the necessary "causal gaps" in nature, and it is meant to be supplemented by some positive account of self determination. But the positive accounts of self determination suggested by these thinkers point to the other side of the libertarian dilemma.

1.5   Identifying freedom with indeterminism is a confusion. But when libertarians go beyond indeterminism, trying to explain what they mean by self determination, they usually escape confusion only to embrace mystery. To explain how the self might fill causal gaps, or intervene in the natural order, or rise above its circumstances, including past character and motives, they have posited spiritual or noumenal selves, or transempirical power centers outside the order of natural causes, or factors of special kinds, like volitions, reasons or final causes, that can influence choice and action without themselves being subject to antecedent determination or causation in the normal ways, or special forms of agent causality that cannot be interpreted in terms of the natural causality of states, processes, and events.[12] Invariably libertarians have left the manner of operation of these special causal factors or agents a mystery, rarely explaining in detail, and never successfully, how the factors fill causal gaps in nature or how they influence choices and actions without themselves being influenced in objectionable ways. In the absence of such explanations, libertarian accounts of self determination seem as obscure as related theological accounts of the divine being as a *causa sui*. Theologians from Augustine onward have been aware of this analogy between divine and human self causation and its attendant problems. The libertarian idea of self determination suggests the image of Baron Von Münchhausen pulling himself from a ditch by his own bootstraps.

Kant is a critical figure in this connection. He tried to legitimize the obscurity of the libertarian conception of self determination by arguing that, while such a conception had to be presupposed by practical reason, it could not be made intelligible to theoretical reason. Since freedom is "a power of spontaneously beginning a series of successsive states" (58, p. 412), it is "blind and abrogates those rules through which alone a completely coherent experience is possible" (p. 411).

1.6   Kant is a great thinker. But mystery is like wine. Sipped with a substantial meal, it can make life bearable. But gulped alone, it induces intoxication, followed by nausea. The project of this book can now be simply described. It is to make a libertarian theory of human freedom, much like Bramhall's, intelligible to theoretical reason, by answering the Hobbesian charge that a libertarian conception of a self determining itself must be either "confused or empty." This means, on the one hand, avoiding the confusion of identifying freedom with indeterminism while, on the other, not resorting to mysterious accounts of human agency that are empty of explanatory content.

To meet the second requirement, the book will avoid most of the usual strategems employed by libertarians to explain their view. The view I shall present will not rely on appeals to a noumenal self or non-material ego. It will not appeal to a privileged kind of agent, or what C. D. Broad (62) has called "non-occurrent." causation, a kind of agency not analyzable in terms of the causality of states, processes, and events. It will avoid any reliance on arguments to the effect that reasons cannot be causes of action, or that explanations in terms of reasons are incompatible with explanations in terms of causes, or that choices or decisions or volitions are not events and hence not the kinds of things that can be caused or determined. Nor will the conception of freedom presented require that the so-called identity theory of mind and body be false.

Friends of the libertarian cause may think this project unnecessarily difficult, perhaps even perverse. For the above list includes nearly every standard device by which traditional and contemporary libertarians have made their case. Can a libertarian account of self determination hope to get off the ground if it does not at least try to distinguish reasons and/or volitions from the ordinary run of causes or rely on some special notion of agent or non-occurrent causation? These are good questions and perhaps the proper answer to them is negative. But it cannot hurt to try something new. Many philosophers and modern students of the sciences of man, including some who might otherwise be sympathetic to the libertarian cause, remain unimpressed by the various libertarian strategems mentioned in the previous paragraph. Some of these, like references to noumenal selves and non-occurrent causes involve too much mystery for their taste, and others, like the doctrine that reasons cannot be causes of action, rest on arguments which they do not find compelling.[13] The theory I shall defend does not rule out these doctrines, e.g. it does not rule out a mind-body dualism of a Cartesian or some other kind, or a noumenal order, or the possibility of non-occurrent causation. It simply does not require such doctrines.

One might view the project as an attempt to see how far we can go in constructing a libertarian account of freedom without relying on any of these traditional devices. We cannot go as far as many libertarians would like, but we can go much farther than they and many of their opponents have guessed. The project involves a kind of theoretical construction and is not merely a matter of analyzing ordinary terms relating to human freedom, like "can" and "could," "reason," "choice," etc. Such analysis is important, but ordinary language can only be the first word on these matters, not the last. I do not think a coherent libertarian account of freedom is something we are going to find somewhere, already embodied in an existing human language or conceptual scheme. It is something we shall have to construct out of pre-existing material, as Plato's demiurge did the cosmos.

1.7   In a recent essay (73), David Wiggins writes:

One of the many reasons I believe why philosophy falls short of a satisfying solution to the problem of freedom is that we still cannot refer to an unflawed statement of libertarianism. Perhaps libertarianism is in the last analysis untenable. But if we are to salvage its insights we need to know what is the least unreasonable statement the position can be given. Compatibilist resolutions to the problem of freedom must wear an appearance of superficiality, however serious or deep the reflections from which they originate, until what they offer by way of freedom can be compared with something else, actual or possible, . . . which is known to be the best that any indeterminist or libertarian could describe (p.33).

And later he adds,

The free-will dispute has reached a point where real progress depends . . upon a more precise and much more sympathetic examination of what the libertarian wants, of why he wants it, and of how his conception of metaphysical freedom is connected with political and social freedom. Whether or not it is our world— that is another question—we must continue to press the question, 'What is the possible world which could afford the autonomy of thought and agency the libertarian craves in this one?' (pp. 53-4)

I quote these passages because they clearly describe the problem I had been working on before I read Wiggins' essay, and the problem for which I believed I had a solution, Moreover, the solution has implications concerning political and social freedom just as Wiggins requires, as well as for ethics and religion. If talk of a "solution" seems immodest, let me say more modestly that I am going to put another option in the field, different from any existing compatibilist and libertarian alternatives.

This description of the problem is clear enough for introductory purposes, but not clear enough for the purposes of Part II. The remaining three chapters of this part make up the difference. They deal with the will (chapter 2) and with arguments for libertarian theories of freedom (chapter 3) and against them (chapter 4).

Notes

1. Bramhall (44) and Hobbes (62) contain the respective contributions of each author to the debate, though each of these works includes selections from the other author's responses.

2. Nor do I want to suggest that it is a good debate by modern standards. It is repetitious and filled with unnecessary personal attacks and polemics. Bramhall's responses are more typically libertarian than they are original. It is Hobbes' position, I believe, that gives the debate its historical significance. His uncompromising defense of compatibilism and his insistence that the libertarian view is unintelligible both foreshadow later trends.

3. This is the standard textbook definition. See, e.g. Berofsky (66), G. Dworkin (70), Morgenbesser and Walsh (62), O'Connor (71), and R. Taylor (74).

4. See Bramhall (44, p. 24-5). This line of reasoning will be pursued further in 3.5ff.

5. E.g. Berlin (69), C. Campbell (67), Chisholm (67), van Inwagen (74), and R. Taylor (74).

6. Hobbes, like the other pre-twentieth-century writers mentioned here, is a "soft determinist," which means that he is both a compatibilist (affirming that freedom is compatible with determinism) and a determinist. But many twentieth-century writers, who agree with Hobbes that the libertarian view is unintelligible, remain non-committal about the truth of determinism, They are compatibilists without being soft determinists. Since my main concern in the book is the problem of the intelligibility of the libertarian view, I speak throughout of the opposition between "libertarians" and "compatibilists." The latter term covers both traditional soft determinists like Hobbes, Hume, *et al.* as well as modern thinkers who argue that compatibilist accounts of freedom are the only intelligible ones without committing themselves to the truth of determinism. There is another group, namely the hard determinists, who agree that the libertarian view is intelligible, but think it is false, because determinism is true. My response to hard determinists is contained in the arguments of chapter 9.

7. Representative modern compatibilists include Schlick (66), Ayer (54), Hobart (66), and Nowell-Smith (54), among many others.

8. References to many of Berlin's critics are contained in the Introduction to Berlin (69).

9. For a discussion of this matter and possibly relevant exceptions regarding the free will issue, see Compton (35) and Munn (60). The matter is discussed further in the next section, and in greater detail in chapter 9.

10. For general discussion of these trends, see Hook (58), Berofsky (71), Hospers (61), R. Taylor (67), O'Connor (71), Grünbaum (53, 71). Rose (76) and Smith (72) summarize the relevant brain research and both seem inclined toward a Hobbesian position. B. F. Skinner (71) and E. O. Wilson (79) state the determinist case from behavioral and sociobiological perspectives respectively.

11. In addition to those cited in note 7, others to take this position include Berofsky (71), Broad (62), Frankfurt (71), Hospers (61), Nielsen (71), Thalberg (64), and Smart (70).

12. These different views are discussed at length in chapter 4, especially 4.10-17.

13. For arguments against non-occurrent causes, see 4.16-17. For arguments against the view that reasons cannot be causes, see Davidson (66) and Goldman (70).

Will

2.1   Talk about the "will," "free will" and "acts of will" (or "volitions"), which is common in the Hobbes-Bramhall debate and most other discussions of human freedom prior to this century, has fallen out of fashion in recent decades (though there have been attempts to revive it by Kenny (76), Sellars (76), McCann (74), O'Shaughnessy (80), and others).[1] Where traditional thinkers talked about "freedom of will" and "acts of will," many contemporary philosophers prefer to talk about "freedom of action" and "reasons for action" respectively.

This change has some advantages, since talk about the will was often obscure. But it may involve a loss as well. I think the case for libertarian accounts of freedom is weakened by the transformation of the free will issue into an issue about free action and, correlatively, the case for compatibilism is strengthened. Some may doubt this, because, of the thinkers just mentioned who have tried to revive talk about the will, or about volitions, Kenny and Sellars have offered sophisticated defenses of compatibilism, and others either defend a compatibilist position or remain uncommitted. Likewise, Hobbes, Jonathan Edwards, and others talked freely about the will and acts of will without jeopardizing their compatibilist and determinist commitments. Nevertheless, I think a return to the free *will* issue in more than name only is essential to the libertarian cause.

2.2   Thus, we shall take seriously Bramhall's claim that "the freedom of the agent is from the freedom of the will" (44, p. 30). I shall call this "Bramhall's thesis" hereafter, and it will play an important role in subsequent discussions. In practice, it means that the indeterminism, or absence of determination, which is a necessary condition for human freedom according to the libertarian view, is to be located primarily in the will of the agent (in choice and decision) and only secondarily in overt action, through the relation of overt action to the will. In other words, libertarians can in principle accept the claim that the free action was caused or determined by the agent's will or choice, given the circumstances.[2] What they must insist upon is that the will or choice was not caused or determined by the circumstances. They can accept a compatibilist account of the relation between choice and action, but not a compatibilist account of the relation between reasons and choice.

Such a move is suggested by a traditional criticism of views of human freedom requiring indeterminism. Critics like Jonathan Edwards and Schopenhauer argue that indeterminist views suggest the image of free agents sometimes willing to do something and finding themselves, by chance or accident, actually doing something else—finding their legs inextricably moving, for example, when they intended them to be still.[3] As an example of what freedom essentially involves, such an image is indeed absurd, for it leaves out any account of the ability of free agents to control

15

their actions in accordance with their wills. The point is not that chance or indeter-minism might not sometimes "intervene" between will and action, but rather that such intervention is not a necessary condition for freedom of action. To say, however, that it is not necessary to freedom of action is just to say that free actions could in principle be determined by the will. Libertarians may concede this, while insisting with Bramhall that determination *of* the will is not compatible with freedom.

The move represented by Bramhall's thesis does not solve all the problems con-nected with indeterminism. It is only a step. The major problems are only moved backwards from action to will and few further ones are created—about the nature of the will and the possibility of requiring a regress of powers ". . . to will to will . . ." or ". . . to choose to choose . . . .". But I think libertarians must pay the price of dealing with these further problems if they are to make sense of the free agent's control over action without resorting to the strategems mentioned in section 1.6. The first step of this chapter is therefore to rehabilitate the traditional language about the will, making adjustments where necessary to avoid obscurity, and to avoid some legitimate objections against acts of will, by Ryle and others.

2.3   Traditionally it has been held that a "rational agent" or "person" or "self" (these terms will be used interchangeably throughout the book) is something having both an intellect and a will, where "intellect" and "will" designate powers or capaci-ties of the agent defined in terms of theoretical and practical reasoning, respectively. This is an important clue to the meaning of the term "will" in one of its traditional senses. In this sense, the will is a set of powers (to deliberate, to choose, to act for a purpose, to criticize reasons for acting, etc.) defined in terms of a family of notions whose focal member is that of practical reasoning.

Practical reasoning is, in general, reasoning about what is to be done, as distin-guished from theoretical reasoning about what is to be believed.[4] But we can distin-guish two types of practical reasoning, corresponding to two senses of the expres-sion "what is to be done". "What is to be done" can signify what I (he, she, everyone) "ought" to do, or it can signify what I "will" (in the sense of choose or intend) to do. Reasoning of the latter kind, culminating in choice or decision (expressed exclusively in the first person "I will (i.e. choose to, intend to) do a") is deliberation. Reasoning of the second kind, culminating in judgments about what I or others ought or ought not to do (may or may not do, etc.) has no special name, but I shall call it "normative practical reasoning."

Both deliberation and normative practical reasoning terminate in "judgments of the will," to use the traditional expression (*arbitria voluntatis*), as distinguished from "judgments of the intellect" which terminate theoretical reasonings. In the case of deliberation, these terminating judgments are called "choices" or "decisions." In the case of normative practical reasoning, they may be called "normative judgments." Judgments of the will have a special importance for us because of their relation to the freedom of the will. Freedom of will is to be defined as the freedom of choice or decision (so that free choices and decisions will represent the *libera arbitria voluntatis* of the tradition[5]), while normative judgments play a role in the practical reasoning leading to certain kinds of free choices, namely, moral and prudential choices. So we must say more about judgments of the will in general and about choices and decisions in particular.

2.4   Bramhall and other traditional thinkers often refer to judgments of the will as "acts of will." In what sense, if at all, can choices, decisions and judgments be called acts? To act is to "bring something about" and an act or action[6] is the bringing about of something. That (state of affairs or state or change) which is by definition brought about by an act or action may be called its "result."[7] Thus the result of raising my arm is that my arm goes up; raising my arm is by definition bringing it about that my arm goes up. The result of killing the king is that the king is dead, and so on. What is the result of a choice or decision understood as the termination of deliberation? The answer is quite simple and is the key to understanding the nature of choices and decisions as acts of will. Choice or decision so understood is the formation of intention, or the creation of (the state of having) a purpose or end. The purpose is the aim or goal; in the case of intention, it is that which is intended. So the result of a choice or decision is an intention's being formed, or the coming to be of (the state of having) a purpose.[8] Similarly, normative judgment as the culmination of practical reasoning is the formation of a normative belief. In both cases a previously non-existent state of affairs is brought into existence by the agent.

But these so-called acts of will are elusive entities, and not only because they are mental acts. There is also the problem that they do not take a time to occur. It will be helpful in this connection to refer to the typology of things we do suggested by Kenny and Vendler.[9] Some (like running, swimming or visiting) are "activities" which "go on for a time." Others (like turning a dial, building a house, or walking to a specified destination) are "performances" with specified *termini* which "take a time" to complete. Still others (like winning a race, finishing a book, or finding one's keys) are "achievements" which happen "at a time." All three are changes of some kind and are to be contrasted with "states" (like being heavy or having brown hair) which "last for a time."

One can say that choices, decisions, and normative judgments belong to the category of achievements in this typology. They terminate performances (e.g. deliberations) and happen at a time, giving rise to achieved states, like intention and normative belief.[10] The fact that they happen at a time is no reason to refrain from calling them acts. They have as much right to be called so as other achievements like finishing a book or finding something. Since talk about acts of will has come under attack in recent philosophy, it is worth reminding ourselves that among the phenomena most often referred to traditionally as acts of will were such ordinary phenomena as making choices or decisions, or reaching conclusions to practical reasonings, in short, what we have been calling judgments of the will.

2.5   We can now remove some misconceptions that may arise about choices and decisions in the light of these remarks.

First, when it is said that choice or decision is by definition the formation of intention or purpose, the terms "choice" and "decision" are being used in a specific sense. One is talking about choosing or deciding "to do" something or other.[11] The terms "decide" and "choose" have other uses. For example, one can decide "that" something ought to be done (is the best thing to do, etc.). "Deciding that" in this sense is a form of practical judgment to be contrasted with deciding to do something or the formation of an intention. In the case of "choose," one can speak of choosing or selecting an object from among a set (e.g. a pear rather than an apple from a tray of fruit), meaning to refer to an overt action of some kind (moving one's arm and grasping the pear). In this sense the choosing or selecting is itself an overt action and not the formation of an intention "to do" something further. (That which is chosen is a thing, not an action "to be done.") If the person deliberated for a moment when presented with the tray of fruit and decided or chose *to take* the pear, this would have been the formation of an intention distinct from the overt act of taking. In this "inner" act sense, the choice might have been made and the intention formed without the overt action's taking place. The tray might have been abruptly removed or some other causal factor might have intervened.[12]

So, in general, when I speak of choice and decision hereafter, I shall mean choice or decision "to do" something or other as contrasted with practical judgment, on the one hand, and overt action, on the other. When speaking of choice or decision in these other senses we may specify "a decision in the sense of practical judgment" or "a choice in the sense of an overt action."

Second, choices and decisions may immediately give rise to, or initiate, actions, as when one decides to do something now rather than three hours from now, but they need not always do so. A purpose is formed in any case, whether one decides to do something now or later, but only in the first case is action immediately initiated by the choice. In the second case, the action may be performed three hours later in accordance with the previously formed intention, but there is no need to postulate another decision at the later time, unless one has changed one's mind or has had doubts about the earlier decision in the intervening time.

Third, just as choices and decisions may, but need not, initiate actions, so actions, including intentional actions, may, but need not have been initiated by choices or decisions.[13] In short, we need not make use of the doctrine, criticized by Ryle (49) and other contemporary philosophers, that "whenever an overt act is described as intentional, voluntary, culpable or meritorious" (p. 65) it is asserted by implication that it was preceded by or initiated by an act of will or volition. This doctrine is indeed mistaken if by an act of will we mean a choice or decision in the ordinary senses of these terms. Ryle himself mentions certain familiar processes.

> with which volitions are sometimes wrongly identified. People are frequently in doubt what to do; having considered alternative courses of action, they then sometimes select or choose one of these courses. This process of opting for one of a set of alternative courses of action is sometimes said to be what is signified by 'volition'. But this identification will no do, for most ordinary actions do not issue out of conditions of indecision and are not therefore results of settlements of indecisions (p. 68).

Ryle's "settlements of indecision" are our choices or decisions (to do), and we need not assume that actions are always initiated by them. Choices and decisions (to do) always initiate, or form, intentions or purposes, but they are not always the direct initiators of intentional actions.

A fourth and final point about choices and decisions concerns their relation to deliberation. We shall assume that choices or decisions (to do) as described in 2.2 always terminate some process of reasoning, however brief. But such a process need not always be called "deliberation" in the ordinary sense of that term. There are such things as impulsive, spur of the moment, or snap, decisions.[14] A man walking along the street sees his friends entering a tavern and impulsively decides to join them for a drink. Now one could say there is a minimal amount of practical reasoning going on, even in such cases, in the sense that some option (possible action or plan of action) is considered in the light of background beliefs and memories, and assessed in terms of background wants and desires. The option is found to be attractive and is immediately chosen. What is lacking in such impulsive or spur of the moment decisions is reflection upon and debate over alternatives to the option chosen. Since we ordinarily think of deliberation as involving such a debate over alternatives *in foro interno,* we should qualify our earlier statement and say that choices or decisions to do *normally* terminate deliberations in the ordinary sense involving consideration of, and reflection upon, more than one option. But in certain cases of impulsive or spur of the moment decisions, they may terminate minimal processes of practical reasoning in which only one option is considered and assessed.

Though spur of the moment or snap decisions occur, we ordinarily think of ourselves as being more free in the normal cases in which choices or decisions terminate deliberation, because in such cases we are more likely to feel that we "could have chosen otherwise." If indeterminist theories of freedom were to reduce all free choices or decisions to spur of the moment decisions, as some critics suggest,[15] they would be clearly inadequate. Whatever else it does, a libertarian theory, like any other, must be able to explain how and why our choices and decisions are free and rational in the normal and paradigmatic cases where they conclude processes of reasoning, sometimes quite lengthy and complex, in which more than one possible course of action is considered and assessed.

In summary, choices and decisions "to do" something or other are examples of judgments of the will. They *normally* terminate deliberations about alternative courses of action and *sometimes* directly initiate intentional actions. But what they always do, and do by definition, is to *form intentions or purposes* that may guide actions, now or in the future.

2.6   We have been discussing the term "will" in only one of its traditional senses. In this sense, it designates a set of closely related powers associated with the notion of practical reasoning, the powers to deliberate, to engage in normative practical reasoning, to make choices and decisions, to make normative judgments, and a number of other powers related to these, e.g. to criticize and reevaluate one's intentions or purposes, and so on. In the language of some earlier thinkers, such a set of interconnected powers would be called a "faculty." But use of the term "faculty" in this connection is not fashionable today, and I do not want to multiply unfashionable terms without necessity. Fortunately, the terms "set" and "power" are both very much in fashion. So we can confidently refer to the will, in this sense, as a set of interconnected powers of the above kinds, all conceptually related to practical reasoning. And we can call the will in this sense "rational will," since, along with intellect, its possession distinguishes rational agents (persons, selves) from non-rational agents.

The will in its other traditional sense may be called "natural (or appetitive) will." In this sense, the term "will" signifies one, or a combination of, an agent's desires, wants, preferences, likes, dislikes, hopes, fears, and other attitudes, appetites, aversions, or emotions that can be generally classified as inclinations toward or away from certain objects and states of affairs. Clearly, this is a legitimate meaning of "will," though different from "rational will." When agents are said to do something in accordance with their wills, this may mean in accordance with their choices or intentions, on the one hand, or in accordance with their wants or desires, on the other. Now, natural will is not a power, or set of powers, in the same sense in which rational will is a power, or set of powers. Having natural will at a certain time may designate simply being in certain states at that time (wanting, desiring, liking, hoping, etc.). Insofar as natural will could be said to be a power at all, it would be the general power to be in states of these kinds, to have desires and feelings, as some animals do, but inanimate objects, plants and some other living things (perhaps) do not. Rational will is, by contrast, a set of related powers to do certain things rather than a power to be in certain states. This is another reason why freedom of the will is related to rational will (freedom in all of its senses being a certain kind of power *to do* certain things).

2.7   The distinction between natural and rational will is an ancient one. Aristotle says in the *De Anima* (08), for example, that "there is justification for regarding these two as the sources of movement [*archai tēs kinēseos,* his expression for "efficient causes"], i.e. appetite and practical thought" (433a 17-18), adding that "both of these . . . are capable of originating local movement, mind and appetite: (1) mind, that is, which calculates means to an end, i.e. mind practical (it differs from mind speculative in the character of its end); while (2) appetite is in every form of it related to an end" (433za 14-15). In the *Metaphysics,* where he is discussing the four causes and the history of Greek thought, Aristotle again speaks of appetite and mind as examples of sources of motion, crediting Empedocles with the recognition of appetite (Empedocles' Love and Strife), and Anaxagoras with the recognition of mind, as fundamental efficient causes (984a 23ff). The idea that love and mind rule nature is an earlier extension of the correct idea that appetite (natural will) and "mind practical" (rational will) are the two "sources of motion" in rational beings.

Though natural will and rational will can be distinguished, they are related in rational beings, and not only because both can be sources of motion. The link between them is once again practical reason. For, as choices, decisions and practical judgments are related to the logical conclusions of practical reasoning, so wants, desires, preferences, and other elements of natural will are related to its logical premises. Practical reasoning involves at least one cognitive premise (asserting something believed or known) and at least one conative premise (asserting that something is wanted or desired), though, in practice, it will usually involve many premises of both kinds. "That which is the object of appetite," as Aristotle says, "is the stimulant of mind practical" (433a 16-17). Related to this is the fact that, in rational agents, desires and wants may have conceptualized objects, and it is insofar as they have conceptualized objects that they can play a role in practical reasoning.

Recent philosophical writings on the will, including Brian O'Shaughnessy's notable two volume work (80), have focussed on will in a third sense, which O'Shaughnessy has called "striving will." As rational will is associated with terms like "deliberation," "choice," and "intention," and natural or appetitive will with terms like "want " and "desire," so striving will is associated with terms like "trying," "attempting," "endeavoring," and "making an effort of will." These terms can legitimately be regarded as expressing a third sense of will, though traditionally striving will was associated with either rational or natural will, depending on whether the trying or making an effort was motivated by reason or appetite. Now I think that striving will, like appetitive will, is important for our purposes. But it is my contention, in line with Bramhall and other traditional writers, that rational will is pivotal for defining the freedom of the will. Striving will and appetitive will come into the picture through their relation to rational will (to deliberation, choice and intention), and we shall be exploring this relation as we go along.

2.8   Having said this much about the will, we are now in a position to define its freedom. As suggested, we define free will with respect to those specific judgments of the will (*arbitria voluntatis*) called choices or decisions (to do) , and we say that an agent is free with respect to such a judgment of the will, if and only if, the agent has simultaneously the power to make the judgment and the power to do otherwise:

> **D1.**   (Freedom of the Will): A rational agent (person or self) S is (was) free at a time t with respect to a choice or decision J, if and only if, S has (had) the power at t to make J at t and S has (had) the power at t to do otherwise at t (i.e. to refrain from making J and/or to make some choice or decision other than J at t).

Free will, so defined, is a dual power, the power to choose (or "efficacy," as we shall call it) and to do otherwise (or "avoidability"). The latter, as indicated, may involve either refraining or making a contrary or contradictory choice or decision.

The definition, be it noted, contains time designations both for the power and the choice ("the power at t to make J at t"). It is now widely recognized that in the general case of having the power to perform a certain action the time of possession of the power may be earlier than, or the same as, the time of the action (though not later than the time of the action).[16] But, for defining the freedom of the will, the special case in which the time designations are the same is the critical one. We tend to assume that a person must possess the power to do and do otherwise with respect to a free choice or decision at the moment when the choice or decision is made. It will not do to say that the person had the power earlier but lost it prior to the moment of choice. (There will be more on the topic of temporal designations as we proceed.)

In the Introduction, free will was defined as the power of persons to originate or bring into existence the purposes or ends that guide their actions. D1 can be seen to express this definition by way of the connection between intentions and purposes, on the one hand, and choices or decisions, on the other. Having an intention or purpose or aim is a state (of mind), according to the Kenny-Vendler typology; and the power of persons to originate or bring into existence the purposes or ends that guide their action is the power to bring such states into existence by choice or decision.[17]

2.9   John Locke (59) argued that there was a confusion in talking about the freedom "of the will" as many previous philosophers had done. His remarks are worth considering in the light of the above definition.

> I leave it to be considered whether [these claims] may not help to put an end to that long agitated, and I think, unreasonable, because unintelligible question, viz. *Whether man's will be free or no?* . . .   the question itself is altogether improper. For . . . when any one well considers it, I think he will as plainly perceive that liberty, which is but a power, belongs only to agents, and cannot be an attribute or modification of the will, which is also but a power (pp. 319-20).

Whatever one might say of the definitions of his predecessors, D1 is not subject to the confusion Locke describes. Freedom of the will as defined by D1 is a power attributed to an agent. What makes it a freedom "of the will" is that this power is defined for the agent with respect to certain kinds of acts, namely, the acts (achievements) of choosing or deciding, which are said to be judgments "of the will" because of their relation to practical reasoning and intention.

If there is a point worth pursuing in Locke's remarks, it would be that the definition D1 does not provide a general definition of what it means to say that an agent is free with respect to acts or actions of any kinds whatever, rather than with respect to specific kinds of acts "of will." One who defines freedom of will must go on to give some account of the freedom of action generally, in order to give a full and adequate account of freedom of agency.

2.10   This is where Bramhall's thesis comes into play. "The freedom of the agent," he says, "is from the freedom of the will." I take this to mean that "true" freedom of agency (that which grounds human dignity) with respect to acts or actions generally must presuppose freedom with respect to certain special kinds of acts, namely, certain judgments of the will. The details of this relationship must await description in Part II, but the general strategy suggested by Bramhall's thesis is a traditional one, and can be described here. Those who defend a "free will" strategy like Bramhall's want to say that an agent who performs an act or action of any kind is free (in the true, dignity-grounding, sense) only if the agent could have done otherwise (refrained or performed some contrary act or action) *by choice or decision,* or, as we sometimes say, "at will." More precisely , they want to say that the agent could have done otherwise by a choice or decision to do so that was free in the sense of D1, or, as we sometimes put it, "of his or her own free will." This freedom of will is only a necessary condition for freedom of action. Absence of internal and external constraints preventing the realization of will in action, such as compatibilists require, must also be present. But free will theorists insist that the absence of such constraints is not sufficient for true freedom of action. Free agents must be able to do and do otherwise, either way "at will," or "by free choice," or "of their own free will."

This is but the outline of a strategy and by no means a finished product. In fact, there is a reasonable doubt that a strategy of this kind can ever be successful. The main problem with such a free will strategy for defining freedom of action is the problem of a potentially infinite regress. If choices and decisions are themselves acts, or bringings about of something by the agent, as argued in 2.4, and if, according to this strategy, an act is free only if the agent could have done otherwise by a free choice or decision to do otherwise, then it would appear that the choosing to do otherwise would be free only if the agent could have chosen otherwise by freely choosing to choose otherwise (and so on for chooosing to choose otherwise, choosing to choose to choose otherwise, etc.).

This problem is a familiar one to students of the free will issue.[18] But it may easily be misinterpreted. According to the strategy described two paragraphs above, we are not saying that the free action must have been preceded by or initiated by an *actual* free choice. This would generate a regress of actual choices such as Ryle criticizes. What we are saying is the agent had the *power to refrain* from doing what he or she did by a free choice, or "of his or her own free will." The power to have done otherwise involves the further power to have freely chosen otherwise. The danger therefore is not of a regress of actual choices, at earlier times or all at the same time, but of a regress of *powers* to choose (to choose to choose, etc.) possessed at earlier times or all at the same time.

2.11   Accepting this qualification, there remain two serious objections to such a free will strategy for defining the freedom of the agent. Hobbes made the first of these objections against Bramhall's view and suggested the second. The first objection is that talk of such a series of powers to choose, to choose to choose etc. requires one to use expressions like "willing to will" and "choosing to choose" which, according to Hobbes, make no sense. ("I acknowledge this liberty, that I can do if I will: but to say I can will if I will, I take to be an absurd speech" (62 p. 39).

Now this objection can be answered, but only in a way that raises the second and more important objection. Whether or not expressions like "choosing to choose" and "willing to will" have any ordinary uses, it is clear that they can be given a meaning within the context of a free will strategy like Bramhall's. Within this context, the power "to choose to choose otherwise" may be viewed as the power "to alter by choice, or at will, one or more of the purposes or ends upon which one's present choice depends." This power might either be ascribed to the agent at the same time as the present choice or it might be ascribed to the agent at some earlier time. In the second case, for example, the agent may be said to now have the power to make choice$_1$ to do otherwise *and* to have had the power at some earlier time to have altered, by a choice$_2$, one or another of the purposes on which choice$_1$ depends. If a businessman now chooses to take a bus in order to meet a client, he may be said to now have, or to have had at an earlier time, the power to alter by choice the purpose (to meet the client) upon which the present choice (to take the bus) depends.

While this is a move libertarians *could* make in answer to the charge that "willing to will" makes no sense, it is a move that most of them (Bramhall included) have been reluctant to make. For it gives rise to a second and more powerful objection to their view, also seen by Hobbes.[19] It leads to an infinite regress of powers ". . . to will to will . . ." or ". . . to choose to choose . . ." otherwise. If the existence of a power to do otherwise were to depend upon the existence of an earlier power to have altered some purpose by choice, then the existence of the power to make the earlier choice would depend upon a still earlier power to alter some purpose by choice, and so on indefinitely. The agent who is said to now have the power to make choice$_1$ to do otherwise must also be said to have had the power at some earlier time to have altered by a choice$_2$ one of the purposes or ends upon which choice$_1$ depends and to have had the still earlier power to have altered by a choice$_3$ one of the purposes or ends upon which choice$_2$ depended, and so on. Or, what seems even more bizarre, the free agent must be said to have an infinite series of such powers all at the same time.

The main problem with this regress of powers, either possessed simultaneously or at progressively earlier times, can be simply stated. The regress is vicious because it *systematically* prevents us from giving a non-circular explanation of the freedom of any act in the series, including the first one. As Hobbes would have put it, a free will strategy, like Bramhall's, which defines the freedom of the agent in terms of the freedom of the will, leads either to "confusion or emptiness." Either it forces us to use expressions like "choosing to choose" or "willing to will" which make no sense (confusion), or, if such expressions can be given sense, it leads to an infinite regress of powers which provides no explanation of what we set out to explain, i.e. the freedom of the agent (emptiness). The problem is further compounded for libertarians, because such a regress provides no clue (and seems to exclude the possibility of providing any clue) to the role of *indeterminism* in their account of freedom of action. It appears that freedom of action is being defined in terms of the power of *determination* by a certain kind of act of will and freedom of the act of will in terms of a power of determination by a further act of will, and so on.

2.12   How can one escape this familiar regress of powers without giving up the free will strategy embodied in Bramhall's thesis that the freedom of agency is from the freedom of the will? Somehow the regress must stop at the level of free will as defined by D1. The freedom of acts or actions other than choices and other judgments of the will could be interpreted conditionally or hypothetically in the sense that it would depend upon a further power in the agent to freely choose or decide to refrain or do otherwise. But this further power to freely choose or decide to do otherwise, as defined by D1, must be interpreted as an unconditional or categorical power, at least in the sense that it would not depend upon any further power to choose to choose, or to alter by choice any of the reasons upon which the free choice depended. This is clearly the move Bramhall wants to make (though what he means by an unconditional or categorical power to will is not so clear). It is also a move that brings us back to the theme of the first section of this chapter: libertarians can in principle accept a compatibilist account of the relation between choice and action so long as they insist upon an incompatibilist account of the relation between reasons and choice.

Now a solution of this kind to the regress problem would be merely arbitrary if one could not explain why the freedom of choices and decisions as defined by D1 should be treated differently from the freedom of acts or actions of other kinds. This is where the difficult work of subsequent chapters begins. The reasons, if there are any, for treating judgments of the will differently in this respect, should have something to do with their unique role as terminators of practical reasoning. And it should also have something to do with the libertarian requirement of indeterminism, that is, with the requirement that free choices and decisions cannot be determined or caused. The indeterminist requirement must be related in a manner yet to be explained to the idea that freedom of will in the sense of D1 is an "unconditional" or "categorical" power.

But then, as indicated in chapter 1, there are problems about unconditional or categorical interpretations of freedom involving indeterminism that are at least as troubling as the regress problem itself. To say that the will is free merely because it is undetermined is the confusion of identifying freedom and indeterminism discussed in 1.3. But notions of unconditional power that go beyond the mere assertion of indeterminism tend to involve appeals to obscure forms or agency or causation that are as empty of explanatory content as the regress itself.

In sum, free will theories like Bramhall's face a two-fold dilemma that may be diagrammed as follows:

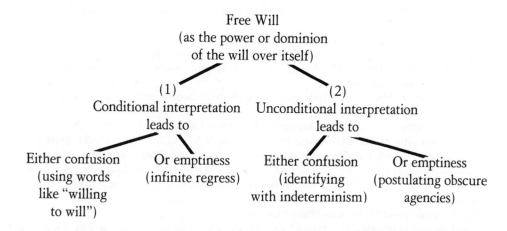

Free Will
(as the power or dominion
of the will over itself)

(1)   (2)
Conditional interpretation   Unconditional interpretation
leads to   leads to

Either confusion   Or emptiness   Either confusion   Or emptiness
(using words   (infinite regress)   (identifying   (postulating obscure
like "willing   with indeterminism)   agencies)
to will")

This dual dilemma summarizes Hobbes' case against the intelligibility of Bramhall's libertarian theory of free will,[20] a case that has become a standard one since Hobbes' time. In an influential essay written in this century, to cite just one example, C. D. Broad (62) presents the same dual dilemma to libertarians and, after examining all of the options, concludes that libertarian theories of self determination cannot be made intelligible.

Note that path (2) represents the distinctively libertarian dilemma described in chapter 1. It applies to libertarian theories of all kinds. Path (1) represents a problem characteristic of libertarian theories of "free will" in particular. The problems of Path (1) have led many to give up on the traditional ideas of will and free will. I have said that this is a mistake. But even so, Path (1) is not very promising for the reasons given; and free will theorists (as we have seen in Bramhall's case) find themselves sooner or later moving over to Path (2) in order to confront the dilemma of an undetermined free will. I think there is more to be learned from the regress problem and shall be returning to it.[21] But the move to Path (2) is inevitable for libertarians (even for free will theorists) if they wish to cut short a regress at some point and exploit their idea that a free choice or action cannot be determined by antecedent causes.

So let us turn from the deep blue sea of an infinite regress to the devil of indeterminism.

Notes

1. Other revivalists include L. Davis (79) and J. Blumenfeld (83). For discussion of the topic, see also Aune (74), Danto (73), Goldman (76), and O'Shaughnessy (73). O'Shaughnessy (80), which is the most thorough recent study of the topic, focusses on what he calls "striving will." For more on this, see 2.7.

2. I am not saying that libertarians must accept this claim, merely that they could live with it. Nor do I wish to say that a person is "locked in" once a decision is made in the sense that last minute alterations of decisions cannot be made. There is a discussion of such alterations, and of weakness of will, in 8.6-7.

3. J. Edwards (69), p. 49; Schopenhauer (60), p. 47.

4. Discussions of practical reasoning to which I am indebted include Gauthier (63), Binkley (65), Sellars (66), (80), Castaneda (75), Aune (77), and Audi (82). Rescher (66), Körner, (74) and Raz (79) are important collections.

5. This claim will be qualified somewhat in 6.5 to accommodate problems about willing to will discussed later in this chapter.

6. For background to this general account of acts and actions see D. Brown (68), Danto (65 and 73), Goldman (70), McCann (74), Care and Landesman (68), and A. R. White (68). Throughout the book I do not bother to distinguish between acts and actions. There are subtle differences in ordinary uses of the terms "act" and "action" as White (68), for example, has shown. But none of my arguments depend on these differences. Both acts and actions are the "bringing about" of states or changes by agents, and this common feature is what is important about them for my purposes.

7. The term "result" is borrowed from McCann (74). He would insist that act and result are the same in the case of mental acts. Though I do not want to make an issue of this, it is consistent with what I say. The formation of an intention and an intention's being formed may be said to be the same event.

8. This is a widely held view about the relation of choice and decision to intention, though some controversies about it persist. Cf. Meiland (70) and Raz (75). Hall (78) claims it is generally true that choices form intentions, but argues that choices sometimes reaffirm intentions already made. See Aune (78) for critical remarks on this view. Others insist that intentions are always forward looking, so that it can be said that one intends to do something only before one does it, not while one is doing it; though, if the action is intentional, it can still be said that one has a purpose or aim of some kind while doing it. Cf. L. Davis (79). By speaking of choices or decisions as forming intentions *or creating purposes,* I mean to indicate that even in cases where choices immediately initiate actions some purpose is formed (to complete the action), even if it cannot properly be said that one intends to perform the action.

9. Kenny (63, chap. 8); Vendler (67, chap. 4). Kenny's distinction is threefold: he does not discuss achievements. For further discussion of the Kenny-Vendler typology see Mourelatos (78).

10. Someone might quarrel with these claims, saying that choices may take a small, but finite, time to occur and therefore could be regarded as performances. I could accommodate such a view without substantially altering my position and will, in fact, take this suggestion seriously in 6.6. But to introduce it now would complicate the arguments of the next several chapters with no compensating gain.

11. Though the terms "choice" and "decision" have some divergent uses in ordinary language, as this section shows, when they refer to choices or decisions "to do," they are almost always interchangeable. Since this is the meaning of interest in subsequent chapters, I use the two terms interchangeably throughout this book. It is convenient to have both terms at our disposal since some authors like to talk about "freedom of choice" and others about "freedom of decision."

12. For useful discussions of these and other points about choosing and deciding, see Oldenquist (67), Daveney (64), Audi (73), and Raz (75).

13. Intentional actions, as understood here, are those the agents intended to perform or were performed as a result of the agent's trying to perform them. Cf. Malcolm (68). In both cases they are purposive, or guided by purpose. See note 17 of this chapter for further references on intention and intentional action.

14. I am indebted to Audi (73) for a discussion of these.

15. See 4.8 and the sections leading up to it for a discussion of this and related criticisms.

16. See Chisholm (67 and Lehrer (76).

17. For helpful discussions of intention as disposition or state of mind, see Anscombe (58), Gustafson (68), Meiland (70), Langford (71), Lawrence (72), and Audi (73). To ascribe an intention to an agent is, among other things, to say that the agent is disposed to act in certain ways in certain circumstances, as all of these authors insist. But this dispositional character of intentions is consistent with saying that having of an intention is a state. See Armstrong (68). I have more to say about states in 3.2.

18. The regress is mentioned by Hobbes (62, pp. 34-5, and more clearly on p. 51), and is discussed at length by later critics of the libertarian view like Jonathan Edwards (69), Schopenhauer (60), and J. S. Mill (62). Most twentieth century critics also discuss it, including Schlick (66), Ayer (54), Broad (62), and Hobart (66).

19. Hobbes merely suggests in the passages cited in the previous note that this regress is lurking in Bramhall's view without pursuing the issue as other writers mentioned in the previous note were to do. This, I think, is because Bramhall does not take the bait and make the move that would lead to the regress argument. Bramhall's actual move, described in the next section, leads to a different set of problems.

20. Hobbes (62). For the Path (1) dilemma see esp. pp. 39, 34-5, 51. For the Path (2) dilemma, pp. 35, 77, 113.

21. In chapter 6, I argue that the freedom of certain kinds of free choices, namely free practical choices, must be interpreted in terms of a willing to will. But the willing to will is interpreted differently than in 2.11 and the regress is not infinite. Moreover, this is only true of free practical choices, not of free moral and prudential choices.

Indeterminism and Power

3.1   If indeterminism is the devil it is alleged to be, why do Bramhall and others insist that it is a necessary condition of free will? Why must the atoms "swerve" if there is to be room in nature for human freedom? The answers to these questions, described briefly in chapter 1, will get a closer look in this chapter before we turn in chapter 4 to the problems created by indeterminist theories of freedom.

Reasons for thinking that indeterminism is required for freedom of will have to do with the dual power ascribed to the free agent by the definition D1. If, according to D1, the free agent simultaneously has the power to choose and the power to do otherwise, it seems to many persons that both the choosing and the doing otherwise must be "genuinely possible" or "open" alternatives in a sense that is precluded if either alternative is determined or necessitated by the past. Many arguments have been offered to support this alleged incompatibility of free will and determinism, including some challenging arguments by recent philosophers.[1] But all such arguments, if they do not fail in other ways, tend to founder over disagreements about the nature of the agent's power to do otherwise. Debates about the nature of this power, or, equivalently, about the meaning of the expression "could have done otherwise," persist, in their turn, without resolution.[2]

There is much to be learned from current debates about the alleged incompatibility of free will and determinism. But the literature on this topic is now so vast that it is easy to miss the forest for the trees. The approach taken in this chapter is somewhat unusual by modern standards and is designed to bring the forest back into focus. It is inspired in part by reasoning of Bramhall, briefly described in section 1.2, and affords some needed insight into the historical roots of the free will issue.

Since the argument of the chapter is complex, the reader is due an explanation of its place in the overall plan of the book. The case for incompatibility will not be completed in this chapter because the question of whether or not free will is compatible with determinism cannot be entirely separated from the question of whether an incompatibilist account of freedom can be made intelligible; and this latter question is the major one of Part II. In consequence, the arguments for incompatibility begun in this chapter are not completed until chapter 9, after the libertarian view has been developed in the intervening chapters. This chapter plays the additional role of introducing some key notions, like "covert non-constraining control" and "sole or ultimate dominion," that have an important place in the theory of the intervening chapters.

There is another reason for this two step approach to the incompatibility issue (chapter 3 and then chapter 9). Years of thinking about the free will issue have convinced me that it involves not only questions of fact and conceptual analysis (as important as these may be to its resolution), but also questions of value. The clash of intuitions between compatibilists and incompatibilists is difficult to remove not only because the conceptual issues are complex, but also because competing images of the self are involved, and these in turn involve evaluative as well as cognitive commitments. I think this point was seen most clearly by Williams James among traditional writers on the subject, though others have taken note of it. Frithjof Bergmann (77), for example, has drawn attention more recently to the connection between conceptions of freedom and images of the self. Since questions about value play an important role in Part II, this aspect of the debate must wait until chapter 9 as well. We shall find that the discussion of values in Part II has a dual role. It is essential to the construction of the libertarian theory developed in Part II and, at another level, it provides some clues for dealing with the evaluative issues involved in the debate about compatibility.

For all that, the present chapter is an important step in the argument. It seeks to lay bare the intuitions that motivate libertarians like Bramhall, and it introduces notions that are indispensable to the arguments of Part II.

3.2   The first task is to say something about the terms "determinism" and "indeterminism" as they enter into the debate. Determinists (or necessitarians as they were called in Hobbes' day) generally hold that whatever is or happens at any time, must be or happen as it does, given the past, or given the past and nature's laws. They ascribe a kind of necessity to all that is or happens, but the necessity is a conditional, or as Hobbes' says, an "antecedent," necessity. The determined occurrence must take place on the condition that something else has taken place earlier and certain laws of nature hold. By contrast, indeterminist intuitions about free will are nicely expressed, if a little fancifully, by William James (56) when he objects that, according to determinists, "the future has not ambiguous possibilities hidden in its womb." For James , as for Bramhall, a free choice must be an "ambiguous possibility" in the sense that it might not have occurred as it did, given the laws of nature and all that preceded it in time.

To define these views more accurately, we need a standard vocabulary for talking about what "is" or "happens" at a time and for talking about "the past." Let us first distinguish *states* an object may be in from *changes* it may undergo. For an object to be in a state or to undergo a change at a time is for it to possess some attribute (have some property or stand in some relation) at the time. The difference between states and changes lies in the nature of the attribute possessed. Attributes signifying changes (moving, expanding, stopping, colliding) possessed by an object at a time t presuppose a difference in some other attribute of the object before and after t.[3] Thus, if an object is *moving* at t, then its *position* is different before and after t; if it is expanding at t then its size is different before and after t; if it stops at t then it was moving before t, but is at rest after t. This criterion captures what we take to be characteristic of change in general: for something to change is for it to be different in some way over time. (Needless to say, the criterion is also satisfied by choosing at t, which presupposes the possession after t of an intention or purpose the agent did not possess before t.) By contrast, possession of attributes signifying states (having a certain mass, being red, being next to b) at t does not presuppose a difference in the object before and after t, though it is, of course, compatible with a number of differences over time of other attributes of the object.[4]

We shall speak of states and changes "occurring" at various times and, in the manner of D1, the primary references to time will be to moments of time. A state or change that occurs throughout an interval of time is one that occurs, or is occurring, at every moment on the interval; and such a state or change will be determined if and only if it is determined at every moment of the interval.[5] Finally, a "past circumstance (or a circumstance belonging to the past) relative to a time t" will be the occurrence of a state or change at a time earlier than t.[6]

3.3   Now determinists want to ascribe a certain kind of necessity to the determined occurrence, called "antecedent necessity" by Hobbes, and variously call "historical necessity" or "physical necessity" by modern writers. They want to say that a state or change E which is determined *must* occur at t, *given* that certain circumstances belong to the past relative to t, or certain circumstances belong to the past relative to t and certain laws of nature hold. The determined occurrence in this sense need not be logically necessary—the supposition of its non-existence need not involve a contradiction. What *is* logically necessary for determinists is rather the condition expressed by the hypothetical claim that *if* certain past circumstances, or past circumstances and laws of nature, obtain, *then* the occurrence takes place. In short, the rubric "it *must* be that Y, *given* X" means "it (logically) *must* be that *if* X *then* Y." If the occurrence of E at t is determined by virtue of past circumstances and laws of nature, then it is logically necessary that if these circumstances *and* laws obtain, then E occurs at t. Or, in the language of possible worlds favored by many today, though E need not occur at t in every logically possible world whatever, E will occur at t in every logically possible world in which certain further conditions are present, namely worlds in which the relevant past circumstances and laws of nature obtain. We can thus express the relevant notion of determination in the following way:

> **D2.**   (Determination): The occurrence of a state or change E at a time t is determined if and only if there is some combination of past circumstances relative to t, or past circumstances relative to t and laws of nature, whose joint existence is a logically sufficient condition for the occurrence of E at t (where "X is a logically sufficient condition for Y" means "it is logically necessary that if X then Y.")[7]

The kind of logical necessity involved in this definition, to be more specific about it, is what Plantinga calls necessity in the "broadly logical" sense.[8] In this sense, it is logically necessary that p, if "p" is true by virtue of the laws of logic or of the meaning of its constituent terms. The latter condition ("by the meaning of its constituent terms") is important for dealing with traditional versions of logical or theological determinism, as we shall see.

Some modern writers on determinism[9] prefer to define determination in terms of propositions, sentences, or statements, and such definitions can also be related to D2. Let P be a proposition (or sentence or statement) asserting (saying) that $C_1 \ldots C_n$ are past circumstances relative to t and Q a proposition asserting that E occurs at t. If the occurrence of E at t is determined by virtue of the circumstances $C_1 \ldots C_n$ and laws of nature, $L_1 \ldots L_m$, one should be able to derive the proposition "if P then Q" from propositions expressing the laws, $L_1 \ldots L_m$. It will then turn out that the proposition "If (P and (if P then Q)) then Q," which expresses the relationship between the past circumstances and laws, on the one hand, and the occurrence of E at t, on the other, is a logical truth. This corresponds to the fact that the existence conjointly of the circumstances and laws is a logically sufficient condition for the occurrence of E.

It will thus be helpful to work with several equivalent ways of expressing what D2 asserts, a "standard" formulation (D2 itself) in terms of circumstances and laws of nature, a "semantic" formulation in terms of possible worlds, as in the first paragraph of this section, and a "propositional" formulation, as in the preceding paragraph. One of the advantages of a propositional formulation, and one of the reasons it is favored by many writers, is that it provides a way of characterizing laws of nature.

Our preanalytic views about laws of nature are based upon what we know of certain propositions of the natural sciences that purportedly express such laws. A law of nature exists whenever such a proposition is true. Despite some debate about how propositions expressing laws of nature are to be characterized, there is widespread agreement about the following necessary characteristics, which are the important ones for our purposes. Propositions expressing laws of nature must be universal, saying something about all entities or systems of entities of certain kinds at all times;[10] they must be conditional or hypothetical, saying, or implying, that if entities or systems of the specified kinds are in certain states and/or undergoing certain changes at a time they will be in some other state or undergo some other change at the same or a later time. They must be true propositions, though not logically nor analytically true, and they must support counterfactual conditional assertions (to the effect that if (contrary to fact) an entity or system had been in certain states and /or undergone certain changes, it would have been in some other state or undergone some other change). There is considerable discussion of these conditions in the literature on laws of nature, especially the last condition.[11] But rather than pursue these discussions here, I intend to deal with specific issues regarding laws of nature as subsequent arguments demand.

It should be added that D2 is so stated that it also covers those versions of determinism, like ancient doctrines of fatalism or logical determinism and later doctrines of theological determinism, which do not mention laws of nature at all. These doctrines usually specify that the existence of some past circumstance alone is a logically sufficient condition for the occurrence of E at t. Logical determinists insist, for example, that if E occurs at t, then the future tensed proposition "E will occur at t" must have been true at all times earlier than t. They insist further that the truth of this proposition at any time earlier than t is a logically sufficient condition for the occurrence of E at t. E will occur in every logically possible world in which such a proposition is true at an earlier time. (These claims are controversial, to be sure. But it is their meaning, not their truth, that concerns us for the moment.[12]) Theological determinists make similar claims about God's foreordaining or foreknowing that E will occur at t. Given certain (allegedly necessary) truths about God (namely, that God is omnipotent and the divine will is unchangeable) the fact that God foreordains that E will occur at t is logically sufficient for the occurrence of E at t; and given the infallibility of divine cognition (or simply because knowledge entails truth), God's foreknowing that E will occur at t is logically sufficient for the occurrence of E at t. E will occur at t in every logically possible world in which its occurrence is divinely ordained or known at times earlier than t.

Such views seem to be saying that occurrences can be determined by the existence of certain past circumstances alone (the truth of propositions, divine states or acts) without mentioning laws of nature. One may object, particularly in the case of theological determinism, that laws of nature are presupposed, though not mentioned. God it might be said, can infallibly foreordain and foreknow only by virtue of creating and knowing certain laws linking past and future. But even this would be a controversial claim in the light of the differing ways in which divine willing and knowing have been described in the theological tradition.[13] So, to avoid begging the question, and to accommodate logical as well as theological determinism, I have written D2 in such a way that occurrences can be determined by virtue of past circumstances alone *or* by virtue of past circumstances and laws of nature. The main point is that libertarians object to a free choice's being determined in either case. They object to the claim that free choices must occur, given the past, or given the past and nature's laws.

3.4 Determinists of all kinds, logical, theological, and scientific, may be said to hold that every occurrence is determined in the sense of D2. This statement should be regarded as an implication of determinist views, however, not as a definition of every determinist view. Determinists use different terms to define their view and some define it in stronger terms, e.g. specifying the kinds of laws and circumstances that must be involved (like the laws of mechanics and antecedent positions and momenta of particles).[14] But the varying statements of determinists all imply that every occurrence is determined in the sense of D2, and this statement therefore represents a core commitment of determinists. Moreover, it is a commitment that is critical to the free will issue because it is invariably rejected by libertarians. They want to deny that free choices or actions can be determined in the sense of D2; and denying that all choices or actions are determined in this sense, they must deny any more specific or stronger view having such an implication, in short, any form of determinism.

The relevant libertarian intuitions were expressed earlier in the words of William James, who objected that according to determinists "the future has no ambiguous possibilities hidden in its womb." For James, as for Bramhall, a free choice had to be an "ambiguous possibility" in the sense that it might not have occurred as it did occur, given the laws of nature and all that preceded it in time. We can now translate this claim into an "indeterminist condition" for free will, using the definitions D1 and D2: if an agent S is free at a time t (in the sense of D1) with respect to a choice of decision J, then

(The Indeterminist Condition—First Form): Neither S's making J at t nor S's doing otherwise at t can be determined in the sense of D2;

or using the language of D2,

(The Indeterminist Condition—Second Form): Given all past circumstances relative to t and all laws of nature, (i) it can be the case that S makes J at t, and (ii) it can be the case that S does other than make J at t (where "given X, it can be that Y" means "it logically can be that X *and* Y").[15]

This condition in both forms will play an important role in subsequent discussions. For libertarians it is only a necessary , not a sufficient, condition for free will in the sense of D1. But it is a crucial, and moreover, an extremely problematic, condition. There is, first of all, the problem of explaining why such a condition should be regarded as necessary for free will at all. And, second, there is the problem of explaining how a theory of free will can accommodate a condition of this kind without making free choices arbitrary, capricious, and irrational. The first of these problems will concern us in the remainder of this chapter. The second will be taken up in chapter 4.

3.5   Why do libertarians believe that truly free choices cannot be determined in the sense of D2? I said that our search for an answer to this question would be somewhat unusual by comparison with recent philosophical discussions, but important for an understanding of the history of the free will issue. The leading idea is suggested by some remarks of Bramhall and other traditional writers. (Cf. 1.2.) They hold that, whatever else it might imply, free will, or the dual power of the self to determine or originate its own purposes or ends, must imply that nothing *other than* the self could determine these purposes or ends. As it stands, this claim merely expresses an intuition, not a line of reasoning, and it may seem too vague to be helpful. But I think it is the key to understanding the free will issue in historical perspective and the most important clue to libertarian intuitions.

When Bramhall suggests that nothing other than the self can determine or originate its own purposes, he especially means to rule out the possibility that the free agent might be controlled or manipulated by another agent. Now there are two distinguishable kinds of control of one agent by another, which we may call "constraining control" and "non-constraining control," and the difference between them is of paramount importance for the free will issue. Constraining control takes place when the controlled agent's will is frustrated by certain conditions, customarily called "constraints," imposed by the controller, so that the agent is prevented from realizing certain wants, desires or intentions in choice or action.[16] Compatibilists, like Hobbes, have always been concerned about constraining control, since they tend to define freedom in terms of the absence of constraints. Hobbes says that a man is free when he finds no "stops" or hindrances in doing what he has the will, desire, or inclination to do (62, pp. 171-2). These "stops" or hindrances of which he speaks are conditions, like fatigue, limitations of strength, physical restraint, threats of harm, etc., which are impediments to the realization of desires and intentions. Constraining control is the creation of such constraints by an agent in order to get others to do what the agent wants.

Non-constraining control is another matter. When it takes place, the controlled agent's will is not frustrated. No conditions prevent the agent's wants, desires, and intentions from being realized in action. Nevertheless, the agent is controlled by another who has manipulated past circumstances so that the controlled agent wants, desires, and intends what the controller has planned. The fictional creator of B. F. Skinner's controversial utopian community, Walden Two, gives a clear description of such non-constraining control. In his community, he says, persons can have and do whatever they want or choose, but they have been conditioned since childhood to want and choose only what they can have and do (62, p. 263).

Now libertarians are especially concerned about non-constraining control and they want to emphasize that it also undermines freedom. That is why modern humanists with libertarian intuitions react so negatively to views like Skinner's which call for non-constraining behavioral modification and engineering in human societies. Skinner is the kind of figure libertarians would have had to invent if he did not already exist. For he extols, and promotes as social policy, one of the things that libertarians in Western culture have been most concerned to rule out when they asserted that humans have free will, namely, non-constraining control of the will by another agent.

This is not to say that constraining control does not concern libertarians. They agree that constraint undermines freedom. But this is a relatively non-controversial claim on which libertarians and compatibilists agree. It is over the possibility of forms of control other than constraining control that their views diverge. Libertarians oppose non-constraining control for reasons that are clear in Bramhall's responses to Hobbes. Where non-constraining control exists, the controlled agent is not free in the dignity-grounding sense. It is the controller and not the controlled agent who is ultimately responsible for the outcome. The controlled agent is a "staff in . . . [another's] hands." Someone other than the controlled agent is the ultimate determiner or originator of the purposes or ends that guide the controlled agent's actions. The controlled agent is a means and not an end in himself because he does not ultimately determine his own purposes or ends. He has a "kind of freedom," but not the true freedom of being an end in himself, which confers dignity on human beings.

3.6 The next step in our development of Bramhall's suggestion requires a distinction between two kinds of non-constraining control. Non-constraining control can be either overt or covert. It is overt when the controlled agent is aware of the plans or intentions of the controller (with respect to the controlled agent's choices and actions); it is covert when the controlled agent is not aware of the controller's plans or intentions.[17] In the extreme cases of covert non-constraining control, the controlled agent is not even aware that there is a controller, or that his or her choices and actions are being controlled. The covert non-constraining controller in these cases is a behind the scenes manipulator who brings about certain wants, desires, beliefs, etc., in the agent, so that the agent will choose and act as he (the controller) plans. The controlled agent may not be aware that his behavior is being controlled or even that there is a person attempting to control his behavior. He may suspect there is a controller but not be sure whether or not there is one. On the views of some theological determinists, God would be such a covert controller. Similarly, the behavior engineers in a Skinnerian utopia would be such covert controllers if the inhabitants ceased to be aware of the controllers' plans or of even their existence.

If libertarians are concerned about non-constraining control, they are especially concerned about covert non-constraining control (called "CNC control" hereafter). They want to know how the free agent can ensure against, or guarantee the absence of, CNC control of his or her will by another agent. This is an interesting problem because it is not clear how CNC control could be avoided or thwarted, even if the agent wanted to avoid or thwart it. If the control were overt the controlled agent would know what the controller intended him to choose or do. Then, if he (the controlled agent) did not acquiesce, but wanted to thwart the controller, the only further requirement would be an absence of constraints or conditions preventing him from doing what he wanted. In the absence of these constraints, if the agent wanted to thwart the controller, he could do the opposite of what the controller intended. But in the case of CNC control, even wanting to thwart the controller *and* an absence of constraints would not be enough. For the controlled agent would not know which of the unconstrained options open to him was planned or intended by the controller.

Suppose an agent wants to thwart a CNC controller. Should he make a choice or do A or a choice to do B? Let us assume that no constraints prevent him from making either choice. Nevertheless, he does not know which one to make because he does not know which will thwart the covert controller. Suppose he overwhelmingly prefers to do A rather an B. But just to be contrary, he chooses B instead. Or, hoping to thwart the controller, he chooses B instead. Will this ensure that the controller is thwarted? Not at all. The controller may have planned that he choose B all along by giving him a contrary nature, or by giving him the hope of thwarting control by choosing the least desired alternative. The controlled agent is flailing in the dark. He may try to improve his situation by going in search of the controller, hoping to decipher the controller's plans and methods. But the controlled agent is a finite creature and all his searches are finite. Failure to find a controller in a finite search does not ensure that there is no covert controller out there, beyond the next veil, knowable *perhaps,* but not yet known. How can one ensure against the possibility of such CNC control?

3.7 Fortunately, this question has an answer. There is a way to thwart *any* potential CNC controller without going on a "search and decipher" mission. The answer lies in the indeterminist condition. Suppose that neither the agent's choice or A nor the choice of B is determined by antecedent circumstances given the laws of nature in the sense of D2. This means that no potential controller could manipulate the situation in advance so that the choice necessarily comes out as the controller plans or intends. Given all antecedent circumstances, including the controller's plans and intentions, and all efforts made to carry them out, either the choice of A or the choice of B might occur. The controller could not determine which one would occur. The choice *might* come out as the controller planned or intended, but this would be by chance or accident, as one might intend to throw a six on a die and actually throw a six. It would be limited control at best and what it left open (the actual choosing of A rather than B or B rather than A) would be left to the agent. In sum, if the choice were undetermined, any potential CNC control would be thwarted. The agent would not have to know who the controller was, or even know that there was controller. There would be no need for a potentially endless search for hidden manipulators. The agent would know, *by the very nature of his free choice,* that any potential covert controller would be thwarted.

One may object that a similarly endless search and decipher mission is required to determine that a given choice is not determined, that is to say, a potentially endless search for possible antecedent causes. But there is an important difference. We do not acknowledge that certain quantum events, like electron jumps, are not determined by antecedent circumstances because we have completed an exhaustive search for antecedent causes. We acknowledge it because we have a reliable scientific theory telling us that events *of these kinds* cannot in principle be determined. They cannot in principle be determined because, according to the theory's laws, it is impossible to specify the coordinate variables of time and energy (or position and momentum) with unlimited accuracy. If the functioning of the brain were such that, as Eccles and Munn have suggested (see 1.4), quantum events could influence choices through some amplifier effect, we would have evidence by virtue of physical theory that the choices were not determined. We would in effect be ruling out the possibility in principle of CNC control by appealing to the most reliable scientific evidence at our disposal.

Of course, the scientific theory itself may turn out to be false and may be superseded. We would not have a kind of absolute certainty that is unattainable in science, or perhaps anywhere else. What we would have is reliable belief based on the best available scientific evidence and theory, and it would not require that we have investigated every antecedent circumstance. This is precisely the edge that the indeterminist condition provides in dealing with CNC control. We can establish that *present* occurrences are of such *kinds* that, theoretically, they could not be covertly controlled by other agents. There might be other theories of similar reliability to quantum theory which told us that our choices could not in principle be controlled by a CNC controller. But I suspect that any such theory, if it were scientific, would be a theory like quantum mechanics which told us that events of certain kinds could not in principle be *determined* and *therefore* could not be CNC controlled.

A second objection against the appeal to the indeterminist condition to rule out CNC control is less easily answered. One might object that the indeterminist condition, used for the purpose of ruling out CNC control, is a two-edged sword. If it thwarts control over the agent's will by other agents, it may also thwart control over the agent's will by the agent himself. This threat is a genuine one. To mention it is to restate the standard criticism against indeterminist theories of freedom mentioned in chapter 1. Indeterminism tends to undermine the power or control of agents over their own choices and actions. The problem is one that must eventually be faced. But it is important to see how it arises. In their attempt to ensure against control of the free agent's will by other agents, libertarians endanger the free agent's control over his or her own will. This is the special irony of their position. Throughout history, it has been a curse and a challenge.

3.8 What I am suggesting then (as a first move in a longer argument) is that one important reason why libertarians require the indeterminist condition is to ensure against the success of any potential covert non-constraining (CNC) control of the agent's will by another agent. It should be noted that no existing compatibilist account of freedom—a compatibilist account by definition denies the indeterminist condition—defines freedom so that this result is ensured. Compatibilists will say, for example, that an agent is free when he (or she) is not compelled, coerced, or in general forced or prevented by causal conditions, from doing what he chooses or tries to do, or from choosing or trying to do what he wants or desires. When such preventing conditions, or constraints, are absent the agent is free. But a would-be controller can get an agent to do his bidding in ways other than coercing or compelling the agent against his will. The CNC controller does this by arranging circumstances beforehand so that the agent wants and desires, and hence chooses and tries, only what the controller intends. The agent is never constrained in the sense of being made to do things he does not want or desire to do. So, in the "absence of constraint" sense, the agent would be free. But there is another sense in which the agent is "made" to do things by the controller. What is different is only the controller's choice of means, constraint or coercion vs. CNC control. The end result is the same: the agent does the controller's bidding.

The same remarks hold for compatibilist accounts of compulsive desire or willing (which is another kind of constraint on the will). Recently, there have been some advances in the philosophical treatment of this subject, following upon the work of Harry Frankfurt (71).[18] The idea is to explain cases of irrational addiction (based upon compulsive desires for alcohol, drugs, etc.) as exemplary cases of unfreedom of the will. Frankfurt characterizes the typical case of compulsive desire by saying that in such cases the agent (a) has a *second order* desire not to have the first order desire, say, for a drug and (b) a second order desire not to give in to his (or her) first order desire (for the drug), but (c) cannot resist giving in to the first order desire nonetheless. By contrast, a person's first order desire would not be compulsive if, given second order desires of the kinds (a) and (b), the agent would resist giving in to the first order desire. On this analysis, the presence of free or non-compulsive willing and acting is compatible with determinism, since the higher order desires and other required circumstances may all have been determined, even where the first order desire is resistible.

This analysis is an improvement over most earlier ones. But, precisely because of the relation to determinism, it leaves the problem of CNC control untouched. A would-be controller might proceed by producing compulsive desires in the controlled agent, as some criminals create heroin addiction in those they want to control. But this is not the only way a controller might proceed. A more sophisticated controller might avoid conditioning in terms of compulsive desires, irrational addictions, or uncontrollable cravings, altogether. The controlled agent might be so conditioned that he would resist acting on his first order desires, if he so desired. But he might also be so conditioned that he never in fact has the higher order desire to resist. The controller would get the controlled agent to do his bidding without the accompanying frustrations of the (higher order) will that go along with compulsive desiring, irrational addiction, and so on. In short, the controller would get his results by CNC control, which is compatible with the absence of compulsion, just as it is compatible with the absence of coercion and other forms of constraint.

For similar reasons, any compatibilist analysis of an agent's power to do otherwise which takes a conditional or hypothetical form (e.g. *if* the agent wanted (desired, intended, chose, tried, etc.) otherwise, the agent *would* have done otherwise) is also compatible with CNC control of the agent's will. Such conditional "would...if" analyses of the agent's powers to do and do otherwise are standard among compatibilists and they have been criticized on other grounds in recent years.[19] But I want to focus on the relation to CNC control. It does not matter which volitional term is used in the "if" clause ("want," "intend," "try," "desire" etc.). The truth of such a "would...if" statement will always be compatible with the presence of CNC control. It may be true that the agent would have chosen otherwise, if he had wanted otherwise, or, that the agent would have done otherwise, if he had tried; and it may also be true that a CNC controller arranged the antecedent circumstances so that the agent did not in fact want otherwise or try to do otherwise. It begins to look as if freedom will be compatible with CNC control on any compatibilist analysis, simply *because* on such an analysis freedom is compatible with determinism.

3.9   Compatibilists will have a response prepared to this argument. In fact, there are two possible responses open to them and we should consider both for the sake of completeness. The first—the hard line—is to concede that existing compatibilist analyses of freedom do not rule out CNC control, but to argue that CNC control does not undermine freedom in any significant or clearly definable sense. The second response—the soft line—is to concede that CNC control *does* undermine freedom in a significant sense, but to emphasize the difference between CNC control and *mere* determination, that is, determination by natural causes without purposeful control by another agent. The former takes away freedom in a significant sense, but the latter does not.

The second response is the more plausible one and is most likely to be made by modern compatibilists. It will receive the bulk of our attention. But the first has played a significant role in the history of debates about free will and deserves comment. The first response is in fact the line taken by Hobbes, Jonathan Edwards, and other predestinationists. Hobbes argued that God's foreordaining all of our choices and actions does not make any real difference to our freedoms. Since we do not *know* what God has predestined, we must have concern for our welfare, deliberating among alternatives to choose the best available, and seeking to avoid constraints, just as we would if we were not predestined (62, pp. 174-5). Edwards takes a similar line. To the question of how we could be free and responsible with respect to our sins, since God has made us the way we are, he responds that, while God created our corrupt natures, we are nevertheless responsible for the actions issuing from these corrupt natures because they are *ours* (69, p. 173).

Such predestinationist views are not as popular as they once were, even among religious thinkers. They flatter neither man or God. Bramhall seems to be right in saying that on such a view we can be free and yet a pawn in the hand of another; and this, as he insists, is counterintuitive, whether we imagine the control taking place at a spiritual or at a secular level, and whether we imagine the controller to be a God, a devil, or some very clever behavioral engineers of the Skinnerian type. In theology, there is the additional problem that troubled Bramhall, Milton, and many others, of reconciling such a view with divine justice.[20] Hobbes, be it noted, is no great defender of human freedom, in either politics or theology. He is ready to give to a political sovereign almost as much power over us as he believes the deity already has.

One of the few twentieth-century authors to give CNC control the central place in discussions of free will it deserves is John Wisdom. In a work not often read today, *Problems of Mind and Matter* (34),[21] he says:

> Suppose that all your acts are determined by your decisions and your decisions by your knowledge (no doubt imperfect) . . . together with your desires. . . . But suppose that on the occasion of each decision the strength of your various desires is fixed by the devil. Suppose that you float a bogus company and ruin thousands. Are you to blame? I believe that you are not. It is a question for inspection. I have confirmed what I seem to see from inspection by asking others to inspect the same problem. I have carefully asked this question of more than one person who was highly intelligent but sufficiently ignorant of philosophy to have no axe to grind, and have received the reply that in such a case you would not be to blame (p. 116).

I think that Wisdom is right in saying that, at this level, the matter is one of "introspection," or intuition. If a hard-core Hobbesian, or predestinationist, insists that CNC control does not take away freedom in any significant sense, there is little one can say to argue him out of his position. But *if* the dispute between compatibilists and incompatibilists were to boil down to a difference of intuitions at this point (a big "if"), I think most persons would side with Bramhall, Wisdom, and the incompatibilists. Intuitively, most of us would concede that human freedom is freedom from every kind of control by others, coercive and non-coercive, overt and covert. Most modern compatibilists are likely to agree as well, and that is why the second response to the arguments about CNC control is the one they are most likely to make.

3.10 The second response is to emphasize the difference between CNC control and mere determination (by antecedent circumstances without purposeful control by another agent) and to argue that while the former does undermine, or take away, freedom in some significant sense, the latter does not. The problem with this response is to say what "significant" kind of freedom it is that CNC control takes away, but mere determination does not. This problem is more difficult than first appearances suggest. To illustrate its subtlety, I suggest that we begin with a thought experiment.

Consider two conceivable worlds. The first, call it World 1(W1), is a completely determined world (every occurrence determined in the sense of D2) which has been created by an omnipotent and omniscient being who has planned its every detail. We imagine that in W1 there lives a man, call him Ishmael, whose lifetime begins at a time t_1 and ends at a time t_n. Ishmael makes some free choices and performs other free actions during his lifetime, at least in the usual compatibilist senses of freedom. He makes choices and performs other actions that are not coerced, constrained, or compulsive. This is not always true, of course. Like the rest of us, he sometimes cannot do what he wants. But, in any case, whether constrained or not, his every choice and action, like every other occurrence in his world, is controlled by its creator. The second world, W2, we imagine to be also a determined world, exactly like W1 down to the minutest detail except that there is no creator and designer of it. Scratch the controller

Ishmael, of course, lives in both worlds between t_1 and t_n, and his biography is identical in both. He journeys to New Bedford, listens to a sermon, joins the crew of the Pequod, and so on, in both worlds. All his thought processes, his beliefs, doubts, fears, hopes, all of his choices, intentions and actions, all physical events in his brain and body, in his environment, his genes, everything in his lifetime is exactly the same in both worlds. Moreover, all of his powers in the usual compatibilist senses are also the same. Where he is constrained in one world, he is constrained in the other; where he is unconstrained in one world he is unconstrained in the other. Whenever he has the ability, capacity or opportunity to do what he wills, desires, intends, chooses, or tries to do without interference in one world, he has the similar ability, capacity , or opportunity in the other.

Now the compatibilist who makes the second response is in an uncomfortable position vis à vis these two worlds. On the one hand, he wants to say that Ishmael is not free in an important sense in W1 (because of the CNC controller), while, on the other hand, he wants to say that Ishmael is free in W2 (because the freedom lacking in W1 is compatible with determinism). And he wants to say these things despite the fact that Ishmael's life history between the times t_1 and t_n in both worlds is exactly the same in every psychological and physical detail and all of his powers (in the usual compatibilist senses) to do what he desires, chooses, tries, etc. to do without interference are exactly the same. It is incumbent upon the respondent to say what power possessed by Ishmael in the merely determined world 2 is not possessed by him in the CNC controlled world 1.

3.11 Now what the compatibilist must say here is reasonably clear. The difference between the two worlds is that, in one of them (W1) but not the other, Ishmael's choices are determined by the intentional actions, and hence the will, of another rational agent. Thus, when asked what powers are possessed in the merely determined world 2 that are not possessed in world 1, the compatibilist can reply as follows. Whenever Ishmael has the power in W2 to perform a certain action X (to journey to New Bedford, to join the crew of the Pequod) in the sense that the action is not coerced, compelled, or otherwise constrained, he has the additional power in W2 to perform X-"free-of"- (or,"in-the-absence-of"-) non-constraining-control-by-another-agent, or, the power to perform X-without-X's-being-CNC-controlled-by-another-agent. With respect to every such action X (journeying to New Bedford, etc.) Ishmael has the power to perform X in the CNC controlled world 1 as well, but he does not have this additional hyphenated power to perform X-without-being-CNC-controlled. (Note also that it is covert non-constraining control that is the difference. For it can be assumed, without affecting the argument, that Ishmael has the power to thwart an overt non-constraining controller in both worlds and would do so if he wanted to. It is the CNC controller he cannot cope with.)

On the face of it, this compatibilist answer seems *ad hoc*. The problem was to explain what kind of power it is that CNC control takes away from the controlled agent and mere determination does not take away. And what the compatibilist is saying in terms of these hyphenated powers is that the kind of freedom in question is "just the kind of freedom that CNC takes away but mere determination does not." Nonetheless, even if compatibilists can do no better in describing the differences in powers between the two worlds (and I think they cannot), they need not be disturbed. For the appeal to these hyphenated powers is merely a device for bringing into the open the bedrock distinction upon which compatibilists must rest their case. In the controlled world 1, all of Ishmael's choices and actions are determined by the actions of a rational agent or intelligent designer, while, in the merely determined world 2, this is not so. The all important distinction for the compatibilist is between "determination by a personal being or intelligent designer" and "determination by impersonal or natural causes." The former takes away freedom for them, the latter does not.

By contrast, libertarians will say that the distinctions, intelligent vs. non-intelligent, personal vs. non-personal, are comparatively insignificant in view of the fact that in both worlds Ishmael's choices and actions are necessitated by circumstances obtaining before his birth. For this means that in both worlds he lacks "dominion over his own will" or the power to "originate the purposes or ends that guide his actions," and *this*, according to libertarians, is the significant power that CNC control takes away.

We are at the vital center of the free will issue at this point. There is a conflict of intuitions here that is not easily resolved. It is a mistake to say that the compatibilist position is simply an "evasion" with no intuitive support. But it is also a mistake to say that incompatibilists are guilty of some obvious error or omission. The familiar charge of compatibilists, from Hobbes and Hume to Schlick and Ayer, is that incompatibilists have failed to distinguish between *constraint* (determination or causation impeding the will) and *mere determination* or causation (not impeding the will). The former takes away freedom, they say, the latter does not. But the distinction between constraint and mere determination, though important, is not the pivotal one for the free will issue. The pivotal distinction is between CNC control and mere determination, and this is a considerably more subtle distinction because *neither* CNC control nor mere determination thwarts the agent's will.

3.12   While the conflict of intuitions over CNC control and mere determination is not easily resolved, there is more to be said about it, on both sides. With this in mind, let us turn to a second thought experiment, one that requires a return to the distinction between constraining and non-constraining control. Imagine a society of primitive animists who believe that, whenever they are constrained, or prevented from doing what they desire by circumstances, these circumstances have been intentionally arranged by invisible gods or spirits. In other words, these people interpret all forms of constraint against their wills as forms of *covert constraining* (or CC) control of their wills by other agents. An interesting analogy can be drawn between CC control and mere constraint (without the gods or spirits), on the one hand, and CNC control and mere determination, on the other.

CC Control	Intelligent Design	Both thwart the will
Mere Constraint	Impersonal Forces	
CNC Control	Intelligent Design	Neither thwarts the will
Mere Determination	Impersonal Forces	

The operative contrast within each pair is the intelligent-non-intelligent, personal-impersonal, contrast of which we spoke in the previous section. The operative contrast between the pairs is that of thwarting vs. not thwarting the agent's will, which distinguishes constraining control from non-constraining control and distinguishes (mere) constraint from (mere) determination.

Now let us suppose that a plague of philosophers descends upon this primitive animist society, corrupting the youth and challenging the traditional belief in the gods or spirits. The philosophers finally convince the populace that the gods or spirits do not exist and that their frustrations are due to natural causes, not to the intelligent design of personal beings. Suppose, further, that one of the populace reasons as follows: "In our society we learned from childhood to use the word 'free' in such a way that a man was free whenever he was not subject to constraining control by another agent, including a god or spirit. Now you philosophers have convinced us that in many cases where we thought we were subject to such control, in fact we were not, because the alleged controllers (the gods or spirits) do not exist. It would appear that we were, and are, a good deal more free (free with respect to many more actions) than we had previously believed."

This reasoning parallels the reasoning of the compatibilist vis à vis CNC control. It is correct in the same way and also, one might argue, irrelevant in the same way. It is correct because *if* you *define* a certain kind of freedom as the absence of CC control (or CNC control), i.e. as the power to act free of, or in the absence of, CC (or CNC) control, then it will follow that an agent possesses this kind of freedom in a merely constrained (or merely determined) world, though not in a CC (CNC) controlled world. It is irrelevant because the additional freedom in the merely constrained world, i.e. the freedom to act "free of" or "in the absence of" CC control is insignificant compared with the freedom that is lacking in both worlds (i.e. the freedom to do what one wants without interference, either by personal or impersonal forces).

To the obstinate animist who wants to go on using the term "free" in the old way, a philosopher might respond as follows: "You have not looked deeply enough into the situation. Covert constraining control by the gods made you unfree *because* it was constraining. If the gods had been bumbling and ineffective in their attempts to create circumstances preventing you from doing what you willed, then you would to that degree have been free. If now we tell you that all along these constraining or preventing circumstances were created by natural forces and not by the gods, you are not to infer that you were more free all along. Your view is overly anthropocentric. You think that a person can be unfree, only because of the actions of another intelligent agent."

Compare the following response: "You (compatibilists) have not looked deeply enough into the situation. Covert non-constraining control by a controller made you unfree *because* it was *determining*. If the controller had been bumbling and ineffective in his attempts to create circumstances *determining what you willed*, then your will to that degree would have been free. If now we tell you that all along there was no controller, but the determining circumstances were created by natural forces, you are not to infer that you were more free all along. Your view is overly anthropocentric. You think that a person can be unfree, only because of the actions of another intelligent agent."

3.13   This is an interesting result: the obstinate animist is using the same line of reasoning to resist the move from

(1) CC control takes away an agent's freedom in some significant sense,

to

(2) Mere constraint takes away an agent's freedom in the same sense (as 1),

as the compatibilist uses to resist the move from

(3) CNC control takes away an agent's freedom in some significant sense,

to

(4) Mere determination takes away an agent's freedom in the same sense (as 3).

Mere determination stands in the same relation to CNC control as mere constraint to CC control, that is, CC control takes away freedom because it is constraining, CNC control because it is determining. But while the obstinate animist's resistance to the move from (1) to (2) is likely to be regarded as reactionary and anthropocentric, the compatibilist's position is likely to be regarded nowadays as the latest in sophistication.

Nevertheless, there is more to the situation than this description suggests. For the move from (3) to (4) is in fact more subtle and problematic than the move from (1) to (2), though the parallels are pervasive and instructive. One difference is that constraint takes away an agent's freedom in a more obvious and understandable way than determination, making the move from (1) to (2) easier to accept, at least psychologically. Against the obstinate animist who is resisting the move from (1) to (2) the philosopher could say: "Take John over there with the club foot. What additional powers of any significance does he have if it turns out that his club foot was caused by heredity or other physical causes rather than by the design of gods or spirits? Can he run any faster, leap any higher? Can he participate in the tribal dances? Can he . . . ?" Such a reply is likely to be effective because it is comparatively easy to see that mere constraint takes away an agent's freedom in an important sense. Where an agent is prevented from doing what he sometimes desperately wants to do, the difference between being so prevented by natural causes or by intelligent design seems relatively insignificant. What matters in both cases is that *he cannot do anything about his situation.*

But this fact about mere constraint does not undermine the analogy. If mere constraint takes away freedom in an obvious sense, this is because it frustrates the agent's will. This feature of constraint, however, distinguishes it from *both* CNC control and mere determination. One cannot very well say that mere determination does not take away an agent's freedom because the agent does not feel frustrated, since the agent does not feel frustrated when CNC controlled either. That is, one cannot say this unless one wants to return to the hard compatibilist line of Hobbes and Edwards, and say that CNC control does not take away an agent's freedom in any significant sense.

But while this fact (that constraint takes away freedom in an obvious sense) does not undermine the analogy, it does point to a deeper difficulty. In the case of CC control and mere constraint, there is a recognizable and definable kind of freedom (to do what one wills or wants) that they both take away, whose importance overshadows the kind of freedom (to do something-without-being-CC-controlled-(by-another-agent)) that one takes away but the other does not. By contrast, in the case of CNC control and mere determination, it is not clear that there is a recognizable and definable kind of freedom that they both take away whose importance overshadows the kind of freedom (to do something-without-being-CNC-controlled-(by-another-agent)) that one takes away and the other does not. This is the crux of the matter and it is the reason why the move from (3) to (4) is more problematic than the move from (1) to (2). The compatibilist objector's introduction of hyphenated powers to distinguish CNC control and mere determination is no less *ad hoc* than the obstinate animist's similar introduction of hyphenated powers to distinguish CC control and mere constraint. But libertarians lack an effective countermove as long as they cannot specify and define the kind of freedom that is taken away by both CNC control and mere determination.

3.14   Libertarians have tried to meet this challenge. They argue that just as both CC control and constraint take away the power to do what one wills, so both CNC control and determination take away a power that is variously described by Bramhall and others as a "dominion" over what one wills, or "over one's own will," a "power to determine oneself, or one's own will," a "power to originate the purposes or ends that guide one's actions," or as a "control over the springs of one's own action."[22] The problem is to explain what such expressions mean and just why they must describe a power that is incompatible with mere determination.

For there is a sense in which, even for compatibilists, an agent can have "dominion over his own will" or "control over the springs of his own action." In a determined world, an agent may have partly formed or influenced his *present* character and motives by *past* choices and actions. This is a favorite theme of compatibilists who are anxious to emphasize that even in a determined world an agent can have considerable control over the formation of his own character and will, as well as having the power to do what he wills, It is a favorite theme of J. S. Mill, for example, who argues as follows against libertarians: "The true doctrine of the Causation of human actions maintains . . . that not only our conduct, but our character is in part amenable to our will; that we can by employing the proper means, improve our character; and that if our character is such that while it remains what it is, it necessitates us to do wrong, it will be just to apply motives that will necessitate us to strive for its improvement" (62, p. 66). Although we have no control over our initial character, Mill admits, we have the power to alter it later, within limits, if we want to.

But these powers of which Mill speaks, to alter our given character or motives, if we want to, are conditional, "would . . . if" powers, and their possession, as Mill readily admits, is compatible with determinism. Indeed, he insists upon the fact. (Compare Hobbes' remark "And if a man determines himself, the question will still remain, what determined him to determine himself in that manner?" (44, p. 51). But what else, Mill asks, could it mean to say that an agent has control over the springs of his own action? Could it mean that the agent has control over the formation of his *original* character traits and motives, those earliest developed in childhood? If this is what defenders of free will have in mind, Mill responds, they are demanding a power no person can in principle have. Original character traits and motives are by definition precisely those we did not choose on the basis of still earlier formed character traits and motives. We may change them later by conscious choices and efforts. But it is a matter of meaning that we cannot have originally formed them by conscious choices and efforts, that we cannot have brought them into being by our rational will.

Mill and modern writers who emphasize this latter point are surely right.[23] By power or dominion over one's own will, libertarians cannot mean the power to form original character and motives. Nor can they mean Mill's conditional powers to alter given character and motives, if we want to. For these are compatible with determinism and *CNC control*. What then do they mean? And how is the indeterminist condition involved? Unless these questions can be answered the libertarians' case must be incomplete.

3.15   These questions do have an answer, I believe, but it will take most of Part II to adequately spell out that answer. The notion of dominion over one's own will that libertarians seek can be interpreted without supposing it to involve power over the formation of original character and without supposing that it is compatible with determinism. What libertarians want to say is that the free agent is the sole or ultimate cause of his or her choices or motives in the sense that the *only* explanation for why the agent made a given choice rather than not is that the agent rationally willed to do so. No explanation can be adequate that does not refer to the agent's rational will. The condition they want to ascribe to a truly free will in the sense of D1, over and above the requirement that it be unconstrained, may be called

D3.   (The Condition of Sole or Ultimate Dominion): An agent's power (or control) over a choice at a time t satisfies the condition of sole or ultimate dominion if and only if (i) the agent's making the choice rather than doing otherwise (or vice versa, i.e. doing otherwise rather than making the choice) can be explained by saying that the agent rationally willed at t to do so, and (ii) no further explanation can be given for the agent's choosing rather than doing otherwise (or vice versa), or of the agent's rationally willing at t to do so, that is an explanation in terms of conditions whose existence cannot be explained by the agent's choosing or rationally willing something at t.

A good deal more will be said about this condition as we proceed; and at least one variation will be rung on it in chapter 6 to accommodate higher order willings or choosings. But the general import of the condition ought to be clear: the agent's choosing or doing otherwise at a time is to be explicable by reference to the agent's rational will (in terms of what the agent "rationally willed at t to do") *and by nothing else*. To say that the agent "rationally willed at t to do so" is to say that the agent "endorsed reasons or motives at t for doing so over reasons for doing otherwise." More will be said about reasons and motives, and about explanations in terms of reasons and motives, in the next chapter, and the notion of "endorsement" of reasons or motives will be discussed in chapters 5 and 6.

Despite the need to clarify some of these terms, I think one can see that a freedom satisfying the condition defined by D3 would be something taken away by both CNC control and mere determination by natural (non-intelligent) causes. If an agent's choice were determined by CNC control or by non-intelligent causes, there would be an explanation for why the agent made the choice he or she did rather than doing otherwise, in terms of antecedent circumstances whose existence was not explained by the agent's rationally willing something at t, an explanation either in the reasons or motives of another agent, or in natural circumstances not expressing the will of any rational agent whatever. In such cases, there might *also* be an explanation for why the agent chose as he or she did in terms of the agent's own will (reasons or motives). But this explanation in terms of the agent's will would not be the *sole* explanation of why the agent chose as he or she did.

I think D3 expresses the requirement Bramhall and other libertarians had in mind when they talked about free agents being the sole or ultimate causes of their choices, or having ultimate control over the springs of their actions. The idea that a free choice must be solely and ultimately one's own product, as G. H. Hardie (57) and Michael Slote (80) have said, is what explains the significance of the expression "one's own" in the longer expression "of one's own free will." Compatibilists often inform us that even if our actions were determined, they could still be explained in terms of our rational wills (as the results of our deliberation and reasoned choices). Libertarians do (or should at least) concede this. The libertarian's concern lies elsewhere—with the requirement that the explanation of our choice in terms of our rational wills not only explain the choice, but be the sole explanation of it. This is the crux of the matter.

In addition, libertarians have often associated this idea of sole or ultimate dominion with a notion of "ultimate responsibility." Now the notion of responsibility in general is complex, and there is an enormous literature on it in moral philosophy and the philosophy of law.[24] But to understand the libertarian position on responsibility, one has to take note of the fact that libertarians are primarily interested in a special sense of responsibility associated with sole or ultimate dominion. An agent is "ultimately responsible" for a choice in this sense, if and only if, the choice is unconstrained *and* the agent has sole or ultimate dominion over it, so that the choice (or the doing otherwise, whichever occurs) can be explained by the agent's rational will and by nothing else. Libertarians do not want to deny that there are other senses of responsibility related to the compatibilist notions of power. In everyday contexts, for example, physical incapacitation, duress, coercion, compulsion, and other forms of constraint can be accepted as conditions excusing a person from responsibility in one or another of these compatibilist senses. But libertarians want to insist that there is also an ultimate responsibility agents may have that requires sole or ultimate dominion in a sense that is not compatible with determinism.[25]

Having arrived at the condition defined by D3, this chapter will end on an uncertain note. For there is a twofold uncertainty associated with the condition of sole or ultimate dominion. First, can a notion of freedom satisfying this condition be formulated without confusion or emptiness? Second, once formulated. would the freedom so described be something we should want to possess? How important is sole or ultimate dominion and why do libertarians think it important? The questions about importance have answers, but it is unwise to try to answer them before having an answer to the first question, about the intelligibility of a theory of freedom satisfying the condition. Hobbes insists against Bramhall that it is presumptuous to talk about the importance of a kind of freedom if you cannot say what it is or even whether it is possible. Thus, debates about incompatibility tend to stalemate over the intelligibility issue, and the latter must be faced if progress is to be made.

3.16 The argument of this chapter may best be reviewed by returning to the sequence of statements in 3.13: (1) CC control takes away freedom in some significant sense; (2) mere constraint takes away freedom in the same sense (as 1); (3) CNC control takes away freedom in some significant sense; (4) mere determination takes away freedom in the same sense (as 3). I have been arguing that we may look upon these statements as representing increasingly sophisticated stages of knowledge about the kinds of circumstances that can undermine an agent's freedom. Each state presupposes earlier ones but goes further. The first is the primitive animist stage in which coercive control by other agents alone is recognized as undermining freedom. The second stage is one of refined common sense, in which mere constraint by natural causes is also recognized as undermining freedom. Agreement is widespread about these two stages and it certainly exists among most compatibilists and libertarians.

The move from (2) to (3) is pivotal and more controversial. Introducing the idea of covert non-constraining control by another agent raises issues that are not dealt with by common sense talk of freedom solely in terms of absence of coercion, compulsion and other forms of constraint. CNC control is a key to understanding the free will issue in its historical context and the most significant clue to libertarian intuitions. Its importance explains why the free will issue took on a special urgency in Western culture with the rise of Christianity and the widespread acceptance of Judaeo-Christian monotheism. Such a monotheism presupposed the existence of an actual being who had the necessary power to play the role of a CNC controller. Whether this being did actually play such a role became a matter of continuing controversy in Western culture and in other cultures with monotheistic beliefs (in Islam, for example, and among those schools of Indian philosophy in which the ultimate reality, or Brahman, was understood in personal terms).

But the free will issue is not merely a monotheistic, or even merely a religious, issue. It takes on a special urgency in monotheistic cultures because of the belief in being capable of CNC control. But the need to move beyond (1) and (2), to (3) and (4), can be, and has been, recognized without benefit of monotheistic belief. Libertarian and incompatibilist views of freedom have been defended without benefit of theistic beliefs among the ancients, for example by Epicurus and Carneades, and among the moderns by non-theistic humanists like Sartre and by hard determinists who are trying to prove that humans are not free in any significant sense. The point is that while reflection on CNC control represents an important clue to libertarian intuitions it must point beyond itself to a kind of freedom that determinism itself would take away. The move from (2) to (3) is pivotal for the free will issue, but it is not the final move. The final and still more controversial move is from (3) to (4).

The bridge from (3) to (4) is the *pons asinorum* of the free will issue. But, in this case, it is hard to decide who the fool is, the one who crosses (the incompatibilist) or the one who stays behind (the compatibilist). Some compatibilists, like Hobbes, Edwards, and other predestinationists, refuse even to make the move from (2) to

(3). They may be called "hard compatibilists." The claim that CNC control does not take away freedom in any significant sense is indeed a hard saying, and most persons, including present day compatibilists, are likely to reject it as argued. By contrast, those who concede (3), that CNC control undermines freedom, while refusing to accept (4), are "soft compatibilists." The soft compatibilist view is more plausible, I argued, and more difficult to deal with. I tried to deal with it in several stages, first discussing the thought experiment about Ishmael and the two worlds (3.10-11), then drawing the analogy with CC control and constraint (3.12-13), and finally defining a kind of power that both CNC control and mere determination take away (3.15). These discussions were designed to show that the move from (3) to (4) is no less reasonable than the move from (1) to (2), *if* one thinks the kind of power defined by D3 is intelligible and significant.

Notes

1. E.g. by Ginet (66), R. Taylor (62), Wiggins (73), van Inwagen (74 and 75), Lamb (77). For a criticism of the strategy of these arguments see Slote (82). Boyle *et al.* (76) offer a different sort of argument, but it also leads to questions about the interpretation of "could have chosen otherwise." Some other recent arguments bearing on the issue are mentioned in the following note.

2. One line of defense of an incompatibilist interpretation of this expression was initiated by J. L. Austin (66) and developed at length by M. R. Ayers (68). Another line is taken by Chisholm (66a and 67) and Lehrer (63-4 and 76), among others. For discussion and criticism of these lines of argument see Ofstad (67), Nathan (76), L. Davis (79), R. Bradley (62), D. Locke (62), Whitely (62-3), Aune (67), Mayo (68), Hunter (68), Graham (72), and the essays in Brand (70). These works have useful bibliographical references to other works in the large literature on this subject.

3. The criterion as stated is in need of some refinement, but the basic idea of change expressed by it is sufficient for our purposes. The main refinement (required to deal with problems of continuity and periodicity) would involve saying that the changed object possesses an attribute during some finite continuous interval immediately after t that it did not possess during some finite continuous interval immediately prior to t. The intervals are "immediately" before and after t in the sense that there are no moments between any moment on the intervals and t itself.

4. Ascriptions of state may also be dispositional in the sense that they may imply a difference in an object, if certain circumstances were to obtain. But they do not imply an actual difference.

5. It should be clear that states and changes as understood here correspond to what many call states of affairs, and occurrences of states or changes to facts or existing states of affairs.

6. As I use the term "circumstance" in general, it is a synonym for "occurrence." But I use it mostly to describe past, potentially determining occurrences because many writers on free will so use it. There are some subtle problems about the ways we describe past occurrences that can cause trouble here. Consider for example, the two sentences (a) "Moses Mendelssohn was born in 1723" and (b) "The grandfather of Felix Mendelssohn was born in 1723." The former is true after the birth of M. M. in 1723, but the latter does not become true until F. M. is born in 1791. We do not want to say, therefore, that (b) correctly describes the past until F. M. is born, or in general, that sentences like (b) with future reference correctly describe past circumstances until such time as they can be truly asserted. For more on this see Gale (67) and Rescher and Robison (66).

7. A question may arise here about the requirement that *all* of the determining circumstances must be past or prior circumstances. Since scientific laws allow simultaneous causal circumstances, some definitions of determinism merely require that no determining circumstance can come after

the determined occurrence. Cf. Berofsky (71). But this will not do unless one adds that all simultaneous causes essential for the occurrence of a given state or change E must be determined by some other circumstances *all* of which are past. If this were not so, some simultaneous cause essential for the occurrence of E might either occur or not occur given the entire past, and thus E might occur or not occur given the entire past. But this possibility of occurring or not occurring given the entire past is precisely what determinists want to disallow and libertarians want to affirm for free choices or actions. If, on the other hand, every simultaneous cause essential for the occurrence of E is determined by circumstances all of which are past, then E will be determined by circumstances all of which are past. Thus, while simultaneous causal circumstances, and laws expressing functional relations between simultaneous conditions, are important in scientific explanations, it is the ability to trace all causal circumstances back into the past that is essential for determinists. On this point, see Kim (71) and Lamb (77). Both of these papers also suggest the need for a further requirement concerning past circumstances (something like the requirement that all determining circumstances must be earlier than t by some fixed finite time interval, however small). I have avoided this addition in D2 because it would merely complicate subsequent arguments without changing their outcome in any substantial way. The problem it addresses, discussed by Kim and Lamb, is a rather peculiar one, and no one, to my knowledge, has shown that it tips the balance one way or the other in the free will debate.

8. For the record, we can assume (also following Plantinga) that necessity in this broadly logical sense is most reasonably formalized in a standard system of modal logic like C. I. Lewis' S5. But no subsequent argument depends upon a detailed knowledge of this system. Nor would any arguments be substantially affected if one assumed a weaker standard modal system like T or S4. On these modal systems, see Hughes and Cresswell (68); and for some general points about logical necessity assumed here, see Plantinga (74), chap. 1. D2 expresses what some would call "historical necessity." Interesting formal treatments of this idea are given in Thomason (70) and Kamp (74).

9. The most elaborate effort along these lines is Berofsky (71), which provides much useful background to this section. A similar approach is taken by those who, like Montague (63), define determinism in terms of "deterministic *theories.*"

10. This condition is not meant to be interpreted so that it rules out statistical laws. A law may be universal—about all entities and all times—and yet say that if the entities are in certain states at certain times, there is some probability less than certainty that they will be in some other state at the same or a latter time. In short, statistical generalizations, like those of quantum physics, may express laws of nature, if they hold for all entities of certain kinds at all times. But, of course, if some occurrences are explicable only in terms of statistical laws, determinism will not be true.

11. While almost all writers on laws of nature agree that they support counter factuals, there remain differences about (a) why laws of nature do so and (b) how counterfactuals are to be analyzed. Concerning (a), the main differences revolve around the longstanding controversy between "necessity" and "regularity (or Humean)" theories of laws. For a discussion of this in relation to counterfactuals, see Berofsky (71) and Mackie (74), chap. 8, both of which have references to other works. My plan is to revert to these discussions only if and where subsequent arguments demand. On the analysis of counterfactuals, we shall follow the approach of Stalnaker (75) as developed by D. Lewis (73). Though there are controversies over the particulars of the Stalnaker-Lewis approach, these do not substantially affect our arguments.

12. There will be further discussion of theological determinism in this chapter and later ones. See, especially 5.10 and 9.8.

13. It has been held, for example, that God knows all occurrences immediately and non-inferentially, and is in this respect unlike a Laplacean demon who knows the future by knowing past circumstances and laws of nature, and drawing inferences on the basis of this knowledge. Cf. 9.8.

14. D2 requires only that there be some combination of past circumstances, or past circumstances and laws, logically sufficient for the determined occurrence. Many doctrines of determinism, including logical and theological ones, imply that every future occurrence is necessitated by occurrences obtaining at any given past time.

15. I.e. for any set of actual past circumstances, $C_1 \ldots C_n$, and laws, $L_1 \ldots L_m$, it is logically

possible that $C_1 \ldots C_n$ and $L_1 \ldots L_n$ obtain and S makes J at t, and it is logically possible that $C_1 \ldots C_n$ and $L_1 \ldots L_m$ obtain and S does other than make J at t.

16. When discussing certain kinds of constraint, notably coercion and compulsion, one must take care in specifying the wants or desires frustrated or "prevented." In the case of coercion, for example (which is a kind of constraining control) the controlled agent is faced with a threat of harm or prospect of hardship making some option less desirable that would otherwise have been preferred. See, e.g. Nozick (69) and Frankfurt (73). In the case of compulsion, the frustrated desire must be a "higher order" desire. For more on compulsion, see section 8 of this chapter.

17. This covert-overt distinction also applies, of course, to *constraining* control. More will be said about covert constraining control in sections 12 and 13 of this chapter.

18. Similar views are developed by Neely (74), Watson (754) and G. Dworkin (70). For critical discussion of the approach see Slote (80).

19. See the references in note 2 of this chapter.

20. Bramhall (44, pp. 80-1, 104-5, 308); Milton (36, pp. 927 ff).

21. This reference to Wisdom was brought to my attention by Wilfrid Sellars during a discussion of the arguments of this chapter. Subsequently I found a brief, but approving, reference to Wisdom's discussion in Shaw (79). Gendron (77), ch. 6) also deals with the problem in a somewhat different context.

22. Bramhall (44, pp. 24, 150-51). See also Reid (70), C. Campbell (67), R. Taylor (74), Farrer (58), and Franklin (70).

23. Broad (62), P. Edwards (58), Hospers (58 and 61), Nielsen (71).

24. Generally speaking, responsibility is accountability or answerability to certain norms or normative principles of behavior. To be responsible is to be deserving of merit or blame for conforming or not conforming to these norms or principles. Thus there are different kinds of responsibility (legal, moral, etc.) depending upon the different kinds of norms involved. Important general discussions of legal and moral responsibility along these lines include Hart (73), Glover (70), Roberts (65), and Kaufman (67). Ofstad (61) emphasizes issues about responsibility in his book on free will. Useful papers relating free will and responsibility include Feinberg (65), Fingarette (66), and Audi (74).

25. More will be said about this notion of ultimate responsibility in Part II, especially in chapters 8 and 9. I am assuming that ultimate responsibility presupposes ultimate power (or dominion) over the choosing *and* doing otherwise. Of late there has been a controversy inspired by Frankfurt (69) about whether moral responsibility for an action always implies the power to do otherwise. Frankfurt imagines a peculiar kind of controller who wants an agent to do A, but waits to see if the agent will do A on his own before interfering. Only if the agent is not going to do A will the controller intervene and make him do A. (This controller, Frankfurt assumes, is powerful enough to make the agent do A without fail.) Frankfurt argues that in this situation, the agent cannot do other than A. Yet the agent can be responsible for doing A, if he does A on his own without interference from the controller. The agent is responsible even though, strictly speaking, he cannot do otherwise. It is interesting to ask what would happen to a Frankfurt controller if the conditions for sole or ultimate dominion were satisfied. We would have to talk about choices, first of all, rather than actions. The Frankfurt controller would wait to see if the agent was going to choose A on his own before intervening to make him choose A. But if the agent has sole or ultimate dominion over the choice of A, then neither the choosing of A nor the doing otherwise can be determined. This means that Frankfurt controller cannot tell until the moment of choice itself whether the agent is going to choose A or do otherwise. If the controller wants to ensure that the choice of A is made he must act *in advance* to bring it about. But if he does this the agent will not be responsible because the agent's choice will have been controlled by the controller. Thus, if sole or ultimate dominion, and hence also the indeterminist condition, are satisfied, the Frankfurt controller is thwarted in his plans. If he alters his plans, controlling the choice of A in advance so that the indeterminist condition fails, then the agent is not responsible because his choice is controlled by another. For useful discussion of Frankfurt's paper, see D. Blumenfeld (71), van Inwagen (78) and Fischer (82).

Special Cause Strategies

4.1 In chapter 3, we asked why indeterminism is thought to be a necessary condition for freedom of will. In this chapter, we turn to the problems created by the requirement of indeterminism for any theory of freedom. This means returning to the Hobbesian path 2 dilemma described at the end of chapter 2, according to which any account of the will's ultimate dominion over itself presupposing indeterminism will lead either to the confusion of identifying freedom with indeterminism or to the emptiness of postulating obscure or mysterious forms of agency or causation. This chapter looks at both sides of this dilemma, beginning with the alleged confusion of identifying freedom with indeterminism, and it considers various libertarian attempts to resolve the dilemma. A number of ideas of the chapter will reappear in Part II. For, while I think all previous libertarian theories fail to resolve the Hobbesian dilemma, many of them have something to contribute to its resolution. They are pieces of a larger puzzle, as we shall see.

The charge that confusion is involved in identifying freedom with indeterminism is heard more frequently after Hobbes. It is repeated by Edwards, Hume, Schopenhauer, J. S. Mill, Brentano and F. H. Bradley, and more recently by Schlick, Ayer, and Nowell-Smith, and many others. Bradley, for example, says that, according to theories of free will that presuppose indeterminism, "the will is not determined to act by anything *else*; and further it is not determined to act by anything *at all*. . . . Freedom means *chance*; you are free because there is no reason which will account for your particular acts, because no one in the world, not even yourself, can possibly say what you will, or will not do, next" (59, p. 11). Others make similar claims. The undetermined choice is variously called "arbitrary," "capricious," "random," "irrational," and "inexplicable"; and it is said that, as a consequence of this arbitrariness, the agent lacks control over the undetermined choice and cannot be held accountable for it.

What sort of an argument lies behind these charges? Assume, first, that the indeterminist condition is satisfied for a free choice in the sense of D1. This means that the agent may either make the choice or do otherwise given all the same past circumstances and laws of nature. Assume further that the past circumstances include the entire psychological history of the agent prior to choice (as well as a complete account of his or her physiology and environment) and thus all of the agent's earlier formed character traits, prior decisions, processes of reasoning, experiences, motives, and so on. We shall see that many libertarians would deny this second assumption. One of the most common libertarian strategies is to exempt from the category of "past circumstances" certain features of the agent's prior psychological history (items, for example, like volitions, or choices, or reasons for action) because they are not the sorts of things that could determine (cause) or be determined (caused) in the sense of D2. Such a strategy has its problems, as we shall see. But our task at this stage is to understand the initial charges of arbitrariness and irrationality against the indeterminist condition, before considering more or less sophisticated libertarian attempts to respond to these charges. We must first ask what consequences are alleged to follow if this assumption about the psychological history of the agent is made.

Some awkward consequences do seem to follow. If the agent might either make a choice or do otherwise, given all the same past circumstances, and the past circumstances include the entire psychological history of the agent, it would seem that no explanation in terms of the agent's psychological history, including prior character, motives and deliberation, could account for the actual occurrence of one outcome *rather than* the other, i.e. for the choosing rather than doing otherwise, or vice versa. The occurrence of one outcome rather than the other would be "inexplicable," "arbitrary," or "irrational" *relative to* the agent's psychological history prior to choice, and would be neither predictable nor controllable by prior motives and deliberation. The indeterminist condition seems to sever the connection between a present choice, on the one hand, and the person that the agent has become prior to choice, on the other,[1] or the connection between the present choice, on the one hand, and the rational deliberative processes that may have preceded choice, on the other. For the outcome may be different (choosing or doing otherwise), though the psychological history is the same. Hence, the difference of outcome (the choosing rather than doing otherwise, or vice versa) cannot be explained by a difference in the psychological history.

This is a powerful argument, but a deceptively simple one, deserving more careful analysis than it usually receives. There is a tendency, not confined to textbook discussions of the free will issue, to make the charges of arbitrariness and irrationality against indeterminist theories of freedom with rhetorical flourishes (like Bradley's just quoted), and then to move quickly on to criticize libertarian responses in terms of agent causation, transempirical power centers, and so on. We must proceed more cautiously. Since the claim is that the indeterminist condition severs the connection between the choice outcome, on the one hand, and such things as prior deliberation and prior reasons or motives, on the other, I want to say something further about the process of deliberation (in 4.2) and about reasons and motives (in 4.3). This will allow us to state the case against the indeterminist condition more accurately in 4.4 and then to assess it.

4.2   Deliberation as defined in 2.3 is not a simple process of deductive reasoning, though it may involve deductive reasoning. It is similar in some respects to the thought experimentation that is characteristic of processes of scientific discovery, as the following example will show. For some days now I have been deliberating about whether to send my youngest son by airplane across the country to visit his grandmother this summer, or whether to go with him. I have been considering the possible and probable consequences of each option, the conditions that must be satisfied if either is to be realized, and assessing these consequences and conditions in terms of my wants, preferences, other intentions, concerns for my son and mother, etc. This means considering, among other things, the cost of airfare, the difficulties of a child traveling alone, my own alternative plans for the summer and the possible conflicts that might arise between a headstrong young boy and a headstrong older woman, without a mediator who knows them both. Often the process involves the mental construction of possible and probable scenarios which are then assessed. For example, I have been imagining situations that might lead to difficulties for my mother in caring for, or disciplining, the boy if I am not there. To construct and assess such scenarios, I must draw upon background knowledge of, and beliefs about, the persons and places involved, including knowledge of their capacities, tendencies, characters and inclinations, factual and causal beliefs, estimates of probabilities, and so on.

In general, this deliberation, like others, involves the consideration of postulated *options* (sending the boy alone or going with him) in terms of conditions (*means*) required to realize the options (money for airfare) and possible and probable *consequences* of the options. Background knowledge and beliefs are involved in the determination of means and consequences, and the means and consequences are then the subjects of *assessments* in terms of wants, preferences, purposes, normative beliefs, etc. Imagination is often involved in the construction of scenarios that define and allow one to assess the means and consequences of the different options.

The entire process may be compared to the thought experimentation characteristic of processes of scientific discovery, with the options corresponding to hypotheses considered, and the means and consequences of the options corresponding respectively to the presuppositions and consequences of the hypotheses. The major, though not the only, difference between the two processes has to do with the nature of the assessments. Personal wants, desires, concerns, purposes and values play a more important role in the assessments of options, means and consequences in deliberation than they are supposed to play in the assessments of hypotheses in theoretical reasoning. We shall have more to say about this difference later.

4.3 Throughout the process just described, various reasons or motives of the agent are presupposed. The term "reason" (for choice or action) has had two kinds of referents in its previous uses and the time has come to distinguish between them. In one sense, the term "reason" refers to one or another of the agent's *psychological attitudes*, volitional or cognitive, that may be cited in answer to questions of the forms "Why did he (she, you) choose to do X?" or "Why did he (she, you) do X?" In this sense, the term "reason" refers to one or another of the agent's wants, desires, preferences, likes, dislikes, interests, intentions (expressing goals or purposes), hopes, fears, and other emotions and similar attitudes expressive of the agent's will. In this sense also, the term "reason" may refer to one or another of the agent's cognitive mental attitudes, that is, states of knowledge and beliefs, including not only factual beliefs (that such and such is or is not the case) but also normative beliefs (that such and such ought to be, is permitted, forbidden), evaluative beliefs (that something is good or bad in some respect), and beliefs about what is possible, probable, and necessary.

Psychological attitudes of each of these volitional or cognitive kinds may be cited as reasons for choice or action in the sense that they may be cited in answer to "why"-questions of the forms mentioned above ("Why did he (she) do (choose to do) X?") I may say that I chose to accompany my son because I wanted (or desired or intended) to avoid certain dangers or conflicts, or because I believed that my mother could not adequately care for him in her present state. Though we often cite a single volitional or cognitive reason in answer to such "why"-questions, other background reasons are usually assumed. It has been acknowledged since the time of Aristotle that at least one volitional and one cognitive reason must be presupposed in every deliberation (cf. 2.7) and, in most situations, many of both kinds are presupposed. Cognitive reasons are involved in the construction of scenarios and the determination of means and consequences, while both volitional and cognitive reasons are involved in the assessment of means and consequences.

We must distinguish here between the reason, as psychological attitude, that the agent "has" at a time (the want or desire to do A, the belief that p), on the one hand, and the agent's "having" that psychological attitude at a time (the agent's wanting or desiring to do A, believing that p), on the other. The former is what we mean by the "reason"; it is a psychological attitude the agent has. The latter is a psychological *state* of "having the reason." The psychological attitude may be thought of as an attribute that different agents may have at different times, while the having of the attitude is a state in the technical sense defined in 3.2; that is, a particular subject's having some (state-like) attribute at some time or other. I shall therefore sometimes refer to the havings of reasons as "reason states" to distinguish them from the reasons had.

In addition to the sense of "reason" as psychological attitude that the agent may have, there is a second sense of "reason" in which it refers to the object or content of the psychological attitude. In answer to the question "Why did you choose to accompany your son?" I may say "Because I wanted to avoid certain dangers or conflicts," or simply, "In order to avoid certain dangers and conflicts." In the one case, I cite as a reason my psychological attitude, in the other, I cite the object or content of the attitude, that which is wanted. Similarly, I may cite an intention, or its object, a goal or purpose or end, or I may cite a factual belief, or the (possible) fact believed, a normative belief or the principle believed, an evaluative belief, or the value held. Although this object or content sense of "reason" for choice or action is important in ordinary usage, there is a significant sense, for our purposes, in which it is derivative. The choices or actions of agents can be explained in terms of goals, ends, (possible) facts, principles, and values, only if, and insofar as, these goals, ends, (possible) facts, principles, and values are wanted, intended, believed, or held by the agent, that is to say, only if, and insofar as, the goals, ends, etc. are the objects or contents of psychological attitudes which the agent has at one time or another. For this reason, I shall follow the practice, tacitly followed until now, of using the term "reason" when unqualified to refer to the psychological attitudes of the kinds mentioned in the first paragraph of this section. On those less frequent occasions when the term "reason" is used to refer to the objects or contents of these psychological attitudes, I shall make clear that the term is being used "in the object or content sense."

Uses of the terms "reason" and "motive" (for choice or action) overlap to a considerable degree. Psychological attitudes of most of the diverse kinds mentioned at the beginning of the section can also be cited as motives for choice or action. In addition, the term "motive," like "reason," can refer either to the psychological attitude or to the object or content of that attitude. Anscombe (58) calls intentions "forward looking motives." She also distinguishes two other classes of motives, backward looking ones, like revenge, and motives in general, like love and greed. Motives in these two classes can be referred to as reasons as well, either in the object sense (revenge as opposed to the desire for it) or the psychological attitude sense (love as an emotion, greed as an excessive desire for material gain). The term "motive," like "reason," will therefore be used to refer, in an unqualified sense, to the psychological attitudes that may be cited in answer to "why"-questions about choice and action, and in a secondary sense to the objects or contents of these psychological attitudes. The purpose of having two words to cover the same ground will become evident as we proceed in this chapter and in Part II. Many authors writing on free will have used one or the other in crucial arguments, sometimes both interchangeably. I am not saying the two terms, "reason" and "motive," do not have other meanings or that there are no subtle differences in their ordinary uses. I am merely making clear how they will be used, here and in subsequent chapters.[2]

4.4 We can now return to the argument against the indeterminist condition described in 4.1. This argument is most strikingly formulated in terms of prior deliberation. The charge is that the indeterminist condition severs the connection between the choice outcome and the process of deliberation that proceeded it. Let us say that, as a result of my deliberation, I chose to accompany my son. If my choice satisfied the indeterminist condition, then it could have been the case that I chose otherwise (chose to send him alone) given all the same past circumstances. And if the past circumstances included my psychological history prior to choice, then it could have been the case that I chose otherwise, given exactly the same prior process of deliberation.

This is strikingly counterintuitive. The problem is not that I cannot imagine how the outcome may have been different. I chose A (accompanying my son) rather than B (sending him alone) because, all things considered, A seemed the more desirable option. But there may have been facts unnoticed, or scenarios and consequences never considered, that may have tipped the balance the other way. One of the important features of the process of deliberation described in 4.2 is that such a process has no clearly defined limits. How many options should I consider? When have I considered enough possible consequences? When do I stop imagining further scenarios and simply decide? There are no general answers to these questions because the possible consequences and scenarios are limitless.[3] I can therefore understand how the outcome of my deliberation may have been different, if I had known other facts, considered other consequences, imagined other scenarios, etc. But what I cannot understand is how I could have reasonably chosen to do otherwise, how I could have reasonably chosen B, *given exactly the same prior deliberation* that led me to choose A, the same information deployed, the same consequences considered, the same assessments made, and so on.

This way of stating the argument shows what is at stake in the charges of arbitrariness, irrationality, etc., made against the indeterminist condition. If the choice of A was the reasonable outcome of my deliberation, then the choosing otherwise (the choice of B), which may have occurred given the same past circumstances, would have been "arbitrary," "capricious," "irrational," and "inexplicable," relative to my prior deliberation. Similarly, if the choice of B had been the reasonable conclusion of my deliberation, then the choice of A, had it occurred, would have been arbitrary relative to the prior deliberation, In general, where the indeterminist condition is satisfied, and the outcome is the result of prior deliberation, *at least* one of the outcomes (choosing or doing otherwise) must be arbitrary or irrational *in relation to* the prior deliberation.

The conclusion must be stated in this way, because there is a sense in which the choice of A could have been rational and also undetermined. Suppose that the choice of A was the reasonable conclusion of my deliberation and did in fact occur. Suppose, however, that it was undetermined, so that the choice of B could have occurred in the same circumstances, but did not. Since the choice of A was the reasonable one, there is a clear sense in which it would have been explicable in terms of my prior reasons or motives and hence neither arbitrary, capricious, nor irrational in relation to prior deliberation. I would have had reasons for making the choice I did make (of A) even though the choice I did make was not determined by my having these reasons or by any other past circumstances. In the light of this possibility, critics of the indeterminist condition cannot simply say that the undetermined choice must be arbitrary, irrational, and so on, in terms of the agent's psychological history prior to choice, including deliberation. What they must say is that *at least one* of the possible outcomes, the choosing *or* the doing otherwise, would be arbitrary in relation to the prior psychological history.

4.5   The argument of the preceding paragraph is related to a move often made by libertarians in the history of the free will controversy. Against charges that the indeterminist condition would render free choices arbitrary or capricious, libertarians (including Bramhall) have often insisted that reasons can explain choice or action without determining choice or action.[4] To use Leibniz' phrase. they have insisted that reasons may "incline without necessitating" (i.e. without determining).

This point is usually made in response to a familiar claim made by compatibilists and soft determinists that choices or actions must always be determined by the "strongest motive." Libertarians have consistently denied this claim, arguing, as did Bramhall (44, p. 150) and Thomas Reid (70, p. 88), that it cannot be proved except in a trivial form (where the strongest motive is defined as the one that in fact prevails). In its nontrivial form ("the strongest motive always antecedently necessitates (or determines in the sense of D2) the choice or action"), the claim is an unproven empirical one that begs the question of whether determinism of choice and action is or is not true. The stronger motive *may* merely incline without necessitating, and this possibility cannot be ruled out by assumption. Traditionally, libertarians have rejected the simple dichotomy foisted upon them by their critics, between a determination of choice by the having of reasons or motives, on the one hand, or an arbitrariness, or randomness, in the sense of the absence of good reason for choice, on the other. There is a middle way, they insist; reasons or motives may incline without necessitating.[5]

Now this was precisely the situation imagined in the last paragraph of the previous section. The choice of A was the reasonable outcome of my deliberation but, by assumption, it was undetermined. Reasons, therefore, inclined me toward the choice of A without necessitating (i.e. determining) that choice. As we saw, the indeterminist condition does not exclude such a possibility. The problem created by the indeterminist condition is of a different order. If my choosing A *was* rational and explicable in relation to my prior deliberation, then the choosing *otherwise* would have been arbitrary, irrational and inexplicable in terms of the *same* deliberation. Had I chosen otherwise at the end of my deliberation, it would have seemed a fluke or accident, not something I would intuitively recognize as a deliberate free choice.

Thus the observation that reasons may incline without necessitating does not resolve the problem. Indeed, it creates the problem; for the arbitrariness that attaches to the choosing otherwise (choosing B) is due to the fact that the reasons incline toward the choice of A. The observation that reasons may incline without necessitating undermines the strongest motive argument (one of the weakest of compatibilist arguments), but it does not salvage the indeterminist condition.

4.6   Another move that is familiar to students of the free will issue is suggested by the arguments of the previous section. Suppose that my deliberation up to a given time did not provide me, all things considered, with good reasons for choosing A rather than B *or* for choosing B rather than A. I may have had some reasons for preferring A and some for preferring B, but neither set of reasons at the given time was stronger than the other. This would be a case of a so-called "liberty of indifference" (*liberum arbitrium indifferentiae*) sometimes mentioned as a corollary of indeterminist theories of freedom.[6] The agent chooses between two (or more) options with respect to which he or she is indifferent in the sense that the agent does not possess at the time of choice stronger reasons for choosing one of the options over the other (or over any of the others). This idea, known and discussed in the Middle Ages, is mentioned by Dante(32) in the following lines of *The Divine Comedy* (*Paradiso*, 4):

> Between two foods, equally tempting, placed
> Equally near, a man, though free to choose
> Would starve before deciding which to taste.

Schopenhauer (60, p. 61) traces this theme back to Aristotle, who, in the *De Caelo* (295/32), speaks of "the man who, though exceedingly hungry and thirsty, and both equally, yet being equidistant from food and drink, is therefore bound to stay where he is." It became familiar in modern times through the example, perhaps wrongly attributed to Buridan, of the ass that starved between two equidistant bales of hay.

In the light of the arguments of the previous sections, it is easy to see why the idea of a liberty of indifference sometimes appears in the history of debates about free will. But it is also easy to see why the idea has been an object of ridicule among critics of indeterminist theories of freedom. The appeal to a liberty of indifference does not solve the problem described in previous sections. Indeed, it makes matters worse. Instead of one of the alternatives, the choosing or doing otherwise, being arbitrary relative to the prior deliberation, both would be arbitrary in the case of a liberty of indifference. The deliberation would not provide the agent with good reasons for choosing A over B, or B over A. Given the indeterminist condition, either choice might occur, but whichever did occur could not be said to be the rational outcome of the deliberation.[7]

4.8   We have now traced the familiar charges of arbitrariness, etc. made against the indeterminist condition to the following problem. If the indeterminist condition were satisfied, then at least one of the alternatives, either the choosing or the doing otherwise (or both, in the case of a liberty of indifference), would be arbitrary, capricious, irrational and explicable in relation to the process of deliberation and the reasons or motives that may have preceded choice. But why exactly is this a problem and how is the problem related to the definition of free will, D1? These are relevant questions because D1 speaks only about the "powers" to make choices or decisions and to do otherwise, without mentioned deliberation, practical reasoning, reasons or motives.

The answer, I think, is this. According to the charges made by its critics, the indeterminist condition undermines the dual power of the free agent to choose and to do otherwise *in the normal way*, that is, in such a way that the choosing or doing otherwise, whichever occurs, occurs as the conclusion of a process of practical reasoning in which more than one option is reflectively considered. Recall that choices and decisions normally terminate processes of practical reasoning in this sense (2.5). The indeterminist condition would limit all free choices and decisions to impulsive or spur of the moment choices or decisions arbitrarily related to the processes of reasoning that may have preceded them. It would make paradigmatic an abnormal kind of choice over which the agent has limited rational control. Reference to the powers to choose and do otherwise in D1 must include within its scope the powers to choose and do otherwise in the normal way, that is, as a result of prior practical reasoning in which more than one option is reflectively considered. Any theory that cannot account for free choices or decisions made in this way must be considered inadequate.

At a deeper level, the argument is related to the notion of *self* determination, in the sense of determination by a rational agent, *as* rational. The choosing or doing otherwise, *whichever occurs*, must "flow from" myself, with my "mind directing," as Locke says (59, p. 315). It is the need to clarify such expressions that has led to talk of the "rational will" in traditional discussions of human freedom. Rational will, as defined in chapter 2, is a set of interrelated powers associated with practical reasoning, the powers to deliberate, to engage in normative practical reasoning, to make choices or decisions, etc. In general, it is the power to make judgments of the will which are rational in the sense that they result from, and are controlled by, prior processes of *reasoning* and prior reasons or motives entering into those processes of reasoning. The traditional assumption was that the free agent could not be moved this way or that by natural causes alone, or even simply by desire, or natural will. For higher animals have natural will, but they do not have free will. The dual power of free will must be the power to determine one's choosing and doing otherwise, whichever occurs, in the manner distinctive of selves or persons or rational agent's, i.e. in accordance with, and under the control of, one's rational will, which means, as the reasonable outcome of a deliberative process.

We may call this power to choose *either way* as the reasonable outcome of a deliberative process, the power of "dual rational self determination" or "dual rational self control." The argument against the indeterminist condition is that it undermines this dual power, making at least one of the outcomes arbitrary, a kind of fluke or accident, in relation to the agent's prior rational will.

4.9   It may be noted that compatibilists have an easier time explaining dual rational self control than do libertarians, and this is one of the chief attractions of the compatibilist view. If my actual reasons and reasoning inclined me toward the choice of A, compatibilists can say that I could have chosen B in the sense that I *would* have chosen B, *if* at least some of my prior reasons had been different. Thus, they can explain my doing otherwise *rationally* and *deliberately*, but only on the condition that the past had been different in some way.

Such a solution is unavailable to libertarians because it makes free will "dual rational" only by making free will compatible with determinism. But then, libertarians must come to grips with the problem of dual rational self determination on their own terms, reconciling it with the indeterminist condition. In their attempts to do this, libertarians usually shift the strategy of their argument dramatically at this point. They remind us that indeterminism is only a necessary, not a sufficient, condition for free will. The indeterminist condition provides for the causal gaps or ambiguous possibilities in nature that are necessary for the exercise of free will, but it does not by itself explain this exercise. These gaps must be filled by some special form of agency or causation that will provide a positive account of (dual rational) self determination to supplement the ("negative") requirement of indeterminism.

To fill this demand for a positive account of self determination, libertarians have employed many different strategies. But all their strategies have a common pattern. They have looked for factors or entities influencing choice that are not included among the past circumstances or laws of nature referred to by the indeterminist condition . Though the agent may choose or do otherwise, given all the same past circumstances and laws of nature, the choosing rather than doing otherwise, or vice versa, is accounted for by something over and above the past circumstances and laws. I shall call any strategy following this common pattern a "special cause" or "extra-circumstantial" strategy.

The special causes or extra-circumstantial factors appealed to have varied. They have included noumenal selves, non-material egos, agent causes, final causes, acts of will or volitions, reasons for action (in either of the two senses defined in 4.3), abstract entities, like ideas, concepts or theories, the Will (or the Reason) of the agent, conceived as a kind of agent cause within, moral principles, simultaneous causes, acts of attention, and so on. In each case, it is argued that these factors may influence choice without being counted among the past circumstances in the relevant sense required by the indeterminist condition, either because they are not "past," or not "circumstances," in the sense of occurrences of states or changes, or because their influence on choice cannot be interpreted in terms of laws of nature. If such extra-circumstantial factors exist and influence choice, the indeterminist condition can be satisfied, while the outcome of the choice situation in either direction is regarded as rationally self determined.

In chapter 1, I mentioned many of the above listed factors traditionally cited by libertarians to explain their view and argued that they fail to do the job intended. Special cause strategies lead, in Hobbes' terms, either to confusion or emptiness, and, in particular, they fail to solve the problem of dual rational self control. In the remainder of this chapter I want to show why I think the major special cause strategies fail in this regard. There is another motive for doing this, beyond the obvious one or showing why I think alternative theories fail. For, many of these strategies do have something positive to contribute to the libertarian view and will enter into the arguments of Part II. They are pieces of a larger puzzle, as I said earlier, but they fail to solve the libertarian's problems by themselves.

4.10   Special cause strategies are numerous and we shall have to be creatively selective in dealing with them. Fortunately, the discussion can be limited by two considerations. First, we are mainly concerned with how special cause strategies deal with the problem of dual rational self determination or control. If the argument up to now has been correct, this problem is critical for indeterminist theories of freedom, since it underlies the familiar charges of arbitrariness and irrationality made against the indeterminist condition. Second, we can be guided by the assertion that all special cause strategies appeal to factors that may influence choice without being counted among the past circumstances (of the indeterminist condition) either because they are not past, or not circumstances, in a relevant sense. With this in mind, the different special cause strategies can be placed in a limited number of categories, depending upon the reasons given for saying that the factors appealed to are special; and we can then deal with representative theories in each category. Proceeding in this way, I shall discuss special cause strategies in the following categories: (1) Simultaneous Reason States and Bootstrap Theories, (2) Content Theories, (3) Two Level Theories and (4) Non-Occurrent Cause Theories.

(1) *Simultaneous Reason States and Bootstrap Theories*: The indeterminist condition refers to all the same "past" or "prior" circumstances. It does not mention simultaneous circumstances, those occurring at the moment of choice, which might provide a reason for the agent's choosing rather than doing otherwise.[8] While the agent might choose A or choose B, given all the same prior circumstances, including the same prior reason states, the actual occurrence of the choice of A at t might be

explained by the agent's having a certain reason (e.g. a want or desire), or a set of reasons R, at the same time as the choice of A at t, while the choice of B at t would be explained by the agent's having an alternative reason or set of reasons R' (differing from R in at least one member) at t. The difference in choice would be explained, not by a difference in prior reason states, but by a difference in simultaneous reason states.

This suggestion accomplishes little by itself. But it is mentioned here because it is related to other historically significant theories and the difficulty with it carries over to these other theories. The difficulty is that the arbitrariness relative to the agent's prior psychological history is simply transferred from the choices (of A and B) to the simultaneous reason states accompanying these choices (unless of course the reason states are determined—an assumption that would be self defeating). The choice of A at t would be explained by the presence of one set R of simultaneous reason states and the choice of B by another set R'. But if the indeterminist condition continues to hold for the choices, and the appropriate reason states accompany the choices they explain, then the agent's being in one set of reason states rather that the other (R rather than R', or vice versa) would be as arbitrary relative to the prior psychological history as the occurrence of one choice rather than the other. Or, putting it another way, the occurrence at t of one complex, reason-states-in-R-plus-the-choice-of-A, rather than the other, reason-states-in-R'-plus-the-choice-of-B, would be as arbitrary relative to the prior psychological history as the occurrence of the choices themselves. If, by chance, the reason sets need not accompany the choices they explain, the arbitrariness would be compounded. If the reason states in R, whose presence explains why A is chosen rather than B, should instead be accompanied by the choice of B, then the choice of B would be arbitrary relative to both past *and* simultaneous reasons.

The appeal to simultaneous reason states is related to some historically important libertarian theories which may be called bootstrap theories. Bootstrap theorists argue that an agent making a free choice is simultaneously choosing ("adopting," "accepting," "sanctioning," etc.) the very reasons or motives that explain the choice being made. Perhaps the most familiar modern proponent of such a view is Sartre, though the bootstrap idea is only part of his theory. He says that, in the exercise of freedom, "the motive, the act and the end are all constituted in a single upsurge. Each of these three structures claims the others as its meaning. But the organized totality of the three is no longer explained by any particular structure. . . . It is the act which decides its ends and its motives and the act is the expression of freedom" (62, p. 100). In this way, according to Sartre, the free agent transcends his past, including the influences of past character and motives, by accepting or making his own at the moment of choice, the motives that explain the choice.

Others have taken a similar line, including some of Sartre's countrymen. Charles Renouvier (12) says that a "*motive* is always *willed*, that is, singled out at the moment [of choice] among other equally possible motives," and he adds that, once this is realized, "the argument for determinism is instantly overthrown" (p. 315). Émile Boutroux (16) says that "in the resolve that follows the consideration of motives, there is something more than the motives themselves: the consent of the will to some particular motive in preference to some other" (p. 140). A similar line is taken by G. E. Hughes (44) responding in *Mind* to W. D. Ross's critique of indeterminist theories of freedom: "In order to make a potential motive my reason for acting, I select it from others and 'adopt' or 'sanction' . . . it; and in so doing I confer upon it an entirely new status" (p. 317).

Bootstrap theories are often combined with other libertarian strategies, and with good reason. For, by themselves, they do not dispose of the charge of arbitrariness. In a genuine bootstrap theory the "accepting." "making one's own," "adopting," or "sanctioning" of one set of motives rather than another is something that takes place simultaneously with the choice, in which case it is either identical with the choice or a separate event occurring at the same time. The problem is the same in either case. The accepting or making one's own of one set of motives rather than another is no less arbitrary relative to the agent's prior psychological history than the choice itself. Instead of wanting to know why the agent chose A rather than B (or B rather than A) given prior motives and processes of reasoning, we would want to know why the agent accepted, adopted, or made his own a set of motives R for choosing A rather than an alternative set R' for choosing B (or vice versa). Or, in Sartre's language, we would want to know why there was an "upsurge" at t of the complex, motive-states-in-R-plus-choice-of-A,, rather than of motive-states-in-R' -plus-choice-of-B (or vice versa). Just as in the case of simultaneous reason states, the arbitrariness is transferred to the motive-choice complexes.

Bootstrap theorists might respond that, in some way or another yet to be explained, the agent *makes* one simultaneous motive-choice complex prevail at the moment of choice (by acting, for example, as a non-occurrent cause). But this means that bootstrap theories will not stand on their own and must be supplemented by other strategies yet to be considered. Thus, while bootstrap theories may have something important to contribute to the free will problem, they do not solve it on their own.

4.11 (2) *Content Theories*. Bootstrap theories appeal to factors that may influence choice without being counted among the past circumstances, because they are not past. Content theories appeal to factors influencing choice that cannot be counted among the past circumstances because they are not *circumstances*, in the sense of actual occurrences of states or changes. The factors cited by content theorists are such things as conceptions, theories, conjectures, hypotheses, information, policies, rules, norms, or principles (e.g. moral principles), and the like. These are abstract entities, possible objects of thought, but not the sorts of things that could be said to "take place" at some time, or during some interval of time (except as contents of thoughts which may take place). In more traditional Aristotelian terms, they are "formal causes," not "efficient causes." Another class of such contents sometimes said to influence choice in unique ways includes purposes, goals, aims, ends, and the like. These are sometimes classified as "final causes," where this expression does not refer to actual future occurrences, but to abstract (conceptual or propositional) contents of present thoughts which refer to possible future occurrences.

Now, no one would deny that abstract contents of all these kinds do influence choice and action in some manner; and their influence is related to rationality and rational control in a unique way. So it has been tempting for many thinkers to try to account for the mysteries of undetermined free choice or action in terms of the influence of these abstract contents, or formal causes.[9]

An interesting contemporary example of a content theory is the view defended by Sir Karl Popper in his provocative lecture "Of Clouds and Clocks" (72). In this lecture, Popper argues that incompatibilist theories of freedom can only be given sense if their partisans come to grips with "the problem of the influence of the *universe of abstract meanings* upon human behavior (and thereby upon the physical universe)" (p. 230). Included in this "universe of abstract meanings," for Popper, are such things as aims, purposes, moral rules, theories, and hypotheses—various abstract entities belonging to what he calls World Three, a domain of real entities in his ontology that is something like, but not exactly like, Plato's ideal world of Forms (pp. 1533ff.). (World One, in Popper's ontology, is the world of physical occurrences and World Two, the world of mental *occurrences*.) Despite the abstract nature of World Three entities, Popper insists, they can influence behavior and hence the physical universe, by becoming the objects of mental attitudes; and he tries to explain human freedom in terms of this influence.

We may note here that content theorists may, but need not, postulate the real, independent existence of such abstract entities or Forms, as Plato does (and Popper also, though with certain qualifications). Such entities may be regarded as possible objects of thought having actual existence only when they are the contents of the actual mental attitudes of existing persons. For, as it turns out, each of the entities cited by content theorists like Popper is potentially a reason or motive, or a conceptual part of a reason or motive, in the second sense defined in 4.3, that is, a reason or motive "in the object or content sense." In answer to the question "Why did you choose to do this rather than that?" one may cite a theory or hypothesis, a purpose or plan, a rule or principle, as one's reason or motive.

But therein lies the problem with content theories of all kinds. They do not really come to grips with the problem of dual rational self control,[10] and they cannot do so unless they are supplemented by special cause theories belonging to the next category we shall consider, i.e. "two level theories." To see why this is so, let us consider what must be done if the problem of dual rational self control is to be solved by a content theory. The indeterminist condition requires that the agent may choose A or otherwise, given all the same past circumstances. Special cause strategies in general try to locate some factors or entities that are not included among the past circumstances and are therefore not required to be the same by the indeterminist condition. A difference in these special factors would then explain the difference between choosing and doing otherwise. For example, if the special factors are simultaneous reasons, then a difference in simultaneous reasons would account for the difference between choosing A and doing otherwise, though all *past* circumstances remained the same. To deal with the problem of dual rational self control by way of a content theory, a similar move must be made with respect to abstract contents (hypotheses or theories, purposes or principles, etc.). Though all past circumstances (in the sense of occurrences of states or changes) remain the same, the difference between choosing A and doing otherwise must be accounted for by the influence of different abstract contents on choice.[11]

But once the matter is put this way, it is easy to see what is wrong. Abstract contents cannot influence choice unless they are the contents of psychological attitudes which the agent has at some time or other. Hypotheses or theories cannot influence choice unless they are believed, held or accepted; purposes, aims, or plans must be the contents of actual intentions of the agent; rules or principles cannot influence choice unless they are the contents of normative beliefs, i.e. unless the agent believes he or she, or everyone, ought to do this or that, and so on. In general, as argued in 4.3, reasons or motives in the object or content sense can influence choice only if they are the abstract contents of psychological attitudes, or reasons or motives which the agent has at some time or other. Moreover, the contents help to individuate the attitudes. If the agent has two thoughts (or beliefs, or wants . . .) with different conceptual or propositional contents, then the thoughts (or beliefs . . .) are different.[12]

Now, while abstract contents are not themselves circumstances, in the sense of occurring states or changes, the agent's *having* a particular psychological attitude at some time or other is classifiable as a circumstance, in the sense of an occurring state (of mind) belonging to the psychological history of the agent. If one were to assume, therefore, that such havings of particular psychological attitudes at particular times were among the past circumstances of the indeterminist condition, the content theorist who tried to save the indeterminist condition would be in the untenable position of saying that the agent's choosing and doing otherwise could be influenced by different hypotheses or theories even though the agent had all the same beliefs, or by different purposes or aims, even though the agent had all the same intentions, or by different principles even though the agent had all the same normative beliefs, and so on. To avoid this, content theorists would have to make the further point that the agent's having a particular reason or motive at a particular time is also something that could not be counted as a past circumstance of the ordinary kind required by the indeterminist condition, perhaps by arguing that reason states cannot cause and be caused in the normal way by virtue of laws of nature. To make this move, however, is to move beyond a mere content theory to what I call a "two level theory," the next kind of special cause theory to be considered

4.12   Before leaving content theories, I want to make some remarks about a particular content theory that will reenter the discussion of Part II.[13] Kant and others have identified a libertarian freedom with the power to act on a special kind of abstract content, namely a moral principle, or the Moral Law, against one's self interested desires or inclinations. Such theories have appeal because ordinary experiences of acting on moral principle, or acting from duty, are particularly striking experiences in which we have a feeling of freedom, or of rational control over our actions. It is tempting to interpret such experiences by saying that one rises above the influence of one's wants, desires or inclinations in order to act on something that is not an inclination at all, something outside, or above, the natural, causal order, a moral rule or principle.

But here again, it must be noted that a moral rule, like any other abstract content, can influence choice and action only if it is the content of some actual psychological attitudes of the agent. The point is nicely made with respect to moral law theories by W. D. Ross in his *Foundations of Ethics* (39, pp. 226-7): "Duty tends to be represented as something standing over against all objects of desire. But a little reflection shows that . . . an act's being our duty is never the reason why we do it. For however much an act may be our duty, we shall not be led on that account to do it, unless we *know* or *think* it to be our duty . . .. But even this is still elliptical . . . the fuller and truer answer would be . . . 'I did the act because I knew or thought it to be my duty, and because I desired to do it as being my duty, more than I desired to do any other act.' " Ross then adds that thinking something to be one's duty and desiring to do it are matters having to do with the agent's psychological history, so that if one wants to rule out determinism, one must say something about how these psychological attitudes are influenced by, and how they in turn influence, behavior. Appeals to duty or the moral law are not enough unless they are supplemented by further libertarian strategies. The situation is not substantially changed, he adds, if one substitutes for the desire to act from duty a specific emotion, like Kant's respect or reverence for the moral law. Our having or not having such an emotion, and its strength in different persons, could also in principle be determined by environment and upbringing.

It is worth noting that Kant himself would not have denied these claims. He argued that the exercise of practical reason presupposes the assumption that actions done from duty are not determined. But when theoretical reason tries to explain how such actions can be rational and undetermined, it confronts limitations. A theoretical study of such actions, from the point of view of an empirical (or, in Kantian terms, a phenomenal) psychology would have to include references to psychological attitudes of the agent, like belief in the moral law and the desire to act from duty; and the existence of these attitudes would have to be explained as determined features of the agent's psychological history, i.e. under the form of inner sense, which is time. Thus, acts presupposed as free by practical reason are viewed as determined by theoretical reason. Kant, of course, resolves this antinomy by appealing to a noumenal self as the source of free actions, a cause outside time whose activity cannot be explained in terms of occurrences or history, psychological or otherwise. In short, his final solution to the libertarian puzzle is not a content theory at all, but a non-occurrent cause theory.

4.13   (3) *Two Level Theories.* Special cause theories falling into this third category are those that deny the controversial assumption stated in 4.1, where the argument against the indeterminist condition was first formulated. These theories deny the assumption that the past circumstances referred to in the indeterminist condition must include "the entire psychological history of the agent prior to choice" (in the sense of all occurring psychological states and changes of the agent prior to choice). One kind of two level theory, the kind anticipated in the discussion of content theories, would assert that the havings of reasons in the psychological attitude sense cannot be causes of choices or actions, not because they are not circumstances in the technical sense of occurring states or changes, but because they are not the sorts of circumstances whose influence can be accounted for in terms of laws of nature. Thus, the indeterminist condition would require that all past *causal* circumstances remain the same (i.e. all circumstances whose influence can be accounted for in terms of laws of nature). But the category of causal circumstances would not include the having of reasons.[14]

A more traditional version of a two level theory would appeal to a mind-body dualism of the Cartesian kind. Mental occurrences, one might say, are not states or changes of a physical substance and do not enter into laws of nature, which concern only the states and changes of physical substances. yet mental occurrences can and do influence states and changes in physical substances. Thus, the indeterminist condition would require that the agent might choose A or do otherwise, given all the same past *physical* circumstances, but mental occurrences would not be included among the past physical circumstances.[15]

Still other kinds of two level theories appeal to special kinds of acts, e.g. volitions or acts of attention, which are considered to be acts *sui generis*, capable of influencing behavior, but not themselves part of the causal order and not subject to natural laws. The choosing or doing otherwise is then identified with, or explained in terms of, the occurrence or non-occurrence of these special kinds of acts, which are not included among "the same past circumstances" of the indeterminist condition.[16]

The common element of two level theories is the denial that certain psychological circumstances can cause or determine choices or actions by virtue of the existence of laws of nature. Two level theorists argue that if laws of nature do govern human behavior, they are likely to be formulated in the language of physics and chemistry, as employed by the biochemist and the neurophysiologist. They will refer to physical states and changes of the agent's brain, body, and physical environment, but will not refer to mental states and changes (to wantings, desirings and the like, or to practical reasoning) *as* these mental states and changes are ordinarily described.

Some opponents would respond to this claim by saying that mental occurrences and occurrences in the brain might nevertheless be identical occurrences "under different descriptions." But two level theorists must deny this. Indeed, to make their strategy work, as we shall see, they must also deny the following "correlation thesis" between mental and physical occurrences. They must deny that to every difference in the mental states or changes in some agent (e.g. the difference between and agent's being in vs. not being in a certain mental state) there corresponds some physical difference in the agent's brain or body.

4.14 To see this, note that the aim of two level theories vis à vis the indeterminist condition is to explain the difference in choice (choosing A rather than doing otherwise, e.g. choosing B, or vice versa) in terms of a difference in some feature of the agent's psychological history. Certain prior reasons, or a prior process of deliberation, or effort of will, would explain the choice of A, while a different set of reasons or deliberation or effort of will would explain the choice of B. We may diagram the situation as follows:

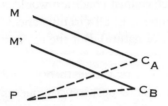

Figure 4.1

M and M' are different sets of prior mental states, activities, or acts (the sets may have only one member) whose presence would rationally explain the choices of $A(C_A)$ and $B(C_B)$ respectively. "P" represents the set of all past causal or physical circumstances, including all prior occurrences in the agent's brain. The branching broken lines from "P" indicate that either of the choices may occur given all the same causal or physical circumstances.

It is evident why such a strategy requires a denial of the correlation thesis. Different sets of mental occurrences, M or M', may have obtained prior to choice, given exactly the same physical occurrences, including the same physical states and changes in the agent's brain. The point is not that anyone who argues that reasons are not causes of actions must make such a denial (of the correlation thesis), nor that anyone who argues that mental occurrences are not identical with physical occurrences must make such a denial. (There are parallelist dualists, after all.) The point is that anyone who uses such claims about reasons or mental phenomena *to defend the indeterminist condition* against the charges of arbitrariness, must make such a denial. For the advantage gained by a two level strategy, vis à vis the indeterminist condition, is that some features of the agent's psychological history can be exempted from the category of relevant past circumstances. Dual rational self control can then be explained in terms of a difference in these exempted conditions.

Suppose, for example, that I chose A (accompanying my son on his trip across country) rather than B, because I had a desire (D) to visit a medical specialist in Boston, near my mother's home. And suppose this desire was decisive in the sense that, in its absence, other things being equal, I would have chosen B (sending my son alone). I can say that a certain set of reasons that I had prior to choice, including the desire D, led me to choose A; yet I could have rationally and deliberately chosen B (not as a fluke or accident) in the sense that I would have chosen B, if my relevant prior reason set had not included D and, thus, had been different in some way. (My havings of reasons, including D, would be represented by "M" in Figure 4.1 , and those without D, by "M'.") Such an account mimics the compatibilists' (conditional) interpretation of dual rational self control (4.9). But the compatibilist is not committed to the indeterminist condition. To reconcile such a conditional approach to dual rational self determination with the indeterminist condition, one must assume that the having of prior reasons or other mental occurrences may be different, while all the states and changes in my brain are the same. The difference between my having and not having the desire to visit the medical specialist and the corresponding differences in my deliberation cannot be reflected in any physical differences in my brain prior to choice, or the indeterminist condition would be violated.

This is a particularly strong denial of correlations between mental and physical occurrences. Many philosophers today who deny that correlations can be found between mental and physical occurrences in the brain do so on the grounds that the ordinary language in which we describe mental phenomena, on the one hand, and the biochemical language of the neurophysiologists, on the other, have such different purposes that we are unlikely to find systematic matches between *types* or kinds of mental occurrences and types or kinds of biochemical occurrences in the brain.[17] This is a defensible claim. But allowing the absence of such type-type correlations between physical and mental occurrences is compatible with saying that particular differences in mental occurrences would be reflected by *some* differences or other in the brain. (Indeed, the absence of type-type correlations is compatible with some physicalist theories of mind.)[18] One takes the anti-correlationist stance a radical step further, if one allows that my having vs. not having a certain desire, or engaging vs. not engaging in a certain process of deliberation, or making vs. not making a particular effort of will, would not be reflected by any corresponding biochemical difference in my brain whatever.

One problem that arises when such a move is made is that it becomes difficult to explain how the mental occurrences influence physical changes in the brain and behavior. Or, if the choices themselves, C_A and C_B, are not correlated with changes in the brain, it becomes difficult to explain how the mental occurrences in M and M' influence the choices, and how the choices "cause" changes in the brain. These problems of "interaction" are well known problems for dualist accounts of the mental and physical, and I think they will arise for any two level theory that tries to reconcile dual rational self determination with the indeterminist condition.

4.15 Beyond these issues of correlation and interaction, two level strategies have other problems. Curiously, despite all the ontological stresses they create, two level theories fail in the end to resolve the problem of dual rational self determination. What exactly is the relationship in the diagram between the prior mental occurrences, in M and M', and the corresponding choices, C_A and C_B? "M" stands for a set of prior psychological states and/or processes of reasoning and/or mental acts whose occurrence allows one to explain why the choice of A was made rather than the choice of B; and the same is true of "M' " in relation to the choice of B. The mental occurrences therefore stand in some sort of rational or conceptual (logical?) relation to their respective choices. But the mental occurrences supposedly do not cause the respective choices; they do not stand in a causal or determining relation defined by laws of nature. This gives rise to a question. Could the mental occurrences in M, which explain why A is chosen rather than B, be followed by the choice of B instead of the choice of A? If so, we have recreated, without solving, the problem about reasons inclining without necessitating, discussed in 4.5. Given the prior mental occurrences in M, the choice of B (i.e. choosing otherwise, or other than A) would be arbitrary and irrational relative to the agent's prior psychological history. Given prior occurrences in M', the choice of A would be arbitrary. In either case, at least one of the outcomes would be arbitrary, and dual rational self control would be absent. Introducing a level of reasons or other mental occurrences distinct from physical causes does not remove the problem of arbitrariness. The problem arises anew at the higher level.

The problem can be avoided by saying that occurrences M are always or invariably followed by C_A and M' by C_B. But what is the source of these invariant connections between mental occurrences? They are not supported by laws of nature, according to the theory. Are they perhaps logical or conceptual connections? Are occurrences in M logically sufficient conditions in themselves for the occurrences of C_A, without benefit of laws of nature? Then the choice would be determined by past circumstances alone in a sense allowed by D2. The view would be a kind of logical determinism as objectionable to libertarians as determination by circumstances and laws of nature. In both cases, it is impossible, given the past, for the agent to do otherwise at the time of choice.

A further problem would arise if the mental occurrences necessitated their respective choices in some non-natural or non-causal way. The libertarian condition of sole or ultimate dominion would then require that the agent had rational control over the earlier mental occurrences. If the occurrence of C_A rather than C_B is necessarily connected in some way with the prior occurrences of M rather than M' (and so for M' and C_B) then the question of the agent's dual rational control over the choices would depend on whether the occurrence at the earlier time of M rather than M' (or vice versa) was under the control of the agent's will. If two level theorists follow their usual strategy, they would explain this earlier control in terms of a difference in still earlier mental occurrences. An infinite regress of the kind described in chapter 2 would threaten. If the regress were cut short by saying that occurrences in M (or M') simply took place, undetermined and unexplained, the problem of arbitrariness would arise anew. In short, two level theories leave us with the same Hobbesian dilemmas described at the end of chapter 2, while adding further problems about correlation and interaction between two levels of phenomena. This is not a bargain.

4.16   (4) *Non-Occurrent Cause Theories*. The difficulties of theories in previous categories suggest to most libertarians that a theory of agency, or of non-occurrent causation, represents the only viable solution to the problems created by the indeterminist condition. The expression "non-occurrent causation" comes from Broad (62), who uses it to characterize the agency of a self with respect to its free choices or actions which satisfies the following conditions. (a) The self (or person or rational agent) is the sole cause of its free choices or actions; (b) its causation can be exercised in two directions, to choose (or do) and to do otherwise; and (c) its causation of free choices or actions is the causation of an occurrence by a *thing* or *substance* which cannot be explained as the causation of an occurrence *by other occurrences*, either simultaneous with, earlier than, or later than, the choice or action.

Conditions (a) and (b) correspond respectively to the libertarian requirements of sole dominion and dual power. It is condition (c) that distinguishes a non-occurrent cause theory from other libertarian theories. (In this section and the next, I shall speak for convenience of "N-O cause theories" and "N-O causation.") Condition (c) requires that the self or agent cause its own free choices in a way that cannot be explained in terms of past or presently occurring states or changes (*physical or psychological*) involving the self, or in terms of past or presently occurring states or changes of any kind. According to N-O cause theorists, we must recognize another kind of causation alongside the usual kind of causation of occurrences by other occurrences. We must recognize the possibility of direct causation of an occurrence by an agent or substance. "Some . . . causal chains . . . have beginnings," as Richard Taylor says, "and they begin with the agents themselves" (74, p. 56).

Broad, who is critical of N-O cause theories, thinks that libertarians are driven to them by the indeterminist condition. At the moment of choice a free agent must be able to act in either of two opposing directions. But acting in one direction rather than the other cannot be accounted for in terms of the circumstances, either past or present, physical or psychological. An account in terms of past circumstances, physical or psychological, is ruled out by the indeterminist condition, since a two level strategy will not work. An account in terms of present circumstances is ruled out by arguments like those we gave earlier in discussing simultaneous reasons. Causation by (actual) later occurrences, Broad regards as absurd. So the agent's causation of its free choices must not be explainable at all in terms of circumstances (i.e. occurrences involving it).

It has often been noted by N-O cause theorists themselves that the conception of causation to which their reasoning leads is an unusual one. We do in fact regularly speak of things or substances causing occurrences. "The stone caused the breaking of the window." "The cat caused the lamp to fall." But these statements are recognized as being elliptical. It is the stone's moving, and its striking the window, that caused the breaking, the cat's leaping that caused the lamp's falling. Causation of occurrences by substances can usually be interpreted as causation of occurrences by other occurrences. This must be denied in the case of N-O causation. "The agent caused his or her choice" cannot be an elliptical way of saying that the agent's being in some state or undergoing some change caused the choice.

All N-O cause theories satisfy Broad's three conditions, but the thing or substance that causes non-occurrently is differently described in different theories. Recent N-O cause theorists like Taylor and Roderick Chisholm[19] follow Thomas Reid in identifying the N-O cause as the agent, or the man himself, a substance in space and time having both mental and physical attributes. Kant and others identify it with a noumenal self or transempirical ego outside space and time. Still other thinkers, before Reid and Kant, speak of that which causes non-occurrently as something within the agent, like the agent's Will or Reason. Duns Scotus expresses a common medieval theme when he says that "nothing other than the Will is the total cause of volition in the will" (62, p. 38). The tendency suggested by such statements to reify the Will, making it a non-occurrent cause within the agent, can perhaps be traced to Aristotle's conception of *Nous*, or active reason—that obscure source of activity in the rational soul which may fairly be regarded as the primitive ancestor of all N-O causes. The reified Will of some later thinkers is Aristotle's active reason manifesting itself in the practical sphere.

4.17   It is not surprising that critics of libertarian views, like Broad, find the notion of N-O causation mysterious, and argue that it is essentially mysterious. Many defenders of N-O causation themselves concede that it is obscure, but argue that some such notion is presupposed by our experiences of choosing and acting freely. For example, Richard Taylor (74) says: "One can hardly affirm such a theory of agency with complete comfort . . . and wholly without embarrassment, for the conception of men and their powers which is involved in it, is strange indeed, if not positively mysterious" (p. 57). Yet Taylor thinks that such a notion of N-O causation is the only one consistent with the presuppositions of free agency, namely that we are the sole cause of our free actions and these actions are not determined by prior circumstances: "If I believe that something not identical with myself was the cause of my behavior— some event wholly external to myself, for instance, or even one internal to myself, such as a nerve impulse, volition, or what not—then I cannot regard that behavior as being an act of mine, unless I further believe that I was the cause of that external or internal event "(p.55), To avoid an infinite regress of causings of events (i.e. occurrences) by the agent, one must suppose that some occurrence is directly caused by the agent but not by virtue of any further occurrence involving the agent. A similar line is taken by N-O cause theorists like Reid, C.A. Campbell,[20] and, of course, Kant when he says that freedom must be presupposed by practical reason, but cannot be made intelligible to theoretical reason.

The consequence of the "strange, and perhaps mysterious" nature of N-O causation which concerns us most is that N-O cause theories fail to provide a solution to the problem of dual rational self control or determination. Indeed, the conception of agency proposed by them seems to preclude in principle any resolution of this problem. To provide an answer to the problem of dual rational self control, one must be able to answer the question "Why did the agent rationally or deliberately choose (or do) this rather than that?" for both of the opposing outcomes that are open to the agent. But N-O cause theorists want to disallow any explanation of the agent's free choices or actions in terms of the occurrences of states or changes, physical or psychological, past or present, involving the agent. Now, all libertarians disallow an explanation of free choice or action in terms of physical causes. But N-O cause theorists must also disallow an explanation in terms of reasons and mental occurrences, like deliberation, as well. They are aware of the dangers of two level theories and they reject all conditional or hypothetical interpretations of the agent's powers to do and do otherwise that would make the exercise of these powers depend on past differences in the agent's psychological history.

But the question "Why did the agent *rationally* or *deliberately* choose this rather than doing otherwise?" (call it "Question Q") fairly begs for an answer in terms of the agent's reasons and/or processes of reasoning. N-O cause theorists must say that an answer in these terms is not forthcoming. The agent simply acts, one way or the other, and in doing so rises about the influence of past character traits, motives and other states and changes, physical and psychological. N-O cause theorists can say that reasons may have inclined the agent to the choice made without necessitating it, and some, like Chisholm, do say this.[21] But they are well aware that this does not solve the problem of one-way arbitrariness. At some times, but not at others, the agent acts against his inclining reasons. Why does the agent do this at some times, but not at others? Again, the answer is that the agent simply does it, non-occurrently. One cannot ask for any further explanation in terms of occurrences, physical or psychological. For then one would have to explain how these occurrences arose. Some causal chains must simply end in the agent.

N-O cause theorists may try to legitimize this failure to solve the problem of dual rational self control by arguing that the question Q itself is illegitimate. Once we understand that N-O causation is unique and different from ordinary occurrent causation, we see that the question "Why did the agent rationally or deliberately choose (or do) this rather than that?" cannot even be asked of N-O causation. For the question *does* call for an answer in terms of past or present occurrences, physical or psychological, and this is the kind of answer that is inappplicable to the case of N-O causation.

This is undoubtedly a correct response from the perspective of their theory. But it is only a roundabout way of saying that the problem of dual rational self control is not solvable in the theory. For the question Q is just a way of eliciting some explanation of how the agent can go either way in the choice situation, rationally or deliberately, given exactly the same past, including the same psychological history. Nor is the question Q an esoteric one invented by scientists or occultists. It makes perfectly good sense in ordinary language. Common sense, not merely scientific reason, demands an answer to it. A scientific answer would be in terms of physical or physiological causes. The answer of ordinary language would be in terms of reasons or motives. Bootstrap theorists, content theorists, and two level theorists, all reject the answer in terms of physical or physiological causes, but they are prepared to accept some sort of an answer in terms of reasons (simultaneous, "in the object or content sense," or whatever). But N-O cause theorists, seeing the inadequacies of these other theories, are not prepared to accept an answer in terms of causes *or* reasons. And this leaves them with no answer whatever to the question of how the choice can be two ways rational.

To complicate matters, common sense *does* provide an answer to the question Q. One may say that the agent rationally or deliberately chose this rather than doing otherwise because the agent had such and such reasons or motives, or because the agent deliberated in such and such a way; and one may add that the agent would have done otherwise rationally or deliberately, if the agent had had other reasons or had deliberated differently. But this answer is unfortunately a compatibilist (conditional or hypothetical) answer and it is unacceptable to libertarians because it violates the indeterminist condition. The obscurity of N-O causation is, therefore. not something forced on us by common sense *simpliciter*. It is forced on us only if we accept the indeterminist condition. But acceptance or rejection of the indeterminist condition is precisely what the debate is all about.[22]

Despite their failure, N-O cause theorists see deeply into the needs of the libertarian position. They are right up to a point in suggesting that libertarians cannot satisfy all the demands of common sense in regard to dual rational self control. But libertarians can do a good deal better than N-O cause theories do in meeting these demands; moreover the demands of common sense regarding dual rational self control that can be satisfied by libertarians can be satisfied without postulating N-O causes or employing any other special cause strategies.

4.18   In summary, we have explored Hobbes' path 2 dilemma in this chapter, according to which any account of the will's ultimate dominion over itself presupposing indeterminism must lead either to the confusion of identifying freedom with indeterminism or to the emptiness of postulating obscure or mysterious forms of agency or causation. The confusion was traced to the problem of dual rational self determination or control, and the emptiness to various "special cause" or "extra-circumstantial" strategies employed by libertarians in response to that problem.

This discussion of libertarian strategies was not exhaustive, and it would perhaps take a whole book to make it so. But the strategies discussed are representative of the major options and many of them will reenter the critical discussions of Part II, some as pieces of a larger puzzle.

Notes

1. Cf. Hume's classic statement in the *Treatise* (60, p. 411): "Where [actions] proceed not from some cause in the characters and dispositions of the person who performed them, they . . . can neither redound to his honor, if good, nor infamy, if evil. . . . the person is not responsible for [the action] . . . as it proceeded from nothing in him that is durable or constant."

2. Peters (58, p. 28) says that "motive" is a somewhat narrower term in ordinary language; and Grice (67) says that, "motive" implies some element of desire or inclination, while "reason" does not. These claims have merit, because etymologically the two terms come from different directions. Roughly speaking, motives "move," while reasons "explain." Nevertheless, there is a tendency for their uses to converge, since merely cognitive reasons do not "explain" choices or actions without presupposing some volitional reasons which incline or "move." And motives can explain *because* they move, i.e. incline agents toward certain choices or actions.

3. Cf. Dennett (78, chap. 15), on this point.

4. Bramhall makes this point in (44, pp. 150-51, and again on p.. 414). Cf. also Reid (70, p. 88), Chisholm (66, p. 25), Rem Edwards (67), and Leibniz (51, p. 435).

5. This line of reasoning also refutes the strong view advocated by some soft determinists, including Hobbes, Hume, Hobart (66), and Schlick (66), that freedom is not only compatible with determinism, but presupposes, or implies, determinism. For a criticism of this strong view see the works cited in the previous note and also Philippa Foot (66).

6. Bramhall introduces the idea in (44, pp. 414-15). The notion is discussed (and criticized) in J. Edwards (69, pp. 71ff. and 160ff), and Schopenhauer (60, pp. 60ff). For an account of other historical uses of the notion, see Bourke (64, chap. 4).

7. The remarks of the previous three sections are not the last words on either the liberty of indifference or reasons inclining without necessitating. Like many other notions and views discussed in this chapter, they have something positive to contribute to theory developed in Part II and will be discussed again. (Cf. 5.2). The point being made here is simply that, by themselves, they cannot rescue the libertarian view.

8. We should remind ourselves here that this restriction to "past" circumstances in the definitions of determination and determinism is inescapable, for the reasons given in chapter 3, note 7.

9. In addition to the content theories discussed in this section, appeals to formal and (and final) causes are common in medieval scholastic discussions of free will. (Cf. Aquinas (45, Part II, pp. 226-7), and Scotus (62, p. 36.)

10. This point has been made in a slightly different way against Popper's theory by D. J. O'Connor (71, p. 97). O'Connor says that Popper does not really come to grips with the problems presented by condition X (O'Connor's name for the indeterminist condition). But he praises Popper's "Of Clouds and Clocks" as one of the most important and innovative works on the free will issue in recent times. I think this assessment is correct and we shall be referring to some of the themes of Popper's essay (especially the evolutionary themes) again in Part II. But Popper's failure to come to grips with the problem of dual rational self control is pivotal, since it means that he fails to meet the critics of the indeterminist condition head-on.

11. I do not mean to suggest that content theorists explicitly make this move. Most of them assume that their content theories must be supplemented by further libertarian strategies, either by two level or non-occurrent cause strategies, or both. Thus they never make explicit why content theories will not work on their own and why they must be supplemented. In addition, some content theorists never directly address the problem of dual rational self control at all. (Cf. the remarks on Popper in the previous note.)

12. The assumption that the contents individuate the attitudes is essential to the argument at this point. It is conceivable that someone might deny this assumption, saying that one might have the same belief (or want, etc.) with different conceptual or propositional contents. But this would distort our ordinary ways of individuating states of mind. And, beyond that, any attempt to use such a move for libertarian purposes would fall prey to arguments of subsequent sections against two level theories.

13. The Kantian "moral law" theory discussed later in this section will be discussed again (though not endorsed) in 8.2; and Popper's theory will be discussed again in 6.3 and 9.6.

14. I am not suggesting that everyone who argues that reasons are not causes of actions is committed to such a strategy vis à vis the indeterminist condition. Most of those who argue for the thesis that reasons are not causes (e.g. Melden (61), Peters (58), and Winch (58)) are simply trying to say something about the nature of actions and action explanations, and not trying to defend indeterminist theories of freedom. Also, those who argue that reasons cannot be causes may be making one or more of the following three claims. (i) Reasons in the object or content sense cannot be causal circumstances (of the kind required by the indeterminist condition); (ii) reasons in the psychological attitude sense cannot be causal circumstances (of the kind required, etc.); or (iii) the having of a reason, in the psychological attitude sense, cannot be a causal circumstance (of the kind required etc.). Now (i) and (ii) are true, but they are not of any help to the libertarian unless (iii) is also true. (i) is true because an abstract content is not a circumstance; (ii) is true because a psychological attitude is an attribute of an agent, not a circumstance involving an agent. But the having of such an attitude or attribute at a time is a circumstance, and thus is is important to show that such a circumstance is not the kind to cause or be caused by virtue of laws of nature. Thus, the affirmation of (iii) is distinctive of a two level strategy.

15. Descartes employs this strategy insofar as his account of free will presupposes that human volitions (the mind's "actions" for him) are outside the physical order and cannot by their nature be subject to physical causation. See Descartes (31, I, pp. 232, 360, 401; II, 75, 104). Other (post-Cartesian) thinkers who use a similar strategy include R. Price (Priestley and Price, 78, p. 139) and Mansel (51, pp. 152-3). In the writings of all such thinkers, however, Descartes included, such a dualistic strategy is combined with other strategies, notably with appeals to volitions and non-occurrent causes.

16. In addition to the figures mentioned in the previous note, this line is taken by Renouvier (12, pp. 317 and 325-6), Bergson (44, p. 287), and James (07, pp. 447-8). James, in (07), identifies volitions with acts of attention.

17. See Thorp (80, chap. 3), Dennett (78), Davidson (70), and Harré (70, pp. 209ff.) for discus-

sions of this denial of type-type correlations. Thorp, Dennett and Harré insist that correlations are possible under some non-ordinary classification of mental states.

18. Davidson's "anomalous monism" (Davidson, 70) is the best known example.

19. R. Taylor (62, 66, and 74); Chisholm (66, 67, 76a, and 76b). A more recent theory of this type is that of Thorp (80).

20. C. A. Campbell (66a, 66b, 67, and 70). Campbell restricts libertarian freedom to moral contexts in which the agent is making an effort to act from duty against inclination.

21. Chisholm (66, p. 25).

22. For criticisms of N-O cause theories that take a similar line, see Broad (62), Ranken (67), Thalberg (76), and Bonjour (76).

Part II

Relativistic Alternatives and R-Choice

5.1   Previous chapters should have suggested what is, in any case, almost certainly true—that an adequate libertarian theory of freedom is not something we are going to find somewhere already embodied in an existing language or conceptual scheme. What is needed is a theoretical construction out of some familiar and some unfamiliar materials, a construction that will save as many appearances (ordinary intuitions about freedom) as possible, without merely describing the ordinary. It should be a likely story, but not necessarily a familiar one.[1] This is the task which begins in the next section after three introductory remarks.

First, the construction will proceed in numbered steps or stages over the next four chapters (5-8), each step building upon previous ones. The steps will be labelled "S1," "S2," etc., and will appear at places along the way, often summarizing points already made. The numbered steps provide an overview of the theory; but, of course, they are mere summaries. Their justification, and often an explanation of their meaning, lies in the surrounding texts. I want to emphasize the serial nature of the construction, because some steps, especially in the early going, will seem ineffective and unpromising. It is the cumulative effect, the mosaic, that counts. The notions of this chapter, for example, of relativistic (or R-) alternative and R-choice, are clearly extraordinary ones. But they will tell us something about the ordinary, and will eventually be embedded in a wider context.

Second, what follows is a possibility argument. We are trying to show that a libertarian freedom presupposing the indeterminist condition is possible or conceivable, and so to answer the Hobbesian charge that any account of such a freedom must be "confused or empty." One may ask of any kind of freedom whether it is possible, whether it exists in fact, and whether it ought to exist. The second two questions, factual and normative respectively, will not be dealt with until chapters 9 and 10, when we have some conception of the relevant freedom in hand. The theory will not try to capture everything that every libertarian has wanted. Some have wanted too much and so have courted confusion or emptiness. But we hope to capture more than their compatibilist opponents have thought possible.

The final point concerns the topic of value relativism. We have neglected it since the Introduction. But relativist themes will begin to emerge in this chapter and will play an increasingly important role as the construction proceeds.

5.2   The first three steps involve themes mentioned earlier. Each has played a role in the history of debates about free will, though no one of them is of much help by itself. In immediately succeeding steps they will be given a new twist. The first of the three is Bramhall's thesis, which was the main theme of chapter 2: "The freedom of the agent is from the freedom of the will." We interpreted this to mean the following:

S1. Bramhall's Thesis: The essential indeterminism associated with the agent's freedom is to be located in the will of the agent (in the relation of reasons or motives to choice) and not in the relation of the will to overt action.

The second and third steps dwell on the "relation of reasons or motives to choice." Both are familiar themes of chapter 4. The first concerns "reasons inclining without necessitating," a theme which has played a significant role in the history of debates about free will. Though it leads to difficulties when employed by itself, as we saw in 4.5, it is an important piece of a larger puzzle. We shall call it

S2. Leibniz' Thesis: In the relation between reasons and choice, the reasons which the agent has prior to choice must in some sense incline the agent toward the choice, or the doing otherwise, whichever occurs, without necessitating what actually occurs, i.e. without determining what actually occurs in the sense of D2.

The third step is another familiar theme of chapter 4. Though often ridiculed by opponents of the libertarian view, it is also an important piece of the larger puzzle.

S3. The Liberty of Indifference: The reasons or motives which the agent has prior to choice must also, in some sense, place the agent in a condition of indifference toward the choosing and the doing otherwise.

So persistent are these last two themes in the history of debates about free will, that one might guess they would be part of an adequate solution. But they seem to be at odds with one another. Indifference as to outcome and reasons inclining toward one outcome rather than another are usually regarded as incompatible alternatives, rather than as complementary requirements for free will. S2 and S3 would, in fact, be incompatible if the sense in which the agent's reasons incline toward one outcome were not different from the sense in which the reasons involve the agent in a condition of indifference. The next step explains how these senses can be different. But it requires some preparation.

5.3   To show how S2 and S3 can be reconciled, we turn to a story, or fable, whose leading character will be called "Everyman," in the manner of such stories with a moral. (I am going to attend to some details of this story because it will play a role in several later discussions, in this and subsequent chapters.) Everyman is a searcher who lives in times past on an Earth with more remote and inaccessible regions than its real counterpart. Dissatisfied with his own civilization, he journeys to one of these remote regions in search of "wisdom" and "happiness," vaguely thinking there is some connection between the two. In his travels he comes upon an isolated society, called "Andon," and lives there for several years, learning its language and culture and transmitting information to a group of elders who rule the society. They tell him of only two other societies previously known to them, called "Baltar" and "Careen," each also isolated by high mountains.

Of special interest is Everyman's relation to the Chief Elder, a position elected by the elders and now held by an older woman. She insists that he may be allowed to live in Andon permanently only if he follows the procedures laid down in the sacred books of their ancestors for cases where a person wishes either to leave Andonian society or to join it. The person must visit each of the other known societies and live in each for a period of time, at least for a year, before deciding where to live.

Thus, Everyman embarks upon an arduous journey, first to Baltar, then to Careen, living in each for over a year. The climactic scenes occur when he returns to confront the Chief Elder. She wants to know which society he has decided to live in. But he is unsure. It is clear that he would prefer life in any one of the three societies to life in his own civilization. He also makes clear that he prefers both Andon and Baltar to Careen. The latter's climate is too cold for his taste and the boisterous, argumentative nature of the Careenian people does not suit his retiring temperament.

But the choice between Andon and Baltar presents a problem for him. He likes each, but for different reasons. On the one hand, Andon is preferable to all the other societies, including Baltar, for the greater tolerance accorded there to different styles of life and for its form of government, which is more democratic. The elders are subject to the wishes of the assembly of citizens in more matters. The cultivation of learning, especially of mathematics and science, is greater in Andon, though these are not neglected in Baltar. He has made more lasting friendships in Andon, though he has made some in Baltar, and so on. On the other hand, Baltar is preferable to all the other societies, including Andon, for different reasons. The climate is better, and Baltar borders the ocean, which satisfies some ancient longings in Everyman. The soil is richer, food more plentiful, and hence there is more leisure time. Also, music in its many forms, vocal and instrumental, is cultivated more actively in Baltar, and music is a special interest of Everyman's.

So it goes, Everyman likes both societies, but for different reasons. And though he believes he has taken everything important into account, he cannot decide between them. He fears he will have to ask the elders to help him decide. But the Chief Elder replies:

> C.E. We are not allowed to choose for you. If you asked us to decide by *our* preferences, we would undoubtedly all choose Andon. If you mean that we should help you uncover *your* true preference, then we have been doing that. And we accept your conclusion that you do not have a clear preference. Yet such a situation is not unknown to our sacred books; and they tell us what to do in such cases. If you want to know, we shall show you.

Everyman agrees to be shown, and is taken to their game room.

C.E. The books of our ancestors say that in cases of this kind, we must appeal to the Orola, the spinning wheel, or some other instrument of our games of chance. The method is simply this. You spin the wheel of equal size red and blue spaces; if it comes to rest on red, you stay in Andon, if on blue, you go to Baltar.

Everyman is appalled by this suggestion. He says it describes no rational "method" at all, but simply a way of leaving the decision to chance.[2] To the question of how he can allow it to be made in this way, he receives the following reply:

C.E. The sacred books say that in these circumstances there is no better way available. You said yourself that you could not decide. If we had wished to take the decision out of your hands, we would not have sent you to Baltar and Careen at all. And the sacred books forbid us to influence your decision unfairly in favor of Andon. So they say this is the best method in such circumstances.

E. Yet, to follow this method of your ancestors is also to take the decision out of my hands. I reject it. I want to think more about my reasons and about Andon and Baltar, perhaps weighing other factors until I can decide between them. Will you help me do that?

5.4 The story does not end here. But let us see what lessons may be learned from it thus far. Everyman's refusal to submit the choice to chance is a reasonable one, as is his request to think more about the options. But suppose he were to give in to the Chief Elder's suggestion, submitting the choice to the Orola. What kind of a choice would this be? Would it be a choice at all?

In 2.3, we defined a choice or decision as the formation of an intention or the creation of a purpose, which normally terminates deliberation between competing options, and may immediately initiate action, or guide action at a future time. If everyman were to follow the Chief Elder's suggestion, he would be making a choice in this sense. For the idea of submission required by the sacred texts is that Everyman agree in advance to "accept" this method of terminating deliberation and forming the intention to live in Andon or the intention to live in Baltar, and to be subsequently guided by the intention accepted. This is certainly no ordinary method of terminating deliberation and forming intention. Nothing of the sort is being claimed by the Chief Elder. In fact, she claims that it is extraordinary, and we are not going to claim otherwise. We merely want to say what can be learned about the ordinary by focussing on the extraordinary.

The situation is this. Of the two options, living in Andon (A), or living in Baltar (B), Everyman has prior reasons or motives, $a_1 \ldots a_n$, for preferring A to B in certain respects (more tolerance, preferable form of government, etc.) and different reasons or motives, $b_1 \ldots b_m$, for preferring B to A (the ocean setting, cultivation of music, etc.). Each of the reasons, the particular a_i's and b_i's, is a volitional or cognitive psychological attitude, of one or another of the kinds discussed in 4.3, that provides a preference (perhaps together with other reasons of its set) for one of the options. But, while Everyman has reasons for preferring each of the alternatives to the other, he does not believe that either of the sets of reasons $(a_1 \ldots a_n)$, $(b_1 \ldots b_m)$, provides him with stronger grounds, all things considered, for preferring one alternative to the other because the reasons are of different kinds that he cannot adequately compare.[3]

Let us say that, in such a situation, he has "first order" reasons inclining him toward A rather than B and "first order" reasons inclining him toward B rather than A (the individual a_i's and b_i's). But, because of the nature of the inclining reasons, he does not have a "second order" reason for preferring one option to the other. A second order reason for preferring X to Y would be a belief that the *set* of first order reasons inclining toward X provides stronger grounds, all things considered, for preferring X to Y than the *set* of first order reasons inclining toward Y provides for preferring Y to X.[4] When a situation of this kind obtains, we shall say that the agent believes he is confronted with

S4. R-(or Relativistic) Alternatives: A set of alternatives (possible actions, purposes, plans, goals, etc.), $(A,B,C \ldots)$ is a set of R-(or relativistic) alternatives for an agent S at a time t, if and only if, (i) S has first order reasons, $a_1 \ldots a_n$, prior to t for preferring to choose A to B and C . . ., first order reasons, $b_1 \ldots b_m$, for preferring to choose B to A and C . . ., first order reasons for preferring to choose C to A and B. . . . and so on, but (ii) S has no second order reason prior to choice for preferring to choose any alternative in the set $(A,B,C \ldots)$ to any other in the set, because of the lack of a common measure or standard for comparing reasons of different kinds, and (iii) S has second order reasons for preferring each alternative in the set to every other alternative not in the set that may have been considered.

The sets of first order reasons, $(a_1 \ldots a_n)$ etc., associated with each of a set of R-alternatives will be called "R-alternative reason sets."

Clause (iii) accounts for the fact that the R-alternatives are superior to all other considered options (Andon and Baltar to Careen, for example), though, according to clause (ii), no R-alternative is superior to any other.

5.5 Use of the term "relativistic" in S4 deserves comment. With respect to Andon and Baltar, Everyman is something of a cultural and value relativist. He recognizes that the two societies have different practices, institutions, opportunities and values. But he cannot say that, taken as a whole, either is better for him than the other. Each is good according to standards (first order reasons) provided by his "Reason," represented by his total set of reasons, but his total set of reasons provides him with no objective, higher order standard by which the competing subsets of standards can be compared.

This does not mean that Everyman (or any man) has to be an unqualified relativist about values and ways of life to acknowledge the existence of R-alternatives. His R-alternatives form a restricted set. He does not believe *all* goals or societies are equally good; and even his present attitude toward Andon and Baltar may be temporary, or due to cloudy vision, for all he knows. What is important in regard to S4 is not the *truth* of relativist views of value, but the *meaning* of such views. And it is their meaning I want to discuss.

To understand that meaning, insofar as it is significant for our purposes, we may turn to an analogy between relativity theories in physics and doctrines of value relativism. Physical theories of relativity and doctrines of value relativism are alike in form, though concerned with different subject matter. The physical theories imply (I) that measurements of certain physical quantities, e.g. distance, time or motion, may differ in different physical frames of reference of a certain class, and (II) that no one of these frames is privileged or superior to any others of the class, in the sense that it gives the absolute, or uniquely true or correct, measurement of these quantities. Each frame provides a correct or true measurement from its perspective and each perspective is equally valid. In Einstein's Special Theory, for example, measurements of lengths of objects and temporal durations of processes are relative in this sense to different inertial frames of reference—those moving with constant velocity relative to one another.[5] Different inertial frames may yield different measurements of lengths and times of the same objects or processes, each correct from its own perspective, but none absolutely, or uniquely, true.

Similarly, doctrines of value relativism assert (I') that judgments of value of certain kinds (e.g. about the goodness or badness of actions, purposes, principles or ways of life) presupposed by different persons (or groups or societies or cultures) may differ, and (II') that no one person's (or group's) judgments are privileged or superior to any of the others in the sense that they are the absolute, or uniquely true, judgments. Each is correct from its perspective and the perspectives are equally valid.

In doctrines of value relativism, "judgments of value" correspond to the "measurements of physical quantities" of the physical theories, and the perspectives of different persons or groups correspond to the "frames of reference" of the physical theories. In one kind of value relativism, defined with respect to individual persons, rather than to societies or cultures (a view sometimes called "value subjectivism") the *reason sets* of different persons correspond to the frames of reference of the physical theories. The reason sets of different persons may presuppose different valuations, each correct from its perspective, but no reason set provides a perspective superior to any other. In other kinds of value relativism, applying to societies or cultures, different frames of reference are defined by the shared reasons of the members of the different societies—i.e. by the shared beliefs and other psychological attitudes that must be inferred from actions, practices, institutions, etc. It should come as no surprise that there are evidential difficulties in determining evaluative frames of reference, because there are well-known difficulties about knowing "other minds." But these difficulties do not invalidate the above definition of value relativism as a view that might be held about different persons or societies; nor does it invalidate the analogy to physical theories of relativity.

What does the term "value" mean in the context of such theories? William Frankena says that since "words like 'value' and 'valuation' may be, and are, used in a variety of ways" by philosophers and social theorists, one should "choose a clear and systematic scheme and use it consistently," when using the terms.[6] This is good advice and will be followed. Let us first define a *valuation* as a proposition having the form "X is good or bad, right or wrong, better or worse than something else (in some ways or respects and/or in certain circumstances and/or in itself or for some purpose)."[7] A *value* of a person is then a valuation believed true by the person, or whose truth is presupposed by the person's reason set. Thus it is one of my values *that* justice is good. Or, putting it another way, the valuation (=proposition) that justice is good is believed to be true by me. It is one of Everyman's values *that* living by the ocean is better than living far from the ocean, and so on for other valuations believed true, or whose truth is presupposed, by him.[8]

Values are thus associated with evaluative beliefs, but not uniquely so. A person's desires, likes, dislikes, interests, emotions and other psychological attitudes may presuppose that certain things are good or bad without there being an explicit belief about the matter. We could undoubtedly generate an argument about whether "belief" ought to be defined so that this is possible. But to avoid such an argument, I have defined a value of a person as a valuation either believed true *or* whose truth is presupposed by the person's reason set. This covers the ground without multiplying arguments. Similarly, we can say that a value of a *group* (society, culture, etc.) is a valuation whose truth is presupposed by the practices, customs, laws, policies, etc. of the group. Finally, a person's *value system* will be the aggregate of all valuations, either believed true by the person, or whose truth is presupposed by the person's total reason set. And "value system" would be defined analogously for groups of persons.

5.6 Now let us return to Everyman and the notion of an R-alternative defined by S4. We can understand the use of the term "relativistic" in S4 by reference to the physical analogy and the definition of value relativism just given. Think of the first order reason sets favoring Andon and Baltar, $(a_1 \ldots a_n)$, $(b_1 \ldots b_m)$, as defining different "frames of reference" within the "universe" of Everyman's total reason set. Different valuations are true from the perspectives of these different frames of reference. Thus A is better than B *from* $(a_1 \ldots a_n)$ but B is better than A *from* $(b_1 \ldots b_m)$. Moreover, neither perspective is superior to the other in the universe of Everyman's total reason set, if the conditions of S4 are satisfied. Each perspective is valid, but none is privileged. In this manner, the idea of value relativism—that the reason sets of different agents define relativistic frames of reference—is transposed to the inner life of a single agent, so that different *subsets* of the agent's total reason set define relativistic frames of reference for the agent. The resulting analogy between R-alternative reason sets *in foro interno* and R-alternative reason sets *in foro externo* is crucial for understanding later developments of the theory.

Of course, Everyman's R-alternatives are limited in number, so that what we have is a qualified relativism at best. But relativistic theories *can* be limited in this and other ways, while conforming to the patterns of (I)-(II) and (I')-(II'). In physical theories, measurements of some physical quantities may be relative to different frames (e.g. lengths and times in Einstein's Special Theory), while measurements of other quantities (space-time intervals or the speed of light *in vacuo*) remain invariant. And the class of relativistic frames of reference may be limited, e.g. to sets of frames moving with constant velocity relative to one another. The fact that relativistic theories of value can be similarly restricted is of great importance to the free will issue. S4 is merely the first indication of this fact.[9]

Before moving on, we should note that something like the idea of an R-alternative has surfaced from time to time in the history of discussions of free will. To my knowledge, the first philosopher in the West to employ something like it was Aquinas.[10] The idea gained currency among some of Aquinas' followers thereafter and among other thinkers influenced by scholastic thought. Bramhall mentions it [11] and may have gotten it from Aquinas, through Suarez. Hobbes says that everything Bramhall has to say about free will (which is not of much importance, according to Hobbes) could already be found in Suarez. Thomas Reid (70) also appeals to the idea, but I do not know what, if any, influences there are in his case.[12]

Yet the notion of an R-alternative defined by S4, like the notions defined by earlier steps, can only be a piece of the puzzle. Those who mention it, like Aquinas, Bramhall, and Reid, generally do so vaguely and use it only to counter the charge that the will or agent must be necessitated by the strongest prior motive. This leaves them with the problem of explaining how the actual choice is made and leads, in most cases, to appeals to the "Will" or "agent" which moves itself in a special way, e.g. as a non-occurrent cause, to make one set of motives prevail over the others. In short, the appeal to R-alternatives is a prelude to some special cause, or extra-circumstantial, strategy. Our approach must be different, since no appeal to non-circumstantial causes is to be allowed. S4 is a step along the way. A great deal depends upon where we go from here.

5.7 The sacred books of Andon suggest an alternative route. They appeal to no special powers that Everyman possesses to settle the matter. Instead they require that he submit the selection to chance. They require, in other words, what may be called an

> S5. R-Choice or R-Decision =df. the termination of a process of delibera-
> tion by carrying out a prior commitment to accept and take responsibility for a
> random selection from among a set of R-alternatives.[13] (This accepting or
> taking responsibility amounts to forming the intention or purpose (at the
> moment of selection) to bring about A or B or C . . ., whichever R-alternative
> is selected, and the corollary commitment to take the steps required to bring
> about the purpose, or what is intended.)

This is an extraordinary suggestion as we noted; and Everyman had resisted it at the point where our story left off. But before asking how the Chief Elder will respond to Everyman's resistance, let us consider some of the characteristics such an R-choice would possess.

First, such a choice would satisfy the indeterminist condition. Given all past circumstances relative to the moment of selection, and all laws of nature, including all the Everyman's prior reason or motive states and prior processes of deliberation, it can be the case that he R-chooses A and it can be the case that he R-chooses B. (Do not be distracted, here or elsewhere, by the thought that the wheel's spinning is a macroscopic process that may in fact be determined, though its outcome is unknown to the onlookers. The wheel plays merely a figurative role in the argument, representing some undetermined process. In any eventually true story, its role would have to be assumed by an ontologically undetermined process. This is a factual matter to be dealt with later.)[14]

Second, Bramhall's thesis (S1) is satisfied by R-choice because the indeterminism "intervenes" between prior reason or motive states and the resulting choice, not between choice and subsequent action. Third, Leibniz's thesis (S2) is satisfied in the sense that, whatever alternatives is selected, Everyman would have (first order) reasons for preferring it to every other alternative. We can imagine that if he goes to Baltar and is asked why he chose it over Andon, he will not be at a loss for words. He will refer to his many reasons, $b_1 \ldots b_m$ for preferring Baltar to Andon. Of course, he will also concede, if pressed, that he had many other reasons, no better or worse collectively speaking, for choosing Andon over Baltar. But he might add "I did not say my reasons, $b_1 \ldots b_m$, for choosing Baltar 'necessitated' the choice of Baltar. I merely said that these were my reasons for selecting Baltar rather than Andon, and if I had not had these reasons ($b_1 \ldots b_m$), I would not be here. I would respect for our traditions. But this does not mean you have not agreed out of in an obvious way. Everyman's reasons and motives prior to choice did not incline him, all things considered, to one of the alternatives that might have been chosen rather than the other.

5.8 Thus, the R-choice suggested by the Chief Elder has some interesting features. But it also has a feature that leads Everyman to resist making it. Where the dialogue left off, Everyman rejected her suggestion and asked for more time to think about the options. Let us now continue it:

> C.E. Your request for more time to think about your problem is justified, as is your request that we help you clarify the consequences of your options and your reasons for desiring them. The sacred books do not advise submitting choices to the Orola too quickly. Quite the contrary, they advise caution. The agent must *want* to do so. The books do note, however, that there is no guarantee that such a postponement will necessarily result in a preference for one option over the other. There will come a time when your overriding need will be to terminate the condition of indecision, though no clear preference has been found, and then the suggestion of the sacred books is to be followed.

Let us suppose that Everyman does think about the matter for some more days and weeks, without being able to generate a second order preference for Andon or Baltar. He becomes anxious, wanting to commit himself wholly to some new way of life, and finally agrees to submit the choice to the Orola. But, in doing so, his ego makes one last stand. He emphasizes that this is a move of last resort which he takes only out of respect for their sacred books. He insists that by making the move he is compromising his aim of making a reasonable choice. The choice will be made by chance rather than by reason. With this reservation, he agrees to play their "ancestral game."

The Chief Elder is pleased, but she is too much of a philosopher and too anxious to defend her ancestral ways to let the matter rest there

> C.E. I am glad that you agree. But any condescension is unjustified. For you must not say, without qualification, that if the Orola is used, the decision is "taken out of your hands," or that it is "made by chance," or "not made by reason."
>
> These claims are misleading. For if your reasons for preferring Andon and Baltar were not as strong as they in fact were, you would not have been able to rule out the other options, Careen and your own civilization, as inferior to Andon and Baltar. It was your reasons and your reasoning that determined which alternatives the spinning wheel would choose among, ruling out all alternatives that were not worthy, that were not among the best. You are its master, not its slave.
>
> Moreover, whichever of the two options, Andon or Baltar, is selected, you will have the strongest available reasons for accepting it. It is simply the case that there is no *one* set of "strongest available reasons." If you should go to Baltar, be sure to tell them that. If they are unhappy because your reasons for choosing them do not make them clearly better than us in your eyes, then that is *their* problem, not yours. We all want to be thought superior, especially Baltarians. But your choice will have been rational nonetheless, even if it should wound their pride. Tell them it is so written in our sacred books.
>
> Finally, it is misleading to say that the choice was made merely by chance and not by you, because it is you who have decided to terminate your thinking and to accept the selection of the Orola. You decide not only the options for the wheel, but when it shall be used. I know that you have agreed out of respect for our traditions. But this does not mean you have not agreed out of respect for yourself. Sometimes it is better to get on with the business of living, than not to choose at all.

In sum,

> **S6.** An R-choice (or R-decision) is rational in five ways: First, deliberation, sometimes quite lengthy, may have proceeded it, involving reflection upon various options that are eventually ruled out as inferior to the R-alternatives involved. Second, the agent has (first order) reasons for preferring the selected alternative to *all* other alternatives, including other R-alternatives. Third, the decision to terminate deliberation after a time when faced with R-alternatives is as reasonable as the decision to go on. In fact, indefinite postponement of choice simply on the grounds that one's alternatives are R-alternatives is irrational. It is behavior perhaps befitting an ass, but not a rational animal. Fourth, if a choice is to be made, choosing by chance is as reasonable a method as any other. A case could be made for saying it is the most reasonable method, since it systematically takes into account the equal status of the R-alternatives.

And fifth, the choice is rational because any R-alternative selected, though not "the" best option in the circumstances, since there is no one best, is "a" best option, and hence is one of a set, each of which is an option judged to be most "worth trying" by the agent. Since only one option can be tried at once, it is rational to try any one of them first on an experimental basis.

The last four of these features of R-choice are essential to it. The first is not because alternatives other than the R-alternatives need not have been considered. But, in any case, there is no reason to believe that lengthy deliberation cannot lead up to R-choice or that R-choices must be hasty, ill-considered or spur of the moment choices in the sense of 2.5.

5.9   We may now allow the Chief Elder to conclude her discourse and thereby bring out several additional points of some importance.

> C.E. So do not say the choice was made by chance. Say it was made by reason *and* chance, just as your philosopher Plato said the cosmos was constructed by the interaction of reason and chance. And do not say the choice was taken from you. Say it was *given* by you to the Orola. For the sacred books of our ancestors say that to submit such a decision to the Orola is for reason to recognize its limitations. In the sphere where we make choices and decisions, reason cannot rule by always selecting the best, for it is not always the case that there is a best. To see this and to know when to submit to it, such knowledge and such submission are the beginning of wisdom. So say our sacred books.

There are two important and related themes here. We express the first by

> S7.   An R-choice, like the creation of the cosmos on one interpretation of Plato's *Timaeus*, is the result of the interaction of reason and chance.[15] To realize this about R-choice and to recognize the consequent limitation of reason in the practical sphere is an important step toward understanding what a libertarian conception of free will requires.

The second theme has to do with the source of this alleged limitation of practical reason. The source is said to be related to the fact that, in the sphere of ideals and values—in the practical sphere—reason cannot always select the single best, for there may not always be a single best. Let us pursue this theme further.

There are some who feel that if persons cannot choose between conflicting options or ideals they must be, for the time being at least, in ignorance of their true good. This is to assume that among conflicting options no more than one can be the true good for a person. Such an assumption may tempt us by analogy with theoretical reasoning. If someone is uncertain about two competing (because contrary or contradictory) answers to a theoretical question, he or she will nevertheless assume that no more than one of them can be true. Both may be false (if they are contraries) or both may be irrelevant. But if they imply contrary or contradictory beliefs they cannot, on logical grounds, be simultaneously endorsed. Let us call this the "no more than one truth" doctrine, or the "one truth" doctrine.

It may be thought that an analogue of the one truth doctrine exists for practical reasoning, a "no more than one (true) good" doctrine. If a person cannot simultaneously endorse more than one of a set of competing ideals or values (because they require contrary actions in the same circumstances) then no more than one of them can be the "good" for the person. But there is an ambiguity in the practical case. To "endorse" one of a set of competing ideals may mean to accept it as one's own, and hence to act on it or live by it. In this sense, a man cannot simultaneously endorse more than one of a set of competing ideals requiring contrary actions in the same circumstances. But he can simultaneously endorse more than one set of ideals in another sense of "endorse." Logic does not require that he say the other competing ideals he did not choose to live by are "false" goods for him. Some of them may be relativistic (or R-) alternatives to the one he chose, alternatives that are good for him in incommensurable ways, like Andon and Baltar for Everyman.

J. L. Austin once remarked that in the practical sphere we may need "the grace to be torn between, simply disparate ideals—why must there be a conceivable amalgam, the Good Life for Man?"[16] The denial of such an amalgam has usually been associated with doctrines of ethical and value relativism. But the relativists went too far. They insisted that any functional system of ideals or way of life was as good as any other. I think this is wrong for reasons to be discussed in subsequent chapters.[17] But it does not follow that because judgments of better and worse among systems of values are possible there must be one best for a single person or for all persons. What we have been describing in S4 and S6 is a "relativism at the top," where some alternatives are better than others but no single one is at the apex. And the suggestion is that this modified relativism, with its denial that there is always a one "true" good, is an essential ingredient in a doctrine of the freedom of the will. I do not know whether Austin recognized a connection between his rhetorical question "Why must there be a conceivable analgam—the Good Life for Man?" and his search for a "can" without an "if," but the connection is there.

Let us sum this up in

S8. The Many Goods Principle: There is no analogue in the realm of practical reasoning for the "no more than one truth" doctrine. That is to say, if a man is faced with a choice or decision between alternatives he cannot simultaneously endorse (in the sense of act upon), it is not the case that he must believe that no more than one of them can be the one (true) good for him, or for anyone exactly like him in the same circumstances. A fortiori, it is not the case that he must believe that no more than one of them can be the one (true) good for all persons whatever.

I do not want to argue for or against the (no more than) one *truth* doctrine here, though I think it is plausible. There have been epistemological relativists, like the

Sophist Protagoras, who have denied it, along with the one (true) good doctrine. The point is simply that maintaining the no more than one truth doctrine does not commit one to maintaining the no more than one good doctrine as well. because of differences in the nature of endorsement in the theoretical and practical spheres. So that, if the one truth doctrine is correct, then S8 marks a significant difference between the spheres of theoretical and practical reasoning.

5.10   As a consequence of S8, the failure of a person to decide upon a unique best among competing goods may not be due to ignorance. Such a failure might therefore arise in principle for an omniscient being as well. This bears upon Leibniz' argument for the notorious claim that God must have created the best of all possible worlds. If there is one best possible world, Leibniz argued, an all knowing, all powerful and all good being must have chosen to create it. But is there one best possible world? If some values are incommensurable, not capable of being compared as better or worse than one another by some objective standard, there could have been R-alternatives among the worlds God may have created. Leibniz denies this on the grounds that God could not act without a "sufficient reason" or "strongest motive." If there had been more than one best world, God would have lacked a sufficient reason to choose between them and so (contrary to fact) would have created nothing.[18] But this argument is a version, applied to God, of the "strongest motive" argument criticized in 4.5, and it shares the weakness of that latter argument. The possibility of R-alternatives and the Many Goods principle present a viable alternative. Any R-alternative world is a good world, one that is "worth trying," though not uniquely so. If therefore it would be better to create some good rather than none at all (as Leibniz also seems to have held),[19] then it would be better for God to R-choose one alternative, just as it is better for Everyman to get on with the business of living rather than to indefinitely postpone choice.

To pursue this line of thought, Leibniz would have had to give up the principle of sufficient reason in the strong form in which he held it—something he was not prepared to do. Though his instincts on the free will issue were libertarian, there was no room in Leibniz' metaphysical system, with its principle of sufficient reason, for a libertarian freedom. Once one gives up this principle, with its demand for sufficient causes and sufficient motives, an essential step toward understanding and accepting such a freedom would be acceptance of the Many Goods principle, along with S7.

As a consequence of these principles, genuine freedom would involve a limitation in the sense that not all of what is judged best can always be chosen—a limitation related to Hegel's insight that tragedy is most often the result of a clash between one good and another that cannot be simultaneously realized. Freedom and finitude (limitation), in this (potentially tragic) sense, are inextricably linked. This is one of the lessons of S7 and S8.

5.11   An important aspect of the above argument was the assertion that any R-alternative (world) actually chosen would be "worth trying" ("worth creating"). This was the fifth of the five ways in which an R-choice was said to be rational in S6. Since each of a set of R-alternatives is worth trying and no more than one of them can be simultaneously chosen, it is more rational to choose one of them on an experimental basis than to indefinitely postpone choice.

The idea of an "experiment with values" suggested by this point is another that is closely connected with the freedom of the will. If Everyman R-chooses to live in either Andon or Baltar he will do so as a value experiment. If his expectations should be disappointed, he reserves the option, circumstances permitting, to terminate the experiment and try the other alternative. In fact, the Chief Elder assures him that this is an essential feature of an R-choice—that an action, or way of life, is chosen on a provisional basis, as an "experiment with values."[20]

We are reluctant to use the term "experiment" in connection with values because uses of the term in the empirical sciences have come to seem definitive. But there are many analogies between scientific experimentation and value experimentation. A person who tests a plan of action, or way of life, by living in accordance with it, judges it against the prior expectations, preferences, and desires that led him or her to select it. Everyman may go to Baltar and find it disappointing in any number of unexpected ways not foreseen in his original practical reasoning. Such failed expectations are the analogues of negative results in scientific experimentation, the non-occurrence of predicted consequences of a theory or the occurrence of unpredicted consequences. Now, the point has often been made by historians of science that the occurrence of such negative results does not invariably lead to the falsification of a scientific theory. There is usually room for adjustment in theories to bring them in line with new and even contrary evidence. The tendency to make such adjustments is in part a function of how good the theory is in other areas *and* how good available alternative theories are. But a succession of adjustments can lead to less and less simplicity, as in the case of Ptolemaic astronomy, and when this happens, *if* there is a good alternative available, the contrary evidence is likely to be viewed as a falsification of the theory.[21]

Now there are analogies with each of these points for value experimentation. Everyman is not likely to leave Baltar if he is disappointed to a degree in only one, or even a few, of his expectations, so long as most of them are fulfilled. He will adjust. But if disappointment builds to a greater degree about a few things and/or over a greater variety of things, *and* if Andon remains a viable option, he will judge the Baltarian experiment to have been a failure. As he tries to adjust more and more of his expectations he may find that occasional disappointment is building toward persistent anxiety or despair and these states indicate that a value experiment is failing. His condition is analogous to that of a scientist trying to hold on to an older theory in the face of new evidence and an appealing alternative. There is no clear line between success and failure, yet failure (falsification) is something one can, after a time, come to concede.

Existentialist philosophers, from Kierkegaard to Sartre, are known to be much concerned with such psychological states as anxiety, despair, and the like, that are here associated with the breakdown of a value experiment. Why do these thinkers manifest what many regard as a morbid fascination with such states as these? Part of an answer is suggested by the fact that one of the central themes of existential thought is the breakdown of traditional value systems in the modern Western world. Given this fact, a concern with states of mind that are symptomatic of such a breakdown is understandable. The states that fascinate such thinkers are precisely those indicating that certain values are not working, that experiments in living are failing. In such situations, if one can see no alternative value system "worth trying," the anxiety and despair may be terminal, and suicide may be suggested as the only answer. The other alternative is to do what Everyman did and become a searcher after some new way worth trying, or perhaps creating a new way for oneself. Existentialist philosophers have sometimes suggested the first alternative (suicide), but more often the second (recreating oneself by free choice).[22]

5.12   The above arguments suggest that there are enough similarities between the testing of values by living in accordance with them, on the one hand, and scientific experimentation, on the other, to justify the use of expressions like "value experiment," or "experiment with values." But, of course, there are important differences between value experiments like Everyman's and scientific experiments. A practical value experiment such as Everyman engages in is a more personal matter than a scientific experiment in the sense that success or failure is measured against the experimenter's own expectations, preferences, desires, and other motives that influenced the original choice. This is why apparently subjective psychological states like disappointment, anxiety, and despair can be relevant to the assessment of success or failure. But let us not be misled by the term "subjective" in this context. A value experiment is "subjective" in the sense that the expectations, desires, etc., of the person making the experiment are relevant to the assessment of success or failure; it is not subjective in the sense that the outcome—success or failure—is merely apparent to the investigator and not objectively real. Disappointment, anxiety, and despair are real states of an individual resulting from genuine conflicts between expectations and experiences, and their presence can be symptomatic of a real, not merely an apparent, failure of a way of living.

A second way in which practical value experiments differ from scientific experiments is connected with S8, the Many Goods principle. If Everyman goes to Baltar and happily finds that all of his expectations are fulfilled, he can conclude that the experiment was a success, but he cannot conclude that he has a consequence discovered "the Good Life" for him. All he has proved is that this is a good life for him. Merely to find a good life for oneself is no mean accomplishment. Though a twenty year old may view it as a disappointing conclusion to a life-long search, anyone over forty is more likely to view it as a miracle. In any case, a successful value experiment has a limited outcome. One cannot by value experimentation discover "the Good Life" and demonstrate what the Good Life is for oneself or for Man, because success in living can only show that one has found one good way of living for oneself.

Utopian thinkers systematically ignore this point. They think that if they can provide a utopian community in which everyone is happy, they have thereby proved what the Good Life really is and shown that other alternatives could not be it. But they have shown nothing of the sort, because in value experimentation one cannot show competing alternatives false by showing that one's own is successful. In value experimentation, one cultivates one's own garden; one does not plow the world under.

We summarize with

> **S9.** Value Experiments: The R-chosen alternative is chosen as an "experiment with values," worth testing by acting on, or living in accordance with, them. If it fails, circumstances permitting, the agent can try other R-alternatives. Success or failure in an R-chosen experiment such as Everyman undertakes is measured against the experimenter's own expectations, preferences, desires, and other motives influencing the original choice; and success means that the agent has found a good way or set of values for himself, but not the only good way or set of values for himself, or others.

Like some of the other steps, S9 provides an all too brief summary of the sections leading up to it (in this case 5.11-12) and should be understood in connection with these sections.

5.13   We have seen that the notion of an R-choice brings together a number of themes that have surfaced from time to time in the history of debates about free will, some of which were discussed in chapter 4. There is one more theme of chapter 4 connected with R-choice that deserves to be mentioned: R-choice embodies some fundamental insights of what were there called "bootstrap theories"(4.10).

Bootstrap theorists argue that an agent making a free choice is simultaneously choosing ("adopting," "accepting," "sanctioning," "making his (her) own," or "making to prevail") the very reasons or motives that explain the choice being made. As Sartre figuratively expressed it, "the motive, the act and the end are all constituted in a single upsurge." Now, when the wheel spins for Everyman and one of the alternatives is selected, say, living in Baltar, then the choice to live in Baltar thereby made carries with it an endorsement of the reasons or motives, $b_1 . . . b_m$, for preferring life in Baltar to the other alternatives. Of course, Everyman already *had* the reasons, $b_1 . . . b_m$, prior to choice, just as he had the reasons, $a_1 . . . a_n$, for preferring life in Andon. And prior to choice he had endorsed both sets of reasons in the weaker sense that he viewed the alternatives associated with them as better than all others. But at the time of the R-choice for Baltar, he endorses the selected complex of motives, $b_1 . . . b_m$, in the stronger sense that he will undertake to live by them, i.e. to follow the preference they support to live in Baltar. He "makes them his own" in a special way. Consider this in the light of what some bootstrap theorists were quoted as saying, "A *motive* is always *willed*, that is , singled out at the moment [of choice] among other equally possible motives" (Renouvier 12, p. 315). "In order to make a potential motive my reason for acting, I select it from others and 'adopt' or 'sanction' . . . it; and in so doing I confer on it an entirely new status" (G. E. Hughes, 44, p. 317).

These thinkers, however, do not suggest that the privileged motives are "singled out" by chance. They think the agent does the singling out or makes one or the other complex of reasons prevail, in some unexplained way. Thus they tie their bootstrap strategy to some kind of special cause strategy, in most cases a non-occurrent cause strategy, in order to explain the adopting or sanctioning. (Sartre may be an exception here. I do not know what he would have said about R-choice, but it is possible that the early Sartre would have found the notion of R-choice congenial.) The R-choice suggested by the sacred books of Andon is different. One must bite the bullet and realize that the selection is by chance. But this does not mean, as argued in S6, that the choice is irrational from the chooser's point of view. Thus we may add

S10.   The Bootstrap Theme: R-choice exemplifies the fundamental theme of bootstrap theories: an agent making an R-choice is simultaneously "endorsing" ("accepting," "adopting," "sanctioning," "making his (her) own") in a special way the set of reasons or motives that explain the choice being made. Though the agent already *has* the relevant reasons (e.g. $b_1 \ldots b_m$) prior to choice, these reasons are given a special status by the R-choice itself. The selected reason-choice complex (e.g. $b_1 \ldots b_m$ and the choice of B) upsurges into a context prepared by practical reasoning in the manner described by S6.

5.14   We are now in a position to conclude the discussion of R-choice by noting that it satisfies, in a qualified way, the two chief requirements for free choice discussed in chapters 3 and 4, the requirement of dual rational self control of chapter 4, and the requirement of sole or ultimate dominion of chapter 3. Everyman's R-choice between Andon or Baltar will be rational, whichever way it goes. He will have reasons for making the choice he does make in either case; the reasons will have been possessed prior to choice; they will be the strongest available reasons in either case (though not uniquely the strongest); and the outcome will have been the last step in a long and complex process of practical reasoning. The catch is that this last step is not in his control, so that his control over the final outcome is only partial. Nonetheless, the outcome will be rational in both directions and (this is the key point) it will be as rational as it *can be* given the fact that, relative to his prior reasons or motives, there is no unique best.

S11.   R-choices satisfy the requirement of dual rational self determination in the following sense. The outcome, either way (whether the agent chooses or does otherwise) will be rational with respect to the agent's prior reason or motive states and prior deliberation in all of the senses described in S6; and it will be as rational as it can be given the fact that there is no unique best among the alternatives. The outcome will be in accordance with the agent's *rational will* in either case, and under the partial control of the agent's will in either case.

R-choice thus satisfies the requirement of dual rational self determination with the qualification that the control exercised by the rational will over the outcome is only partial. (The outcome is the result of reason *and* chance, as S7 says.) One of the lessons of R-choice is that partial control of the rational will is consistent with dual rational self control. A second, equally important, lesson is that partial control of the rational will is consistent with satisfaction of the condition of sole or ultimate dominion as defined by D3. To satisfy this condition, two requirements must be satisfied. (i) The agent's making the choice at t rather than doing otherwise, or vice versa, can be explained by saying that the agent rationally willed at t to do so (where "rationally willed at t to do so" means "endorsed reasons or motives at t for doing so over reasons for doing otherwise"). And (ii) no further explanation can be given for the agent's choosing rather than doing otherwise (or vice versa), or of the agent's rationally willing at t to do so, that is an explanation in terms of conditions whose existence cannot be explained by the agent's choosing or rationally willing something at t.

That R-choice satisfies condition (i) of this definition is shown by S10. The agent's making the choice (e.g. choosing B), or vice versa, can be explained by saying that the agent rationally willed at t to do so, in the sense that the agent endorsed ("accepted," "made his (her) own" in a special way) reasons or motives at t for doing so over those for doing otherwise. If the choice is for A, those endorsed reasons are $a_1 \ldots a_n$, if for B they are $b_1 \ldots b_m$. But because, by assumption, the endorsement at t of one of those sets of reasons rather than the other is a random occurrence, in the sense that the two outcomes are equally probable, there is no further explanation of the agent's rationally willing at t to endorse one set rather than the other, and hence no further explanation for the agent's choosing rather than doing otherwise. There is clearly no causal, in the sense of deterministic, explanation as there would have to be in the case of CNC control or determination by natural causes. There is, of course, a statistical explanation. But a statistical explanation will tell us that each alternative is probable to some degree, in the present case that the probability of occurrence of each is 1/2, and this is not an explanation of why one of them actually does occur rather than the other. If a causal, or deterministic, explanation did exist, either in terms of CNC control or prior natural causes, there would be an explanation of the choosing and rationally willing at t to do so that was "in terms of conditions whose existence was not itself explained by the agent's choosing or rationally willing something at t." In the absence of such an explanation, clause (ii) of the condition of sole or ultimate dominion is satisfied.

Now, you will say that a *post factum* explanation in terms of the agent's first order reasons or motives also does not explain why one of the outcomes actually occurs rather than the other. This is true. Nothing will, or can, explain that. But what the reason explanation does tell us is quite interesting and important. It tells us that, since the agent has agreed beforehand to accept the chance selected outcome and to endorse reasons for it in a special way, the selection is going to be "willed to be so" on a provisional basis by the agent, whichever way it goes. What is unique about explanations in terms of the rational will, and hence in terms of reasons, is the possibility of willing either way, making sense of either pathway, though neither is determined. Such a rational explanation is useless for predictive purposes. But that, of course, is just the point. Predictability among other things (e.g. controllability) was to be excluded. Nevertheless, the explanation is important because Everyman can give it with perfect candor to the Baltarians and to others who subsequently ask him why he chose, say, Baltar. It will be an explanation in terms of his reasons; it will be as good an explanation as can be given of the facts of the case; and there will be no explanation beyond it.

> S12.   R-choice satisfies the condition of sole or ultimate dominion in the sense that (i) the agent's making the R-choice at t rather than doing otherwise, or vice versa, can be explained by saying that the agent rationally willed at t to do so, and (ii) no further explanation can be given for the agent's choosing rather than doing otherwise (or vice versa), or for the agent's endorsing the set of reasons he or she did endorse at t, that is an explanation in terms of conditions whose existence cannot be explained by the agent's rationally willing something at t.

R-choice thus satisfies the conditions of dual rational self determination and sole or ultimate dominion, with the qualification that the control of the agent's rational will over the outcome is only partial because the outcome is due to reason and chance. That control can be partial, and yet be both sole and dual rational, is one of the lessons we learn from R-choice despite its extraordinary nature. And there are other lessons—about the relation of libertarian freedom to finitude (S7), about the nature of values (S8) and value experimentation (S9)—that are connected with this possibility in essential ways. What I suggest is that rather than viewing the partial control afforded by R-choice as a concession wholly to be regretted we should consider it a veiled clue to our limited condition as free beings.

5.15   In retrospect, a number of rare birds in the aviary of the free will historian (reasons inclining without necessitating, liberty of indifference, the bootstrap theme, etc.) tend to collect around the notion of R-choice. Unfortunately, R-choice is itself something of a rare bird. It is an extraordinary kind of choice in the sense that persons who claim to regularly make free choices are not conscious of submitting them to chance in the manner of R-choice. If we are to draw nearer to ordinary intuitions, certain features of R-choice must be embedded in a wider context. This is part of the task of the next chapter.

Notes

1. I am aware of the methodological problems involved in such a task, but will not worry about them excessively until chapter 9 when the construction is complete.

2. Do not be distracted by the thought that the wheel's spinning is a macroscopic process that may in fact be determined, though the outcome is unknown to the onlookers. The wheel plays merely a figurative role in the story. In any eventually true story its role would have to be assumed by an actually undetermined process. What that actual process might be is discussed, along with other factual questions, in 9.2ff.

3. This assumption of incomparability, or incommensurability, is important for later developments and must be explicitly made. It means there is no common measure by which the strengths of the competing reason sets can be compared as greater or less, or as equal to one another. Everyman not only lacks grounds for saying that one reason set provides a stronger motive than the other, he also lacks grounds for saying they are of equal strength.

4. In general, a second order reason is a belief about the comparative strengths of *sets* of first order reasons. It should be added that an agent's "having" a first order reason "for preferring" one or another option means only that the agent has a psychological attitude that is relevant to his assessment of one or another option. It does not mean that he must be aware or conscious of the relevance of the reason, or even conscious that he has it. One way unconscious reasons can influence conscious deliberation has to do with particular features of deliberation discussed in 4.2. During deliberation the agent may consider various images, reflect on various memories, and construct various scenarios in order to assess the possible consequences of options. Though the images, memories, and scenarios may be consciously considered, the agent may not be aware of all of the reasons influencing his *assessments* of them. Images of the Baltarian ocean make life in Baltar strongly attractive to Everyman, but he may not be aware of all the reasons for this attraction. Perhaps in youth his parents took him to the ocean and he now associates it with a long lost family warmth, but is not consciously aware of this. He is aware of the attraction, however, and it is one of the grounds for his belief that, all things considered, Baltar is preferable to Careen and is not clearly more nor less preferable than Andon. In short, vagueness about, or lack of conscious awareness of, at least some relevant first order reasons is compatible with having (or believing one does not have) a second order reason for preferring one option to another.

5. Einstein (68).

6. Frankena (67, p. 230).

7. I am not going to try to define "good." For our purposes, it is enough to know that people *do* believe that certain things are good or bad, better or worse in some respects, for some purposes, etc. This means they *have* values and we can identify the values they have if we can identify the beliefs. As for "right" and "wrong," these terms are associated with normative beliefs, which persons also have, about what should or should not be done. Thus a person's or group's values, in the sense defined, include normative as well as evaluative propositions whose truth is believed or presupposed. We shall have more to say about moral senses of "right" and "wrong" in chapter 7, and hence about moral values. Moral value, however, is only one kind of value in the sense defined here. Similarly, moral or ethical relativism is a special variant of value relativism as defined by (I')-(II').

8. Since valuations can say that certain things are bad as well as good, we can also say, e.g. that it is one of Everyman's values *that* living with argumentative people is bad, or *that* cold climates are worse than warm climates. This allows for a certain economy. For when we speak about a person's values, we are including what the person negatively values (or disvalues) as well as what he or she positively values.

9. More will be made of these restrictions on relativistic frames in 7.9-10 and 10.1-3.

10. Aquinas (31, question 6, art. 1; also, less explicitly in 45, Vol. 1, pp. 778-80); see also Suarez (56, 1, XIX, 6, 14). I do not mean to suggest that these authors employ the distinction between first and second order reasons of S4, or relate the idea to value relativism. These are my own twists. In addition, Aquinas follows Aristotle in saying that deliberation is always about means, not about ends. Thus he holds that there may be alternate means for attaining a certain end that are equally good in different respects. But he denies this about ends that are not means to further ends. This is a significant difference from the point of view of this book.

11. Bramhall (44, pp. 414-15). "Where I say, that 'reason cannot give a positive sentence,' [Hobbes] maketh me say, that 'reason can give no sentence.' There is a great difference between these two. The judges name three men to the sheriff-wick of a county; here is a nomination or judgment, but not yet positive. The king picks one of these three; then the nomination or judgment is positive. So reason representeth to the free agent, . . . three means to obtain one end, either not examining or not determining any advantage which one mean hath above another. . . . In this case the will of the free agent chooseth one of these three means as good, without any further examination which is

best. Reason is 'the root of liberty' in representing what is good, even when it does give no positive or determinate sentence what is best" (p. 414). The Hobbes comment about Bramhall and Suarez is in Hobbes (62, p. 37).

12. Reid (70, p. 88).

13. "Random" in this context means that the selections of the relevant alternatives are equiprobable. This feature of R-choice underscores the requirement that the alternatives be treated equally because there are no grounds for favoring one over the other. I realize that "randomness" is usually defined nowadays for sequences of occurrences. But I think it is useful to employ the term here, as many writers on free will have used it, to refer to individual occurrences of potential random sequences — the outcome of each such occurrence being no more nor less probable than any other potential outcome.

14. See note 2 of this chapter for further comment on this point. There are several other features of R-choice that will undoubtedly make the careful reader uneasy at this point. But they also should not be allowed to distract from the argument since each will be addressed as we go along. First, since Everyman and the others must interpret the outcome of the spin in terms of their prearranged conventions, there will be a lapse of time between the wheel's alighting and the formation of intention. Thus, the R-choice is not merely the chance spin, but the chance-spin-plus-interpretation. (Cf. 6.6 for more on this.) Second, Everyman may opt out of his arrangement at any time before finalizing the result. (Of course, he may also change his mind after an R-choice is made. But, in this respect, R-choice does not differ from any other kind of choice.) Third, with the above points in mind, one might reason as follows. R-choice consists of an undetermined part (the wheel's alighting) and a part involving Everyman's reasoning (prior to the spin and after accepting it). If the reasoning part is determined, as it might be, then R-choice would consist of two parts, one undetermined, the other determined, neither of which was ultimately controlled by the agent. So, R-choice cannot be what libertarians want. Each of these complaints is legitimate and will be addressed eventually. Keep in mind that R-choice is *not* ultimately what libertarians want. But it does tell us something about what they want.

15. Actually Plato says in the *Timaeus* that this universe was the mixed result of necessity (*anangkē*) and reason (37, p. 160). but the necessity in question is said to be an errant or wandering cause, "rambling," "aimless" and "irresponsible" (pp. 163-4). Thus Cornford argues (in Plato, 37a, pp. 166ff.), pursuing suggestions of Grote and A. E. Taylor, that the "necessity" of the *Timaeus* is more reasonably conceived as indeterminateness or chance, that which is not subject to any law or purpose. Without arguing the matter we can assume that the Chief Elder learned her Plato from Everyman who learned it from Cornford.

16. Austin (70, p. 203).

17. Sections 7.9-11 and 10.1-3.

18. Leibniz (51, p. 95).

19. Leibniz (51, pp. 92-93). For a discussion of this and related points, see D. Blumenfeld (75) and R. M. Adams (77).

20. It is not essential to the argument that an unchosen R-alternative remain an R-alternative indefinitely. If Everyman chooses Baltar, circumstances may change making Andon less attractive; or the choice itself and his new way of life may so change Everyman that Andon is no longer as attractive to him. The main point is that the unchosen R-alternative is an incommensurable alternative at the time of choice and may remain so for a time thereafter. There is more on this in chapter 6.

21. These points are made with illuminating examples in Kuhn's celebrated *The Structure of Scientific Revolutions* (62). A good discussion of the importance of falsification and its limitations, as emphasized by Kuhn and other critics of Popper, can be found in Lakatos (70).

22. The suicide option is, of course, suggested by Camus (55). The slogan used by Sartre and others that a man must "create himself" by his free choices is pertinent to the second option. Kierkegaard, more directly than any other existentialist, addresses issues about how value systems or ways of life can fail. In *Either/Or* (59) and other works, his characters argue that certain ways of life, the aesthetic and moral, for example, will lead to boredom, anxiety, and despair.

Reason Sets and Practical Reason

6.1 The steps of chapter 5 are preliminary ones. In order to proceed beyond them, a distinction is needed between three kinds of free choice, practical, prudential, and moral. Practical choices will be discussed in this chapter, prudential and moral choices in subsequent chapters.

What I am here calling prudential and moral choices differ from practical ones in the following respect. Both prudential and moral choices involve conflicts between what the agent believes ought to be done and what the agent wants to do. In the case of moral choice, the "ought" has to do with demands of justice, or respect for other persons, which come in conflict with self interested motives. In the case of prudential choice, the "ought" has to do with the agent's own future or long range interests which are in conflict with present wants or desires. By contrast, practical choices, as I shall call them, do not ultimately involve such conflicts between perceived obligation and inclination. Deliberation preceding practical choice may involve consideration of moral principles and long range interests, but in the end the agent chooses one option rather than others because he prefers it, or wants it, more. The choice may be in conformity with, or in accordance with, moral principle or long range interest, as the agent sees it, but it is not in conflict with present prevailing inclinations.

Kant and other libertarians like C. A. Campbell are right in saying that cases of acting from duty against inclination have a special role to play in libertarian theories of freedom. But they are wrong in suggesting that moral choices are the only ones in which we are truly free in the libertarian sense. An adequate libertarian view should be able to account for undetermined free choices of all kinds, practical prudential, and moral. But the treatment of each of the three must be different, because the differences are significant. Let me reemphasize, then, that this chapter is concerned only with practical choices. Moral and prudential choices will be considered in later chapters. And this chapter will not quite tell the whole story of practical choice. A few new twists will be added to the account of practical choice in chapter 8, after the accounts of moral and prudential choice are completed.[1]

Everyman's choice is a practical one in our sense. It comes down to a matter of selecting the society he most prefers, and the selection does not turn on a conflict between perceived obligation and inclination. None of his alternatives is such that he believes he ought to choose it, for moral or prudential reasons, but does not want to choose it—or such that he wants to choose it, but believes he ought not to choose it, for moral or prudential reasons. This is important in the light of Everyman's ultimate agreement to make an R-choice, because R-choices are more closely related to practical choices between different plans of action or ways of life, such as Everyman faced, than to moral or prudential choices. (Though, as we shall see, many of the ideas of the previous chapter associated with R-choice are also relevant to moral and prudential choice.)

But while R-choice is more closely related to practical choice, its extraordinary nature also prevents it from providing a suitable model for everyday practical choices. Persons who regularly make practical choices are not conscious of submitting them to chance in the manner of R-choice. Usually, they would say that they were not faced with R-alternatives at all, but had better reasons, or a stronger motive, for choosing what they did choose, even while insisting that they "could have done otherwise." The theory must be brought in line with such claims if we are to draw closer to everyday conceptions of free practical choice.

To do this, I shall first present two analogies—the first to creative problem solving, the second to natural evolution—that will indicate the general strategy of the chapter (6.2-3). This strategy will then be worked out in greater detail by way of three additional analogies, (i) a micro-analogy to R-choice (6.44-6)), (ii) a macro-analogy to R-choice (6.7-8), and finally, what I shall call (iii) the "Everyman in Baltar" analogy (6.9).

6.2   Near the end of chapter 5, we supposed that Everyman, following the Chief Elder's suggestion, had R-chosen to live in Baltar and gone to live there as a value experiment. Now let us suppose that he comes around to the same result by a different, more normal, route. He rejects her offer to make an R-choice, in order to think further about his options. but in this case, further reflection finally leads him to believe that life in Baltar is, all things considered, preferable to life in Andon, and he chooses to live in Baltar. Thus, he takes a more normal route to practical choice, in which a gradual accumulation of reasons leads to an overall preference, a stronger set of reasons, for one option over others.

Now this assumption, that one finally chooses for the stronger reasons, can be reconciled with the assumption that chance was involved in the accumulation of reasons for choice along the way; and it can be reconciled in a way that would allow for a dual rationality and other properties analogous to those of R-choice. To see this, let us ask what it is for Everyman to "think further" about his options? The process of practical reasoning described in 4.2 is an open ended one. The reasoner must consider various presuppositions and consequences of proposed lines of action, and this usually calls for the use of imagination to construct possible and probable scenarios exempilfying these presuppositions and consequences. Of vital importance to such a process is what gets considered and what does not get considered, what associations are made between thoughts, images, and memories in the course of considering the options, what does and does not come to the deliberator's attention, and, as a consequence, which of the agent's desires, wants, likes, dislikes, fears, hopes, etc., are brought to bear on the deliberation. There are no fixed rules about what to consider, about when one has considered enough possible consequences, and so on. Chance occurrences could in principle play a role in such a process, influencing what is and is not considered without undermining the rationality of the process. In fact, random search procedures for new relevant considerations may actually enhance the deliberative process, as researchers have found in designing machines sophisticated enough to engage in creative problem solving.[2]

These remarks suggest two analogies:

> **S13.** Practical deliberation and creative problem solving have much in common since both are trial and error processes involving thought experimentation about possible options and their consequences. The similarities suggest that, if chance occurrences play a role in practical reasoning at all, the role is likely to be like the role of inspiration to the creative thinker. Chance occurrences would influence the stream of consciousness of the reflecting agent, suggesting new possible options, new consequences of the options, new ways of viewing consequences of the options, etc. Inspiration in creative problem solving is not totally within the control of the reflecting agent. Yet its results are significant only to the prepared mind. As in the case of R-choice, chance occurrences are given meaning only within a wider context of reasoning and reasons; and the agent can be responsible for chance outcomes if he or she *interprets* them and *accepts* them as guides to further deliberation or to experiments in living.

We should not begrudge Newton his achievement if we found that a chance collocation of images and thoughts in his mind produced the insight about gravitation when he saw an apple fall from a tree. To do so would be to forget the struggles that preceded this moment and those that were to follow working out his insight. It would be to forget the necessity of the "prepared mind." We are all inspired, Ned Rorem once said about himself and his fellow musicians, but we are not all great. Nor should we begrudge Everyman his achievement, if he should make a happy life for himself in Baltar, simply because his being there involved a chance selection. Again, we would be forgetting the struggles that led up to R-choice and those that were to follow it, making an experiment work. This would be no less true if chance were involved in practical deliberations in the manner suggested by S13.

One can assume that some of these chance selected considerations well up from the unconscious mind. Freud and other theorists of the unconscious are often thought to be allies of determinists and compatibilists, not of libertarians, But, in reality, theories of the unconscious are two-edged swords in debates about free will. The unconscious may be the source of compelling desires and fears, but it may also be the source of novel insights resulting from chance associations of images and motives. It is odd that in theories of artistic creation the unconscious is often given the role of multiplying and expanding the inventive capacities of the agent, while in theories of freedom of choice the unconscious is usually viewed as limiting our options, determining them to one.[3]

6.3   S13 suggests a second analogy, in this case to natural evolution.

> **S14.** Natural evolution, conceived along Darwinian lines, is a trial and error process in which the results of chance mutations in the genetic makeup

of individuals of a species are tested and selected through interaction with the natural environment. In practical deliberation as described by S13, the role of chance corresponds to the role of mutations in natural evolution, while the role of reason corresponds to that of the selecting environment. Chance occurrences may influence the stream of consciousness of the reflecting agent suggesting new possible options, consequences, etc., and these are then selected or rejected by the agent, first, by way of thought experimentation (i.e. deliberation), and ultimately by living in accordance with their implications as value experiments in the sense of S9.

In this way, practical human freedom may be conceived as an extension of evolutionary processes allowing analogues of genetic mutations to occur in the mind and then to be subject to selection in the mental life of rational agents. Such an extension, however, would make a qualitative change in the evolutionary process. The possibilities for new ways or forms of life within a single species would be indefinitely multiplied and the importance of individuals of the species in the selection process (each with his or her own *internal rational environment*) would be enhanced immeasurably by comparison with natural evolution.

This evolutionary theme has been emphasized by number of thinkers recently, and I believe it is one of the important pieces of the puzzle of libertarian freedom, at least of libertarian *practical* freedom. One such thinker is Popper, in his lecture "Of Clouds and Clocks." I criticized Popper in chapter 4 for relying too heavily on a "content" strategy in this lecture and ultimately failing thereby to answer the critics of the indeterminist condition. But it is time to right the balance here and to note that this lecture contains some important insights for the libertarian view. And the most important of these insights, I believe, concerns this evolutionary theme. The problem for the libertarian, according to Popper, is to explain "how freedom is not just chance, but rather the result of a subtle interplay between *something almost random or haphazard* and *something like a restrictive or selective control*" (p. 237). But this, according to Popper, is the problem of evolution and life itself. Random or chance mutations are trial balloons subjected to the restrictive or selective control of the environment. And "each organism is all the time engaged in problem solving by trial and error; . . . it reacts to new and old problems by more or less chance-like . . . trials which are eliminated if unsuccessful" (p. 245). Human problem solving is a continuation of this process, the added feature being the role of reason in the process. "Deliberation always works by *trial and error, or more precisely, by the method of trial and of error elimination.* by tentatively proposing various possibilities and eliminating those that do not seem adequate" (p. 234).

Similar conclusions are arrived at by some students of the fields of cybernetics and artificial intelligence, who note the importance of computer processes for generating random numbers to initiate trial and error probes in creative problem solving.[4] This theme has been pursued by a number of thinkers, most recently by Daniel Dennett in his important work *Brainstorms* (78). Dennett quotes approvingly the poet Paul Valéry's claim that the essence of invention is the intelligent selection from among chance generated candidates and he goes on to suggest a model of decision making based on this idea. "The model of decision making I am proposing has the following feature: when we are faced with an important decision, a consideration generator whose output is to some degree undetermined produces a series of considerations, some of which may of course be immediately rejected as irrelevant by the agent (consciously or unconsciously). Those considerations that are selected by the agent as having a more than negligible bearing on the decision then figure in a reasoning process" (p. 295). Dennett argues that such a model can help to make sense of the libertarian view. I agree—but with the proviso that such a model is only directly relevant to contexts of *practical* decision making. Moral and prudential choice, as I have emphasized, must be treated differently. Dennett does not suggest, nor could it be justifiably suggested, that such a model would account for moral decision making without major revisions or additions. But he is nevertheless on to something important, a significant piece in the overall puzzle of a libertarian freedom.

6.4 S13 and S14 indicate the general strategy to be employed with regard to practical choice. But if we are to come to grips with problems about dual rational self control, sole or ultimate dominion, and the like, we shall have to attend to details. It is here that the discussion of R-choice will come to our aid.

Suppose that as Everyman reflects further about his options he remembers an evening's walk along the beach in Baltar and the memory reminds him of how much he likes to walk by the ocean in such reflective moments. Or, remembering a picnic in Baltar, his attention is drawn to the papaya someone offered him, and he is reminded of how much he likes that exotic fruit, which is plentiful in Baltar but does not grow in Andon. Now previously, we may assume, these particular likings, which are psychological attitudes with quite specific contents, had not entered into his weighing of pros and cons for Baltar and Andon. Nor had associated beliefs about evening walks and where papayas grow. But, henceforth, these reasons, both volitional (the likings) and cognitive (related beliefs), have a bearing on the outcome of the deliberation. They do not decide the issue, of course, but they are added to his reasons for preferring one option, Baltar (B), over another, Andon (A). (Let us call the set of these reasons the "preference set" for Baltar.)

Now the suggestion of S13 and S14 is that the rememberings and attending that introduced these novel considerations into the deliberation may have been chance selected. Many of the resulting chance selected considerations are passed over as irrelevant, but some, like the evening walk and the papaya, are immediately seen to be relevant to the deliberation. The relevant considerations are separated from the irrelevant by background cognitive and volitional attitudes that he already has. What is interesting, however, is that the chance selected considerations (the remembered walk and the papaya) also pick out these background cognitive and volitional attitudes (the likings and associated beliefs) as relevant to the deliberation. These attitudes, or reasons, may have already been in the preference set of one or another option, in which case they take on a new relevance, or they may not previously have been considered at all and are added to one or another preference set.

We may speak in this connection of the "endorsement" of reasons or motives for choice, meaning by this the acknowledgement on the part of the agent that certain reasons or motives are relevant to deliberation in ways not previously recognized. Such endorsement does not mean coming to *have* the reasons at the moment they are endorsed. Likings, wants, desires, preferences, and similar attitudes are not the sorts of things one normally gets or loses suddenly. But these and other psychological attitudes that the agent may already have (e.g. liking evening walks on the beach) may be seen to be relevant to deliberation in new ways or may be added to the preference set for one or another option.[5] Such endorsement then is something like what happens in the case of R-choice to the selected reasons, e.g. the reasons b_1 . . . b_m for preferring Baltar. The agent does not come to have these reasons at the moment of R-choice. He had them all along. But they are endorsed in a special way as a result of a chance occurrence.

Let us put this more accurately in the following step:

S15. Endorsement of Reasons for Choice: If chance occurrences play a role in deliberation leading to practical choice, they do so by initiating processes of thinking about or imagining, remembering or attending to, possible states or changes that may be relevant to deliberation in some way, as means or consequences of the options. Let us refer to these chance initiated thinkings, imaginings, rememberings, etc., as "chance selected considerings" and to the possible states or changes they bring to mind as "chance selected considerations." Some of the resulting chance selected considerations brought to mind are passed over as irrelevant, while others are acknowledged as relevant to the deliberation. In the manner explained in this section, the acknowledgement of relevance is either the adoption into the preference set for some option of cognitive and volitional reasons not previously regarded as relevant to the deliberation, or it is the endorsement of a new significance to reasons already in one or another preference set (or some combination of these two possibilities).

6.5 With this step in hand, we can relate the general account of practical deliberation suggested by S13 and 14 to the earlier discussion of R-choice. We do this in a series of three steps.

S16. The Micro-analogy to R-choice (I): The endorsement of reasons described in S15 is like R-choice in the sense that certain reasons or motives in the agent's total reason set are singled out, given a special status, by a chance initiated process. In the case of R-choice, the wheel spins to select the intention (to live in Baltar) Everyman will have and, in doing so, selects a set of first order reasons, b_1 . . . b_m, already in his reason set, to be endorsed in a special way. In the case of the endorsements of S15:

(i) the wheel does not select one option or another (Baltar or Andon) in one fell swoop, but rather it selects various first order reasons (say, a^*_1 . . . a^*_j, b^*_1 . . . b^*_k), such as the likings and beliefs about beaches and papayas of the previous section, that will go into, or give greater weight to, the preference sets $((a_1 . . . a_n), (b_1 . . . b_m))$ for one or another option.

(ii) This is done by virtue of chance selected considerings which provide *reasons for* endorsing these reasons (e.g. $b^*_1 \ldots b^*_k$) for preferring to choose one or another option. For example, remembering the evening walk provides Everyman with a reason (the remembered walk, which is a chance selected consider*ation*) for acknowledging the relevance to deliberation of his liking evening walks by the ocean (b^*_1) and associated beliefs about such walks (b^*_2 $\ldots b^*_k$). (Thus, reasons *for* endorsing reasons *for* choice will be possible states or changes that may be thought about, remembered, attended to, etc., and hence items in different logical categories than reasons *for* choice *simpliciter*.)

(iii) In addition, for the case of S15, we must imagine that the wheel has more possible options on it than in the case of R-choice, corresponding to the many possible considerations that might be selected; and a succession of spins leads to a separation of relevant from irrelevant outcomes. It is as if we modified the Everyman example by allowing the wheel to have more options on it than red (for Andon) and blue (for Baltar); and the wheel is spun until a relevant outcome turns up.

(iv) Finally we must imagine this wheel spinning unconsciously in Everyman's mind, so that insofar as he is aware of the process he views it as the coming to mind of certain considerations that are accepted or rejected as relevant to his deliberation.[6]

S17. The Micro-analogy to R-choice(II): (i) In the process described by S16, the *relevant* chance selected considerations are the analogues of the R-alternatives (A,B,C. . .) of R-choice and the sets of reasons ($a^*_1 \ldots a^*_j$), ($b^*_1 \ldots b^*_k$) endorsed into the preference sets by the chance selected considerations are the analogues of the R-alternative reason sets ($a_1 \ldots a_n$), ($b_1 \ldots b_m$), of R-choice. The chance selected considerations that are passed over as *irrelevant* to the deliberation are the analogues of alternatives (like life in Careen) that are dismissed as inferior prior to R-choice. But in this case, irrelevant as well as relevant options may be selected by the wheel because there is no way for the agent to tell in advance which considerations will turn out to be relevant and which not. The relevant are picked out from the irrelevant after chance selection by virtue of certain reasons ($b^*_1 \ldots b^*_k$) already in the agent's total reason set which show them to be relevant.

(ii) This means that there is an interdependence between the chance selected considerations (CSC's), i.e. the states or changes thought about, remembered, attended to, and the reasons they endorse ($b^*_1 \ldots b^*_k$) into the preference set for one or another option (e.g. the likings and beliefs about beaches and papayas). The CSC's pick out the endorsed reasons as relevant to deliberation in a special way, because if the CSC's had not come to mind the endorsed reasons would not have been seen to be relevant. But the endorsed reasons also pick out the CSC's as relevant, because if the agent did not have the endorsed reasons, the CSC's would not have *been* relevant to the deliberation.

(iii) In other words, just as in R-choice, where an R-alternative (A or B. . .) is selected along with its justifying reasons ($a_1 \ldots a_n$ or $b_1 \ldots b_m \ldots$), so here a CSC is selected along with the reasons ($a^*_1 \ldots a^*_j$ or $b^*_1 \ldots b^*_k$) that pick it out as relevant. Suppose we think of a choice as a "first order willing," the endorsement of reasons *for* choice as a "second order willing," and the coming to have a reason (the coming to mind of a relevant CSC) *for* endorseing reasons *for* choice as a "third order willing." Then, for R-choice, the first order willing (the choice) and the second order willing (the endorsement of reasons for choice) go together and explain each other. While, in the present case, the third order willing (coming to have a reason for endorsing reasons for choice) and the second order willing (endorsing reasons for choice) go together and explain each other. In both cases *a potential regress of willings turns into a circle and thereby terminates.*

S18. The Micro-analogy to R-choice (III): (i) The endorsed reasons ($b^*_1 \ldots b^*_k$) that pick out a CSC as relevant are to be regarded as analogues of *first order* reasons in R-choice. This is so, because *prior to selection* the deliberator does not have a belief that one CSC is more worthy of being selected than another. (How could he, not knowing before the considerations come to mind, which of them might be relevant and how relevant each might be?) This is why he engages in reflection or meditation, "fishing around" for further information that might be relevant to his deliberation, and it is why potential considerations can be treated *antecedently* as R-alternatives to be sought out by an undetermined search procedure.

(ii) *After* selection, of course, things are different. The relevant are separated from the irrelevant (the Baltars from the Careens) immediately. Then, even among the relevant considerations, some will seem more relevant than others in the sense of giving more weight to one side or another than other considerations. Now this corresponds in R-choice to the following situation: Everyman selects his R-alternatives (life in Baltar, life in Andon) *in succession* and tries them out as value experiments. *Before* selection, he treated them as R-alternatives, any of which is believed to be "worthy of being tried." But *after* selection and experimentation, they may not turn out to be equally worthy at all. One may turn out to be a better life for him than the other. So it is with chance selected considerations. But the experimentation takes place in thought, not in "living."

6.6 Now step back and look at this process described as a "micro-analogue to R-choice" in S16-18. It begins with a chance initiated considering that brings to mind a consideration acknowledged to be relevant to deliberation by virtue of reasons of the agent which the consideration endorses. Let us refer to the process so described as "the coming to have a reason for endorsing reasons for choice," or "the coming to have an RRC." Such a process takes a time to occur because the chance initiated considering must be interpreted as relevant. Thus, it is a process that involves chance-plus-interpretation. Now the fact that the coming to have an RRC takes a time to unfold may be thought to be another difference from R-choice. But this difference is not as pronounced as it appears. For there was a feature of R-choice that we conveniently overlooked in chapter 5. We assumed that the wheel's alighting on blue *was* Everyman's R-choice of Baltar. But this is misleading. For it takes a finite time for Everyman to recognize the outcome of the spin and to interpret it in the appropriate way.[7] Thus, an R-choice is also a matter of chance-plus-interpretation. The real difference in the micro-analogue is that the interpretation takes longer because relevant outcomes must be separated from irrelevant ones *after* selection.

The fact that chance-plus-interpretation is involved in both cases is related to a fact emphasized in chapter 5. Chance occurrences *per se* can have no meaning in human deliberative processes unless they are given meaning by the deliberating agents, that is, unless they occur in context of reasoning that interprets them in some way. Chance occurrences lie on the interfaces between an agent's psychological past and certain "open" (undetermined) pathways into the future. But the key point is that *each of the open pathways can be reasonable in some way*, and each can therefore be tried as a value experiment, in thought or action.

With these remarks in mind, we now add that

> S19.   The coming to have a reason for endorsing reasons for choice (coming to have an RRC) described in S16-18 satisfies the condition of dual rational self control in a manner analogous to the way in which R-choice satisfies this condition. Coming to have an RRC is like the coming to have an intention in R-choice. Both are the outcomes of undetermined processes. Yet the outcomes are dual rational in both cases. To come to have and RRC during an interval of time t-t' is to interpret a chance selected consideration (call it "c") as relevant to deliberation. This is reasonable by virtue of the existence of reasons ($b^*_1 \ldots b^*_k$) the agent has, which make c relevant to deliberation. But the agent may not have come to have this particular RRC during the interval t-t' and would not, if by chance, consideration c had not been selected. If c had not been selected during t-t', three other things might have happened: (i) Some other *relevant* consideration c' may have been selected. But then c' would be interpreted as an RRC (different from c) and the coming to have this different RRC would have been reasonable by virtue of the different reasons (say, $a^*_1 \ldots a^*_j$) that made *it* relevant. (ii) Some other *irrelevant* consideration may have been selected during t-t', or (iii) no consideration at all may have been selected during t-t'. In the latter two cases, the agent does not come to have an RRC at all during t-t'; and this too is reasonable, since in both cases there are no reasons to acknowledge a new consideration as relevant.

So when an agent engages in a chance search for considerations relevant to deliberation, the coming to have, or not coming to have, such a reason is reasonable, whatever occurs. We must add, of course, that the agent's dual rational control is only partial, as in R-choice, because he or she does not know what will turn up as the result of an undetermined search. The outcome is the result of reason and chance, just as in R-choice.

S20. The coming to have an RRC of S16-18 also satisfies the condition of sole or ultimate dominion in a manner analogous to the way in which R-choice satisfies this condition. (i) The agent's coming to have the RRC associated with c during the interval t-t', rather than not coming to have it, or vice versa, can be explained by saying that the agent rationally willed during t-t' to do so rather than not, where "rationally willed during t-t' to do so rather than not" means "had stronger reasons during t-t' for doing so rather than not." The meaning of this latter expression for each outcome is explained in the preceding step. And, (ii) no other explanation can be given for the occurrence of this process (of coming to have an RRC during t-t', or vice versa) since the process is chance initiated. Even the explanation in terms of the agent's will is *post factum*, as in the case of R-choice, and is useless for purposes of prediction and control. Yet it does explain how the process, though chance initiated, can be rational, and this is what an explanation in terms of reasons is meant to do.

One might object to clause (ii) of this step by saying that the process is determined by the chance occurrence itself at t and hence is explicable in terms of something that is not a willing. The answer to this objection must hark back to what was said at the beginning of this section. Consider first that one could make a similar objection to R-choice. That is, one could say that the R-choice was determined by something that was not a willing, namely the wheel's alighting on blue. But the answer in the case of R-choice was straightforward and it can be transferred to the micro-analogue. It is a confusion to say that the wheel's alighting on blue determines the R-choice, because the wheel's alighting on blue is *part* of the process we call R-choice. The process is a chance-occurrence-plus-interpretation. And what requires explanation is why this entire process, a chance-alighting-on-blue-plus-interpretation occurred rather than some alternative process, a chance-alighting-on-red-plus-(a-different-)interpretation. Similarly, in this case, what requires explanation is why the entire process of coming to have an RRC, which is a chance-selecting-of-c-plus-interpretation, occurred during this interval rather than some alternative process, e.g. a chance-selecting-of-c'-plus-(a-different-)interpretation. And this is what lacks an explanation according to clause (ii) of S20.

Though moral and prudential choice will be treated differently, this line of argument concerning practical choice tells us something of general importance about libertarian intentions. The aim of a libertarian view is to make chance occurrences *ingredients* of processes of rational willing without undermining the (dual) rationality of these processes. The purpose of the chance, as ingredient of such a process, is to "screen out" all complete explanation, prediction, and control in terms of prior circumstances, so that the process can be a "new beginning," unfolding by virtue of its own internal rationality. No doubt, what the objector of the previous paragraph has in mind is that the process of S20 proceeds predictably once the chance occurrence takes place. This is true, if the process is rational. But even then the unfolding is explained not by chance alone, but by chance and reason; for the chance must be given a meaning. And the resulting chance-plus-interpretation *is* the undetermined free willing.

6.7   We now turn to the second stage of the argument, from the micro-analogy to R-choice, to the macro-analogy. The macro-analogy concerns the cumulative effect of more than one of these micro-analogues of R-choice on the entire process of deliberation leading up to a practical choice. In 6.2, we imagined that Everyman did not make an R-choice to live in Baltar, but instead came around to the same result by a more normal deliberative route. He continued to think about his options until a gradual accumulation of reasons led eventually to an overall preference for Baltar. But we said that this normal route to practical choice, in which one feels that one finally chooses for the stronger reasons, can be reconciled with the assumption that chance is involved in the accumulation of reasons along the way.

Let us diagram the situation as follows:

$$(a_1 . . . a_n \text{—————————————} \ ! \ \text{———} \qquad\qquad\qquad [. . . . . C_A]$$
$$(b_1 . . . b_m) \text{———} \ ! \ \text{———} (b_1 . . . b_m, b^*_1 . . . b^*_k) \text{———} \ ! \ \text{———} . . . . . C_B$$

FIGURE 6.1

Everyman begins with reasons $(a_1 . . . a_n)$ for preferring to choose Andon (C_A) and reasons $(b_1 . . . b_m)$ for preferring to choose Baltar (C_B). But, instead of R-choosing on the basis of these reasons, he thinks further about the options, accumulating further reasons, some of them by virtue of chance selected considerations represented by the exclamation marks.[8] Thus, the memory of the evening walk in Baltar leads to the addition of certain reasons, $b^*_1 . . . b^*_k$, to the preference set for Baltar. The other exclamation marks and the dots before "C_A" and "C_B" indicate that any number of other such chance selected considerations may have influenced his preferences for Baltar or Andon. There may have been an ebb and flow in his inclinations, so that at one time he was leaning toward Baltar, at another toward Andon. But in the end, we have assumed, he believes that the reasons for preferring Baltar are the stronger ones, and he chooses Baltar. The brackets around ". . . C_A" indicate that the choice of Andon was not in fact made.

Now compare the above figure to the following one for R-Choice:

$$(a_1 . . . a_n) \text{———————} [. . . C_A]$$

$$(b_1 . . . b_m) \text{———} \ ! \ \text{———} C_B$$

FIGURE 6.2

The initial situations are the same. But, in contrast to the gradual process of transforming the reason sets for one or another option by a series of chance occurrences, R-choice represents the limiting case in which a single chance occurrence endorses one preference set over the other in one fell swoop. The result is the same. One of the options eventually prevails over the other. So that the more lengthy process of practical deliberation is like an R-choice stretched out over time, with many intermittent chance occurrences instead of a single decisive one.

S21. The Macro-analogy to R-choice: If chance occurrences play a role in deliberation leading to practical choice in the manner described in S15-18, then the entire process of practical deliberation can be viewed as an analogue of R-choice stretched out over time. Instead of a single chance occurrence endorsing one of the options and the reasons for it, there are series of chance occurrences endorsing reasons into the preference sets of different options until one option prevails over others. R-choice can then be conceived as an idealization in which this process is collapsed into a single chance occurrence plus its interpretation.

6.8 The most important feature of the macro-analogy, however, is not noted in S21. To be like R-choice in a significant way, the series of chance selected considerations must be capable of *making a difference* to the outcome in the sense that, if different ones had occurred, the agent may have chosen A rather than B. Only in this way would the micro-analogues of R-choice have a more than negligible effect on the overall process of practical deliberation. For these micro-analogues may be negligible in many ways. Many of our practical choices are such that the motives in favor of one option relative to others are so predominant that all, or most, considerations, whether chance selected or otherwise, will only tend to reinforce the overall preference. One can only miss the mark in such cases, so to speak, by making hasty, ill-considered, or impulsive decisions. But this is far from being the case in all practical choice situations. When I was deliberating about whether to send my son by air alone to visit his grandmother or whether to accompany him, there was a time when I had narrowed the viable options to these two, but was not able to say that I favored one of them over the other. Subsequent considerations led to a favoring of one, then the other. In fact, for the longest time I was leaning toward sending the boy alone, the option I did not finally choose. And after choosing I continued to have doubts that I had chosen the best alternative, all things that *might have been* considered.

Such situations, in which one is not sure that one has chosen the best option "all things that might have been considered," are those that conform to the macro-analogy. In such situations a quandary arises for the practical chooser similar to Everyman's. Everyman resisted R-choice because the termination of deliberation in such a way seemed arbitrary. He wanted to keep searching for his "true good." Otherwise the choice would have been taken out of his hands. The practical chooser's quandary is similar, but it involves the element of present preference absent from R-choice. Why choose *now* rather than go on searching? It is true that B seems to be the better option now, but yesterday A seemed better; and further considerations, for all I know, may make A seem better tomorrow. Unless I have allayed all such doubts, choosing now seems arbitrary. I should go on searching as Everyman wanted to do. Sometimes such situations are forced on us. Decisions cannot be delayed. So we choose what seems to be the best at the time, but are not sure that it is the best, all things considered.

Now the macro-analogy suggests that the proper response to this practical chooser's quandary should parallel the Chief Elder's response to Everyman. We may express it in

S22.   In practical choice situations of uncertainty that conform to the macro-analogy, to choose now (whether you have to, or merely want to in order to get on with the business of living) may be arbitrary to some degree, but *it is not therefore irrational*. (The root of "arbitrary," need we recall, is "*arbitrium*.") It is not irrational, because there need not be a (one) true good for a person in every practical choice situation. One may therefore choose an option on the grounds that it seems better at the time, even if one is not convinced that it is better, all things considered. For one chooses the option in such circumstances, not as the true good for sure, but as a good "worth trying" as a value experiment. And this is reasonable in the light of the Many Goods principle and the fact that all practical choosing for finite creatures is experimental.

This step addresses an important theme in some libertarian writings. Libertarians sometimes say that even if one option, A, is preferred, one can still choose the weaker option, B—meaning to emphasize by saying this that the stronger preference does not always necessitate. I think that they are making an important point when they say this, but are expressing it poorly. For if A really is preferred to B at a certain time, then it would be unreasonable to choose B *at that time*. The important idea underlying their statement is that, in the ebb and flow of practical reasoning, the agent can believe that one option is better than another at a time without being convinced that it is the best option, all things that "might have been considered."

6.9   This brings us finally to

S23.   The Everyman-in-Baltar Analogy: Granting the possibility of choices conforming to the pattern of S21-22, we can believe that the lines of our lives have contained in the past, and will contain in the future, nodes with undetermined branching pathways, each of which could be reasonable because each could represent a true good for us. In such cases, we are like "Everyman-in-Baltar" for whom life in Andon was an *unendorsed* R-alternative. Some of our unendorsed R-alternatives are permanently lost (as life in Andon may be lost for Everyman if external circumstances change or he changes). Others may still be with us, as possible purposes or plans to be pursued if present value experiments should fail. Still others may lie in our future. But Everyman's case, as always, is an idealization, because his alternatives were equally poised in his mind *at the time* he chose, and this is not the way it is for ordinary practical choosers. Moreover, unlike Everyman, we practical choosers do not always know what all of our "Andons" are (our unendorsed R-alternatives), lying on the far sides of the mountain ranges of our minds. But if we have libertarian intuitions, we believe they are there; and we believe we can ferret them out by processes of reasoning that are not determined, should present value experiments fail. This is part of our "feeling of freedom."

An actress being interviewed said that, at a certain time in her life, she almost decided to become a lawyer and still believed she would have been a successful lawyer. We all know what that sort of feeling is like—a feeling that our life contains nodal points at which the choice of one practical good means the loss of another that is good in different ways. These points can seem burdensome when they occur. We sometimes wish that all of our practical choices could be simple ones in which a predominant motive was easily discernible. The incommensurability of different values, and the consequent incommensurability of certain choices, can be a great burden to us; and this burden is the burden of practical freedom. (Can animals experience this burden? Buridan's ass may have, but it existed only in the imagination of a philosopher.)

As libertarians like James and Sartre have emphasized, free choices of all kinds impose burdens on us that we often want to escape. The burdens of moral and prudential choice are well known. But the special burden of *practical* choice has to do with the incommensurability of values, which caused Everyman's quandary and the similar quandary of the practical chooser described in terms of the macro-analogy. This special burden is a particular stumbling block for mathematical decision theorists and social choice theorists, who are always looking for strategies to overcome what is called, in measurement theory, "the multi-attribute problem."[9] This is the problem of simply ordering (as greater or less) the values of utility functions defined in terms of different, and not obviously comparable, "goods." Such an ordering is necessary to determine what the best choice is in a given situation. But in many practical choice situations there is simply no non-arbitrary way of determining such an ordering because the "goods" are so different in kind. And even where decision theorists have worked out strategies for doing so, there is often more than one strategy available, each yielding different results, and no non-arbitrary way of choosing between them.

I think libertarians must say that this problem of decision and social choice theories is no accidental one so far as human freedom is concerned. To desire objective, non-conventional, non-arbitrary measures for all combinations of disparate goods is to desire to opt out of the burden of practical freedom. Sartre would undoubtedly call it a form of bad faith, a wanting to escape from freedom. Clearly, this is not an argument against decision theory and social choice theory. They are enormously useful (though one might add "normative") disciplines. But the point does resurrect some old humanist themes often underscored by libertarians, e.g. that quantization of all valuation would undermine freedom and that the failure of such quantization is connected with the fact that the net of explanatory and predictive social science cannot capture all of human behavior.[10]

6.10   It is worth reemphasizing that these remarks, like the steps of this chapter generally, apply only to practical choice. Moral and prudential choice impose their own special burdens on the free agent, shortly to be considered. Though this chapter is nearly complete, it does not, and will not, present the whole story, even about practical choice. There is another sense in which indeterminism is involved in practical choice, more intimately related to the agent's effort of will. But we are not going to be in a position to understand this other sense until chapter 8, after discussing moral and prudential choice. The final step of this chapter, to be presented in this section, will prepare the way for this later development.

The Everyman-in-Baltar analogy suggests that there is an element of *detachment* as well as commitment in the life of a free agent. Our commitment as *practical* (not moral) choosers is colored by an attitude of detachment that comes from believing the way we have chosen may be only one of many good ways. That some degree of detachment from one's practical purposes or goals is essential to "true" freedom has been dimly perceived as a piece of wisdom here and there in human history. It is common theme, for example, in certain Eastern philosophies, like Buddhism and Taoism, which tend to go to an opposite extreme from most Western thought, emphasizing the need for detachment in the free being to the exclusion of commitment altogether. These Eastern views often emphasize that to be truly free one must give up trying to subordinate one's surroundings to one's motives, even if this means detaching oneself from one's motives altogether. In this vein, the Taoist Chuang Tzu says: "No drives, no compulsions, no needs, no attractions. Then your affairs are under control. You are a free man."[11]

Such statements lie purposefully on the fringes of common sense. On the one hand, they may be affirming what common sense affirms, that compulsive desiring takes away freedom. But, on the other, they may be taken to mean (and sometimes are taken to mean) something more radical, namely that all desiring by the self takes away freedom. If a degree of detachment from one's desires and other motives is essential to freedom, then complete detachment from all desires and motives is complete freedom.[12] This logic seems perverse to many Westerners. True freedom becomes the absence of any commitments whatsoever, and its price is the loss of selfhood altogether. Whatever remains, it is not the freedom *of* a self or person.

Yet there is a lesson in the Eastern emphasis on detachment. To understand the practical freedom of a self, one must chart a course between the extremes of complete commitment and complete detachment. True freedom for a self involves both commitment to and detachment from one's practical motives, the latter associated with the belief that the way one has chosen is only one of many good ways. And this element of detachment enters into practical reasoning itself by way of the attitude to chance selected considerations that must come to a receptive and antecedently detached mind (cf. S18). A theme of much Taoist and Zen Buddhist writing is that only when the conscious mind relaxes, and does not try to have complete control over its thinking, does the agent become truly creative and truly free.[13]

S24.   Commitment and Detachment, Creativity and Receptivity: Buddhist and Taoist themes of detachment and receptivity in the life of the free being are associated with many themes in this chapter. True practical freedom, like creativity in the arts and sciences (cf. S13), involves receptivity as well as conscious effort. One must be open to new possibilities, that may come, unforced, to a receptive mind. One must, as a consequence, recognize the limitations of reason in the practical sphere, as the Chief Elder insisted. The process of practical reasoning described in S16-18 and S21 is not under the total control of the rational will. The mind must learn to relax control from time to time in practical reasoning—freely associating, letting things flow—or its present commitments will become obsessions. Zen Buddhists try to foster this wisdom by launching an attack against persons' confidence in their own reason through paradoxes or koans.[14] The ultimate aim is to free the novice for a life of detached commitment, i.e. true freedom. The last temptation of the *free* agent is the temptation of total rational control.

In Western thought, Reason comes close to, and sometimes actually becomes, an object of worship. And reason appears as limitless *power*. It is epitomized in a being which is sometimes said to be omnipotent *because* it is Pure Reason. Eastern philosophies generally tell a different story. They emphasize the limitations of Reason and they have never been tempted by the belief that Reason, exercised through science and technology, can give us total control over our environment *or* ourselves. Libertarians must buy some of this Eastern wisdom. They must say that the tale of reason in the practical sphere is the tale of limited power and partial control. The indeterminism they require makes possible "new beginnings" that cannot be forced by reason, but can be used by reason.

6.11   This chapter began with two analogies—relating practical deliberation to creative problem solving (S13), on the one hand, and to natural evolution (S14), on the other. These provided a general view of the theory of practical choice that was then developed in terms of a micro-analogy to R-choice (S16-18), a macro-analogy (S21), and the Everyman-in-Baltar analogy (S23). The theory was then compared with certain themes in the Eastern philosophies of Buddhism and Taoism (S24), to which we shall return when the theory is completed.

Notes

1. This is done in 8.15.

2. For discussion of some of the implications of this, see Ashby (56), Bateson (790, Dennett (78, ch. 15), and Hofstadter (80, ch. 19).

3. Cf.note 4, ch. 5, for more on unconscious motivation.

4. Ashby (56), Bateson (79, p. 203), Dennett (78, ch 15). It can be argued that such machine processes for generating random numbers may be determined. All that is required is that they generate outcomes that are unexpected by the problem solver, machine or human. This is true as far as the possibilities are concerned. But it is also possible that the generating process be undetermined, and it is this possibility that libertarians must exploit. The point here is not to show that random processes in practical reasoning and creative problem solving must be ontologically undetermined,

but that they could be and still play a positive, constructive role in such reasoning.

5. It is possible that a new, relevant reason state may come into existence at the moment of endorsement. The point being made in this paragraph is simply that this is not required and would be unusual. But we do not want to rule it out.

6. As in the Everyman story, the wheel plays a figurative role here. In any eventually true story, the role played the spinning wheel must be assumed by an ontologically undetermined process. This is discussed in ch. 9.

7. He may even renege on his prior commitment in the interval and not go through with the choice. The process is not complete until he finally "accepts" the intention. And even after that he may change his mind and reverse the R-choice, though in this respect R-choice is like any other choice which might be changed prior to action. Cf. ch. 5, note 15.

8. The diagram necessarily oversimplifies in some ways. Some of the "accumulated" reasons need not be new to the preference sets, but rather reasons already in one or another preference set whose relevance is seen in new ways. Also, it is possible that in a long process of deliberation some considerations may be forgotten, so that the preference sets can lose, as well as gain, members.

9. On this problem, see Roberts (72), (79), Keeney and Raiffa (76), and for background Luce and Raiffa (57, ch. 14).

10. The burden of practical freedom described here is connected with the tragic element of free choice. (See 5.10).

11. Quoted in H. Smith (58, ch. 5).

12. This theme is pervasive in Buddhist writings. See H. Smith (58, ch. 3), and Rahula (59, ch. 4).

13. Of particular interest here is the Taoist ideal of *wei wu wei*, to do without doing, to create effortlessly. Blakney (55), *Tao Te Ching*: A New Translation, pp. 39-40, 54, 100-1, 110. For the theme in Zen Buddhism, see Suzuki (56, ch. 1).

14. See Suzuki (56, ch. 6), and Linssen (58, pp. 252-3), where the relation to freedom is explained by way of a commentary on a particular koan.

Relativism, Empiricism, and Morality

7.1 The theory would be seriously deficient if we stopped here. Up to now, the concern has been with practical choices alone, a kind of "best play" strategy for the individual, with the proviso that there is no unique best. What must be added is an account of moral and prudential choice. As they were defined in 6.1, moral and prudential choice are structurally alike in that both involve a conflict between perceived obligation and present inclination. In the one case (moral choice), the conflict is created by the demands of justice, in the other by the demands of long range self interest. A number of thinkers, most recently Thomas Nagel, have made much of this structural similarity between moral and prudential choice, and we shall exploit it in the next chapter when giving an account of prudential choice. But attention will be focussed in this chapter, and in much of the next, on moral choice, which is by far the more controversial of the two and provides the greater challenge for a libertarian account of freedom. The discussion of moral issues in this chapter provides the necessary steps leading to an account of moral choice in the next.

It must be admitted that the prospects for extending the theory of the previous two chapters to moral choice do not look promising. Moral choice is not the sort of thing one could leave to an Orola. The choice of acting in accordance with a moral principle, rather than for some other reason, could not depend upon a chance selection, or so it would seem. Moral choice, however it is dealt with, must, and will, turn out to be quite different from practical choice. And yet the two are related. A thread connects them allowing us to say that they are both expressions of the freedom of the will.

This thread is described in the following steps:

S25. Despite their differences, free moral choices and free practical choices are alike in that they are both accounted for in terms of R-alternative options (purposes, plans, or ways of life). The difference is that in the case of practical choice the relevant R-alternatives are defined by reference to *subsets* of a single agent's total reason set, whereas in the case of moral choice the relevant R-alternatives are defined with respect to the agent's total reason set and *the total reason sets of other agents.*

S26. The key to the moral point of view, and also to moral choice, lies in this relation of one's own reason set (and hence one's values and ends) to the reason sets of others. To take the moral point of view is to recognize that other persons' reason sets have an equal claim to one's own. One's own values do not have a superior or privileged status in the nature of things. The value

systems of different individuals are incommensurable or relativistic alternatives to it. This is the basis for a principle of equal respect for persons as
persons that is thought by many to define the moral point of view,[1] at least
insofar as that point of view governs our behavior toward other persons.[2] The
same relationship of R-alternativeness between one's own reason set and those
of others is the key to understanding how free will is related to human dignity, a
relation sometimes described by saying that persons are to be treated not as
mere means, but as "ends in themselves" because each one is capable of originating his or her own purposes or ends.

These steps are the pivotal ones of the theory. They describe the connection, mentioned
in the Introduction, between free will (as libertarians must conceive it), on the one
hand, and certain features of a relativist view of values, on the other. Free will, in
its various manifestations, requires the existence of relativistic alternative purposes,
plans, or ways of life, defined for practical choice with respect to subsets of the
reason set of a single agent, for moral choice with respect to the reason sets of
different agents (and for prudential choice in another sense yet to be defined). Thus,
these steps describe the analogy mentioned in 5.6 between relativistic alternative
reason sets *in foro interno* and relativistic alternative reason sets *in foro externo*,
which provides the connection between the theories of practical and moral choice.
The important corollaries of this analogy are, on the practical side, (i) that there
may be more than one incommensurably good way of life consistent with a person's
own total reason set, and, on the moral side, (ii) that there may be more than one
incommensurably good way of life of different persons (and by extension of different societies or cultures) consistent with the dictates of morality. The first of these
corollaries makes it possible to give a coherent libertarian account of practical choice.
The second makes it possible to give a coherent libertarian account of moral choice.
When spelled out in detail, the second implication also provides a link, perceived by
Kant but differently described by him, between human autonomy (free will) and the
moral law.

The aim of this chapter is to develop a moral theory underscoring these claims
along the lines suggested by S25-26. Thus, the chapter is an excursion into ethics,
especially in its first half, but a necessary one, since the libertarian theory of moral
choice presupposes at least the general features of a moral theory. That theory is
presented in 7.2-8, then related to value relativism in 7.9-13, and to a theory associated
with value relativism that I call "value empiricism." These sections, in turn, prepare
the way for a discussion in 7.14-18 of why, if at all, persons should take the moral
point of view in the sense defined. Each of these discussions provides essential steps
for the theory of moral choice.

7.2 Taking the moral point of view, according to S26, requires treating other
persons' reason sets as relativistic, or R-, alternatives to one's own. R-alternative
reason sets, according to S4, define incommensurable alternative purposes, plans of
action or ways of life equally worth trying as value experiments, or, to use Mill's
phrase, as "experiments in living." So to treat other persons' reason sets as R-alternatives to one's own is to regard their purposes, plans, and ways of life as equally

worthy as one's own of being tried. But S26 implies two important qualifications to this general claim, the first of which is related to the analogy with practical choice described in S25.

The first qualification is that *treating* other persons' purposes and plans *as* R-alternatives in this way does not necessarily imply *believing* that their purposes or plans are as good as one's own, or will turn out to be as good as one's own when experimented with. The analogy with practical choice as described in chapter 6 helps us to understand this point. During practical deliberation we may think one alternative is better at a given time, due to the ebb and flow of considerations. But we treat the alternatives as equal in a certain way because we are not yet convinced that the presently favored one will turn out to be the best in the long run. This is like a judge or jury hearing a case, who cannot fail to be moved one way or the other as the evidence is heard. But while they may favor one or another side on the basis of evidence heard up to a given point in the trial, they remain open to evidence from both sides and are ready to give both an "equal hearing" until the final verdict is rendered.

We are asked to do the same by S26 with other persons' purposes and plans. We are not asked to render a final verdict on how good their purposes or plans may turn out to be. We are merely asked to give them an equal hearing, to allow their experiments in living to proceed without interference, as we wish our own to proceed, withholding a final verdict while the experiment goes on.[3] To treat the reason sets of persons as R-alternatives in this way is to treat the persons themselves with equal respect *as persons*, capable of exercising the capacities that define them as persons, of acting upon ("experimenting with") purposes and plans of their own choosing.

7.3 The second qualification presupposed by S26 will take more time to develop and requires some preliminaries. Not *all* purposes, plans, and ways of life are to be treated as R-alternatives. There are limits to the tolerance implied by S26. (If this were not so, one could hardly speak about a "moral" point of view at all.) But the limits emerge as natural consequences of the initial injunction to treat others' purposes and plans as R-alternatives, and not as qualifications added in an *ad hoc* fashion. This is a pivotal point, and it will take several sections (3-8) to show why it is so.

First, let us note that taking the moral point of view in the sense of S26 involves having a baseline belief about how one's own reason set, and hence one's own purposes, plans, and way of life, ought to be treated, and then believing that this treatment ought to be extended equally to the reason sets of others. The baseline belief for each person is that he or she be treated with respect as a person in something like the following sense:

S27. To be treated with respect as a person (or, in Kantian terms, to be treated as an end rather than as a means)[4] is to be allowed to design and pursue one's own experiments in living (to create and pursue one's own ends, purposes and plans of action) without interference, i.e. without being coerced or otherwise constrained, harmed, or controlled without one's consent by some person or other.

To take the moral point of view, as a first approximation, is to extend this belief to all others, to believe that

> **ER***. All persons (including oneself) should be treated in every situation with respect as persons, or as ends, in the sense of S27.

Unfortunately, ER* cannot always be followed in the real world, and this is the source of the second qualification. ER* is made for an ideal world, an ideal "kingdom of ends,"[5] in which there are no impediments to the pursuit of purposes and ways of life, and no conflict between one pursuit and others. In the real world, there are situations in which ER* cannot *in principle* be followed, and consequently a moral view defined in terms of it provides no guide to action.

Such situations are typically, though not exclusively, ones in which some person or group is not treating someone else with respect in the sense of S27, situations in which someone is being coerced, harmed, or controlled by others without their consent, or being treated as a means rather than as an end. If you are witness to an assault or attempted rape and there is something you can do to stop it (by physically preventing it or seeking help), then you have entered a situation of this kind. If you prevent the assault, then you do not allow the assailant to pursue purposes or plans of his or her own choosing. If you do nothing, you do not treat the victim with respect as a person. You do not allow the victim to pursue purposes or plans of his or her own choosing, without being coerced or harmed by others.

Some would argue that if third parties in such situations do not use force to stop the assault when force is necessary, they have not themselves done anything wrong, as they would have if they had been the assailants themselves or had aided in the assault. But while this may be correct in some overly legalistic moral schemes, it is not correct from a moral point of view defined in terms of S27. By doing nothing, by walking on by when one can do something to stop the assault, one fails to treat the victim with respect, or as an end, so defined. It was said that when pirates under the command of William Kidd came into the city of Philadelphia, raping many women, some of the men with pacifist leanings would not protect their women. By allowing the pirates to pursue their chosen purposes these men were not treating their women with respect as persons.

The point is that, in such situations, one cannot *in principle* treat *every* person involved with respect, or as an end. Either the victim or the assailant must be treated unequally with regard to their chosen experiments in living. Thus, one cannot in principle act in accordance with the principle ER*, which requires that one treat every person as an end in every situation. The ideal world, the "moral sphere," as we shall call it, in which ER* *can* be followed, has broken down.

7.4 Since ER* does not tell us what to do in situations in which the moral sphere has broken down, it does not provide us with a general guide to moral action. Nevertheless, treating all persons with respect as persons remains the ideal which ER* attempts to express, and any adjustments to the principle ought to depart from this ideal as little as possible. The problem in other words, is not with the ideal, but with ER* as a guide to actions that would realize the ideal in every situation. And this suggests that where we *must* depart from ER* by treating *someone* as a means, we should do so *in a manner* that shows greatest respect for the ideal of treating all persons with respect as persons.

Two adjustments are immediately suggested by this requirement in the light of the examples: in situations in which one must fail to treat someone or other with respect, or as an end, because someone is being treated as a means (i.e. being coerced or controlled, etc.), (i) it is the guilty party who should not be treated as an end rather than the innocent, and (ii) one should use the minimum amount of coercion necessary to prevent the guilty from treating the innocent as a means. The second of these conditions is easy to justify in terms of the requirement of departing as little as possible from the ideal of respect for all persons in situations in which one must depart from that ideal to some degree. Despite his action, the assailant or coercer remains a person deserving of respect as a person. He forfeits the right to pursue his purposes or chosen experiment in living in the present circumstances, but not all rights to be respected as a person. If the assailant can be subdued by physical force, one does not have the right to shoot him through the heart. One does what is necessary to deter the guilty out of respect for the innocent, but one does only what is necessary, out of a residual respect for the personhood of the guilty. Acting in accordance with this residual respect amounts to departing as little as possible from the ideal of treating every person with respect in situations *in which one must treat someone as a means*. It is violating ER* when we must, but in a manner that shows greatest respect for the ideal of respect for persons in general.

7.5 Condition (i) can be dealt with in a similar way. Our intuition is that the assailant or rapist has "broken" the moral sphere by treating the victim as a means to his ends. In thwarting the guilty, we therefore attempt to "restore" the moral sphere by interfering with the action that has broken it. In doing so, we violate ER*, but in a manner that shows our commitment to the preservation and maintenance of a moral sphere in which persons are treated with respect by other persons.[6]

It might be objected that we would show greater respect for the ideal of a moral sphere by not ourselves violating ER*. But this overlooks the fact that our choice is not between violating or not violating ER*; it is a choice about *how*, not whether, we shall violate ER*—by failing to treat the guilty with respect, or the innocent. And the argument is that by violating ER* in the former way, by failing to treat the guilty as an end, we show greater respect for the ideal of a moral sphere by showing our commitment to its preservation and maintenance.

For a similar reason, this result does not imply a general acceptance of the principle that the end justifies the means. The end (preserving the ideal of a moral sphere) justifies a less-than-ideal means only when the means *qua* less-than-ideal (failing to treat someone as an end) is something that must be done *no matter what we do*.

It might also be objected that the argument presupposes our ability to identify the guilty and distinguish the guilty from the innocent; and this may not always be possible. This is correct. We shall see in a moment that there are cases of moral sphere breakdown in which one cannot easily identify a guilty party, and even those in which there is no guilty party.[7] These cases require separate treatment. But they do not invalidate the above argument for cases where a guilty party can be identified. These latter cases are ones in which some person (or person) is (are) being coerced by another (or others), or controlled without their consent. Now those being coerced or controlled may try to resist, as in the case of the assault or rape victim, and in doing so they are attempting to thwart the purposes of the assailant just as clearly as he is attempting to thwart their purposes. But there is an important asymmetry. The victim, if innocent, has no intention of coercing unless to thwart coercion directed at him or her, whereas the assailant intends to coerce whether or not coercion is directed at him, and whether or not he is resisted. It is in this sense that we can say the assailant's pursuit of his purposes *precipitated* the conflict, and hence the moral sphere breakdown, even in cases where the victim resists.

The victim's resistance can then be justified in such situations by the same argument justifying third party intervention. The assailant has placed the victim in a situation in which the victim must either fail to treat the assailant with respect, by resisting, or fail to treat himself (or herself) with respect, by allowing the assailant to treat him (or her) as a means. Since the ideal is to treat everyone, *including oneself*, as an end, the moral sphere has broken down, and the question is not *whether* to treat someone as a means, but *whom* to treat as a means, the guilty (the one whose actions precipitated the breakdown) or the innocent. In this way, self defense can be justified by an argument similar to that justifying third party intervention. But condition (ii) must be observed as well in cases of self defense: one should use only the minimum amount of coercion necessary to thwart the guilty and thus to restore the moral sphere.

7.6 To summarize, in 7.4 it was said that ER* did not tell us what to do in situations in which the moral sphere has broken down and thus did not provide a general guide to moral action. Nevertheless, it was also said that what really mattered in defining the moral point of view was the ideal of respect for all persons as persons in the sense of S27. ER* was important because it was an attempted expression of this ideal. But ER* tells us how to act in accordance with this ideal only a perfect world in which no one interferes with the pursuits of others. In an imperfect world, one must sometimes fail to treat everyone with respect as a person. But if one keeps the ideal in mind, one will know how to proceed in an imperfect world. In situations in which one must fail to treat someone as an end, one should do so by departing as little as possible from the ideal of respect for all persons as persons. This requirement led us to two conditions on action in "imperfect" situations—conditions having to do with the treatment of the guilty and the amount of force or coercion to be used. With these conditions in mind, we can amend ER* as follows:

ER**. All persons should be treated with respect as persons (in the sense of S27) whenever this is possible. In situations in which it is not possible, one's actions should depart as little as possible from the ideal of respect for all persons as persons. In particular, in situations in which one or more persons is (are) treating another (others) as means, (i) it is the guilty, not the innocent, who should not be treated as an end and (ii) the minimum coercion necessary to prevent the guilty from treating the innocent as a means should be used.

But the amended principle is still incomplete. For it focusses on only one class of situations in which the moral sphere can break down. Thse are situations in which we can identify a guilty party whose actions are the source of the breakdown. But there are other situations of moral sphere breakdown in which it is not possible to identify a guilty party. These are "conflict of interest" situations in which one's person's purposes or experiments in living come in conflict with those of others, so that all cannot be satisfied. But no coercion, harm, or control of one person by another has *yet* taken place. Where ends differ, ends may collide. The resulting conflict of interest situations are a staple of everyday life—a husband and wife debating about how to spend their money, friends differing about how to spend an evening, co-workers arguing about the division of labor—and they invariably have moral overtones. Unless the conflict is otherwise resolved, someone will be treated as a means.

What does the moral point of view require in such conflict of interest situations? I think we would all answer, "a fair compromise, or as fair a compromise as possible," meaning by this a compromise that gives equal weight to each person's interests and purposes, though each will usually have to give up something to resolve the conflict. Now fair compromise in this sense is precisely what is required by the ideal of respect for all persons in the sense of S27. But there are at least two reasons why such compromises are difficult to arrive at in practice, and both are reasons we should expect, given the interpretation of equal respect in terms of treating the reason sets of the different parties as R-alternatives to one another.

First, it is difficult to know for sure whether persons in a conflict situation are bargaining or trying to settle the conflict in good faith, or trying to manipulate others for their own ends. Second, even when all the parties involved are trying their best to find a fair compromise, there is the problem of trying to compare and weigh on a common scale their different values—in short, the problem of incommensurability of values. Is the husband's desire for a night out with friends more important *to him* than the wife's desire to have a certain chore completed is *to her?* There is no doubt which of the two (the night out or the completed chore) is more important to him (from the point of view of his systems of values); and there is no doubt which of the two is more important to her. The problem of incommensurability in this case lies in making the judgment that what he favors is more important to him than what she favors is to her, or vice versa. And there is no guarantee that they will find a common standard for making such judgments; their priorities (i.e. values) may simply differ in incommensurable ways. Thus, they must bargain in trust and love, each one trying to see the importance of the other's desire from the perspective of the other's system of values, not their own, and trying to accommodate it. Various compromises are possible, but the only adequate test of a fair compromise is that both agree to it from their different perspectives, and neither is cheated or manipulated.

7.7 These problems of finding a fair compromise are the problems one would expect if the moral point of view required treating the reason sets of the conflicting parties as R-alternatives to one another. The first problem—determining when others are bargaining in good faith—is related to the problem of knowing other minds. It is a problem of determining whether speech and other behavior truly reflect inner *motives* or *reasons*. There is no theoretical solution to this problem; the practical solution is trust. The second problem—of incommensurability—is related to the relativist themes of chapter 5. Each person's priorities are determined *relative to* his or her reason set, hence value system. (Value systems are understood, as in 5.5, in terms of reason sets. Roughly speaking, a person's value system at a time is the totality of valuations whose truth is presupposed by the agent's total reason set at that time; and valuations are propositions expressing what is good or bad, right or wrong, better or worse, etc.) The second problem arises because the reason sets need not presuppose common standards of value (valuations) by which to judge that one of a set of conflicting purposes is superior or inferior to others. There is no general theoretical solution to *this* problem either. (Cf. 6.9 on the "multi-attribute problem.") Once again, the practical solution, a compromise that seems fair *from* the perspective of *each* of the different reason sets, requires trust.

Given these problems, it is no surprise that the ideal of fair compromise is difficult to realize in a world of conflicting interests. One usually only approximates it, which means in practice that "second best" strategies are often employed. When conflicts of interest cannot be fairly compromised by the parties involved, one resorts to third party arbitrators, judges, juries, majority vote, coin flips, etc.[8] What is important about these second best strategies for our purposes is that they fit the general pattern of "departing as little as possible from the ideal of equal respect when you must depart from it to some degree." The ideal is a fair compromise mutually agreed upon by the parties themselves and judged fair from each perspective. Third party arbitrators try to approximate this ideal, but if left with no other guidelines, they must appeal to their own value systems. Majority vote will produce an unhappy minority, yet it can be shown that in certain "imperfect" situations, no other solution can come closer to respecting the voice of each person equally.[9] Likewise, coin flips are imperfect solutions because they produce winners and losers arbitrarily. Yet they are used as a last resort in some conflict situations because they preserve as best one can in bad circumstances the ideal of equal respect for all parties. In this way, second best strategies can be accommodated to the general account of the moral point of view in an imperfect world.

7.8 Adding these remarks about conflict of interest situations, we can now give a final account of the moral point of view suggested by S26:

S28. (The Principle of Equal Respect (ER)): All persons should be treated with respect as persons, or as ends and not means (in the sense of S27), whenever this is possible. In situations where it is not possible, one's actions should depart as little as possible from the ideal of respect for all persons as persons. In particular,

(a) in situations where one or more person(s) is (are) treating another (others) as means, (i) it is the guilty, not the innocent who should not be treated as an end and (ii) the minimum coercion necessary to prevent the guilty from treating the innocent as a means should be employed;

(b) in situations where all persons cannot be allowed to pursue their chosen experiments in living because interests conflict, but there is no guilty party as yet, one should seek as fair a compromise between the parties as possible, one that recognizes an equal claim for the reason sets (hence the purposes, plans, interests, desires) of all parties involved. Ideally, this would mean a bargained compromise in which all parties agree and none is cheated or manipulated. In practice, second best strategies must be employed which should depart as little as possible from this ideal.

S29. To take the moral point of view toward persons is to believe that one should act in accordance with the principle of equal respect (S28) and to desire to act in accordance with this principle.

To so act would be to treat the reason sets of all other persons as R-alternatives to one's own, whenever possible, and to approximate this ideal as closely as possible whenever it cannot be perfectly realized.

The moral point of view so defined does not give clear directions for action in every human situation. It shows, for example, why the problems of knowing other minds and of incommensurability of values are perennial problems in the moral life, requiring constant effort, understanding, and empathy, and why these problems can sometimes defeat all of our best efforts. Moreover, I would suggest that even in those difficult cases where this account of the moral point of view does not give unambiguous directions, our common moral intuitions also tend to be vague. For I think these moral intuitions do, in most instances revolve around the idea of treating others fairly or justly, which means according equal respect to their reason sets and their purposes, interests, and desires, as long as they accord equal respect to the reason sets of others.

7.9 But it is one thing to suggest that an account of the moral point of view yields judgments in conformity with common moral intuitions, quite another to give convincing reasons why anyone should accept the moral point of view so defined (or endorse the common moral intuitions). We must now address this deeper and more difficult problem because an answer to it is also important for the eventual account of moral choice. But the deeper problem cannot be addressed without some preliminary discussion of value issues in general. And, as a first step in this discussion, I want to say something about the relation of the moral theory just defined to the doctrine of value relativism defined in 5.5.

S30. The moral theory defined by S27-29 might be described as a "potential relativism (or pluralism) qualified by moral principle." For it requires that we take a certain attitude to a restricted class of persons or cultures, like the attitude some relativists have suggested we take toward all persons or cultures (that is, treating their reason sets or value systems as R-alternatives to our own). The restrictions are imposed by the principle of equal respect which rules out of the class of those deserving equal respect those who do not treat the reason sets of others as R-alternatives to their own. Such persons are ruled out of the class of those deserving equal respect temporarily, if their actions are due to weakness of will, or in principle, if their actions are matters of policy directed at others (until the policy is changed). But the reason sets of all others *not* excluded by such considerations are to be treated as relativistic alternatives to one's own. Thus we have a "relativism (or pluralism) qualified by moral principle." The term "potential" captures the qualification mentioned in 7.2. To treat other persons' (morally acceptable) purposes, plans, or ways of life as relativistic alternatives to one's own is to accept them as guides to value experiments "worth trying"; it is not to pass judgment on how they will fare when experimented with.

Thus, the relativism or pluralism is qualified in two ways. It is (a) potential (pending the outcome of value experimentation), and it is (b) restricted by moral principle.

This step reflects themes of some twentiety-century relativists, while qualifying them in certain ways. Some anthropologists who defended relativist views in this century, like Ruth Benedict (46) and Melville Herskovits (47), believed they were making a positive contribution to moral understanding rather than undermining the foundations of morality. As John Ladd has said (73, p. 9), "What these people were trying to say is that moral principles (and moral codes) . . . are binding only on those within a particular group. For that reason, they maintain, no one has the right to pass judgment on another society's ethics or to impose his ethics on another society. That would be ethnocentrism. Instead, one ought to treat the ethics of other societies with tolerance, respect and understanding." But these relativists did not provide any theoretical grounds for qualifying such claims, and so their position came to be viewed as an anti-moral one, rather than a moral one as they intended. Tolerance, respect, and understanding were presumably to be extended not only to societies living at peace with their neighbors and their environment, but also to societies governed by Hitler's National Socialist principles, or to societies that practiced slavery, child sacrifice, or indiscriminate killing at the whim of a leader.

This result was in part due to a philosophical failing. These relativists should, and could, have realized that the requirement of equal tolerance and respect they advocated could not *in principle* be satisfied in an imperfect world. From there they could have reasoned as we did in 7.4-8 to the qualified version of the moral point of view presented in S28 and S29. This was not their only philosophical failing, as we shall see, but it was serious enough. For it led people to overlook the positive contributions to moral understanding these relativists were making, in the flood of moral indignation over the excesses of their view.

The relativism-qualified-by-moral-principle described in S30 takes hold of the positive insights of these relativists, of tolerance and equal respect, without the need to extend such tolerance and respect to the Hitlers, Stalins, slave traders, child sacrificers, aggressors, rapists, and all other persons or groups who coerce, harm, or otherwise impose their wills on others. Such persons or groups are ruled out of the class of those deserving tolerance and respect, temporarily if their actions are due to weakness of will, or, in principle, as in the case of a Hitler or Stalin, if their actions are the expression of a general policy directed at subordinating the desires and interests of others to their own. But once the class of those deserving equal respect is so restricted, those persons or groups remaining in the class, according to S30, are to be treated with the same tolerance and respect for their differing forms of life as the relativists advocated for all persons or societies without restriction.

7.10 In chapter 5, I pointed out that relativist theories can be limited in certain ways. Einstein's Special Theory, for example, limits the class of relativistic frames of reference to inertial frames, those standing in a certain relation (moving with constant velocity relative) to one another. The moral view just outlined exploits this idea. The class of relativistic frames is limited to the reason sets of persons (or cultures) standing in a certain relation—of mutual respect—to one another. Other frames are deviant and need not be treated equally (though certain rules, like using minimum coercion to restrain the guilty, apply when dealing with deviant frames). What marks off the relativistic (non-deviant) frames in the physical theory is that the *laws of nature* are invariant, or retain the same form, in all of them. This is the respect in which they have equal validity. Corresponding to the invariant laws of nature of the physical theory, we have in the moral theory, an invariant *moral law*, or principle of equal respect, which is accepted in all non-deviant frames. In both cases, the relativity and equal validity of frames is related to the invariance of laws. But in the physical theory, laws of nature are *true* in all non-deviant frames. In the moral case, the moral law is *accepted* as a guide to action in all non-deviant frames. The difference should be expected where the relativistic frames of reference are the reason sets of beings possessing free choice.

But there is a difficulty with this analogy that has probably not gone unnoticed. Limited physical theories of relativity are deficient in certain ways. They lack sufficient generality. Thus Einstein sought, and eventually found, a General Theory of Relativity which removed the restriction of relativistic frames to inertial frames. Since relativity theories in physics are a by-product of the search for invariant laws, this move toward greater generality is to be expected. But a similar move in moral theory— from the restricted relativism of S30 to the unrestricted relativism of Benedict, Herskovits, et. al.—would presumably not produce a better, but a worse, moral theory.

Yet here, where the physical analogy seems least appropriate, it turns out to be revealing after all. For the analogue in moral theory for the invariant laws of a General Theory of Relativity is the unqualified moral law ER*. It tells us to treat all persons without restriction as ends. But we know that ER* holds only in an ideal world. In other words, if we lived in a perfect world, in which everyone was treating everyone else with equal respect, a General Theory of moral relativity would hold.

So a General Theory *is* the ideal, in moral as well as physical theory. and would be preferred to a Special Theory, *in an ideal world*. Unfortunately, this world is not an ideal one, morally speaking, and this is the reason why a Special Theory must be preferred in it. To make a General Moral Theory true would be to make a better world.

The main difference in the physical and moral spheres is not that a General Theory is preferred in one but not the other. The main difference is that once again, in moral theory, the relativistic frames of reference are the reason sets of *free* beings. By making free choices, beings with free will can depart from moral laws and create an *imperfect* (moral) world in a way that has no parallel in the relation of physical objects to the laws of nature. And this difference is related to the differences between normative and physical laws in general. In this respect, as in others, both similarities and differences between physical and moral theories of relativity are revealing—for ethics as well as for free will.

7.11 I said that the failure of relativists like Benedict and Herskovits to qualify their view by moral principle in the manner of S30 was in part a philosophical failing. But it was not their only failing. A second one—suggested by the term "potential" in S30—is also important for understanding the theory of moral choice. To understand this second failing, we must return to what was said about value systems and value experimentation in chapters 5 and 6. To say that the reason sets, or correlatively the value systems, of those persons or groups not excluded by moral principle are to be treated as R-alternatives to one's own is not to say that no one of these (non-excluded) value systems is superior or inferior to any other. The remaining value systems are deserving equal respect only in the sense that each one is to be considered "worth trying" as a value experiment in the sense of S9. Some value systems may in fact give rise to failed experiments and thus show themselves to be inferior for the persons involved.

This qualification harks back to a major theme of chapter 5—that value systems guiding ways of life must be tested by experiment and cannot be shown with certainty to be superior or inferior for a given person or group *a priori*. The most one can do prior to experiment is to give more or less plausible arguments that one or another system is more *worthy of being tried* than another, just as one does in ordinary practical reasoning before making a decision, or just as Everyman did with regard to his options. Such antecedent arguments carry weight ("Others have tried this and failed"); but they need not convince ("I understand that others have failed, but I am a different person (we are different persons) and I (we) may succeed"). And, where such arguments do not convince, the proof can only be in the experimenting and failing. This is one reason why equal respect is due to the reason sets of others. Because we cannot be certain *a priori* that a particular form of life will fail for others, that it will not allow them to attain the particular form of satisfaction or excellence they seek, we must give them the right to try their experiment in living, just as we demand the right to pursue our chosen goals or purposes, if others cannot persuade us of the unworthiness of our goals or purposes. Such an attitude is further suggested by the fact, brought out in S9, that successful value experimentation does not show that the one correct or true value system has been found, even for the person or group conducting the experiment. There may in principle be other good ways for the persons or groups themselves and for others like them.

I call the view about values and value experimentation described in the previous two paragraphs "value empiricism." Some of its features were sketched in chapter 5, and they seem to me to capture what is correct in the arguments of value relativists. If we leave aside temporarily the qualificiations imposed by moral principle in S30, then value empiricism can be defined in the following way. (The step following this one will show how the moral point of view can be fitted into the value empiricist perspective.)

S31. *Value empiricism* is the view that plans of action or ways of life must be tested by experiments in living, or value experiments, in the sense of S9. Leaving aside moral considerations temporarily, such experiments are to be judged successful or unsuccessful by whether or not they attain the ends or goals intended by those conducting the experiment, and those ends or goals are tested in turn by whether or not they bring the expected satisfactions of those experimenting. Thus, standards of satisfaction, ends, goals, and plans of action (means) are tested against experience *as complexes* (called "value systems"), and failure of an experiment (marked by conditions of disappointment, despair, etc. as described in 5.11) may lead to an adjustment of different parts of the complex—of the ends or goals, the plans or means, or of the standards of satisfaction. What adjustments should be made is again a matter to be tested by experiments in living, by trial and error.

When it is said that such value systems are "tested against experience," "experience" must be understood in a broad sense to include such emotive states as disappointment, despair, boredom, contentment, joy, and the like, which have evaluative implications. In this way the gap between fact and value, insofar as there is such a gap, is overcome in value experimentation. And value experimentation will differ from scientific experimentation to the extent that such personal psychological states can be relevant to the testing of value theories.[10]

The other side of the value empiricist view is that the goodness or badness of a value system for a person or group (once again temporarily excluding judgments of moral goodness or badness) cannot be known *a priori*, prior to experiments in living. The most one can provide prior to experiment are plausible arguments that the system is or is not "worth trying" as an experiment for a given individual or group, based on past experience of like systems having been tried. But such arguments are inductive, not *a priori*, arguments and they face the normal difficulties of extrapolation from past to future and from one person or group to other persons or groups. And in the case of value experiments, there is the additional difficulty, suggested by S8 (the Many Goods principle) that there is no *a priori* reason to believe that a successful value experiment has shown that the value system tested defines the one correct or true way of life even for the person or group conducting the experiment, much less for others, like or unlike them.

7.12 Value empiricism so defined is obviously an analogue of empiricist theories of theoretical knowledge, with some adjustments made to accommodate special features of value theories brought out in chapter 5. *A priori* knowledge of the correctness or incorrectness of value systems is ruled out. What evidence we do have for judgments about such systems is said to be *a posteriori* and inductive, and to be subject to the difficulties of extrapolation from past to future characteristic of all inductive evidence with the added difficulties imposed by the Many Goods principle.

There is an analogue in the value empiricism of S31 to the claim, made by recent thinkers like W. V. O. Quine, that theories to be tested face the bar of experience as unified wholes, any (perhaps all) parts of which may in principle be adjusted in the light of a failed experiment.[11] In the case of values, the failure of an experiment in living may be answered by an alteration in one's plans or means for realizing one's purposes or goals, by an alteration of one or more of one's more general standards of satisfaction or excellence (ideals, principles, standards of excellence, judgments about what will bring happiness, etc.). What can and should be changed is not something that can be known *a priori*; it must be learned by experiment, by trial and error.

In the case of theoretical knowledge, Quine describes theories as nets touching experience at their outer edges with the more fundamental or entrenched principles nearer to the center. No statements in his view, even logical ones nearest the center, are immune to revision if the theory as a whole does not match up with experience. To appreciate this net analogy for value theory, one does not have to accept Quine's extreme view that no statements are immune to revision or his related denial of the analytic-synthetic distinction. It is sufficient to hold that value systems confront the bar of experience as wholes and that when they lead to disappointment, frustration, despair, and other symptoms of failure *many* different parts of the system may be subject to adjustment, from the more peripheral plans or means or purposes to the most deeply entrenched ideals and standards of excellence. Persons will naturally try to adjust less entrenched plans and purposes first, but they may find at times that only a radical change in their value systems, including deeply entrenched purposes and ideals, will suffice; and this means a change of their ways of life.

Implied by this net analogy is a theory of truth for value systems that is a combination of a coherence theory and a pragmatic theory. The testing of value systems is by experiment or *practice* and the standards of assessment, the ideals and standards of satisfaction and excellence, are *internal* to the theory being tested. This is so because even experiences of disappointment, despair, joy, and the like, can be used to test the system only insofar as they are evaluated as good or bad by the system. (Valuations describing such experiences as good or bad are part of the value system.)[12] It is a view similar to the view of truth and experimentation with respect to values (ends and means) put forward by John Dewey and other pragmatists. (Quine, for his part, has recognized the affinity between his views on evidence and truth and those of Dewey and other pragmatists.)[13]

Now it may be that such a coherence-pragmatic theory is not adequate as a general theory of truth, applicable to the theoretical as well as the practical spheres, to fact as well as value. But I want to argue that such a view *is* correct for value systems. For the problems we normally associate with coherence theories of truth (the possibility of mutually incompatible, but internally consistent, accounts of the real) do not arise in the case of value systems, unless we make an assumption for which there is no *a priori*, or intuitively convincing support, namely, that there is only one true or correct value system, only one good way of life for a particular person, or for all persons. A coherence theory of values, therefore, has the advantages of a coherence theory of factual truth without the major disadvantage. As for the pragmatic aspect of the theory, it is embodied in the claim that value systems cannot be tested in the abstract, divorced from life and practice. They are guides for living, and must be tested by living in accordance with them. And this too is a plausible claim *about value systems*.

7.13 I suggested that the value empiricist view defined by S31 captures what is correct in the arguments of value relativists. The connection with value relativism lies in the fact that judgments of success and failure of value experiments are made in accordance with standards of evaluation *internal to* the value system being tested. This is the consequence of the coherence aspect of the value empiricist view defined by S31; and it is a consequence central to relativist theories of value. Judgments about what is valuable must be made *relative to some system* or other of values which is held by, or could be held by, some person, or culture, or society.

But value empiricism does not imply the more extravagant relativist claim that no value system held by a person or group can be judged to be superior or inferior to any other for that person or group, or for any other person or group. Indeed, value empiricism is consistent with the claim that there is a finite number of value systems or ways of life—or even just one—that is best for all persons and groups. Value empiricists insist only that all such claims about superiority or inferiority must be *based upon inductive evidence and tested by experiment*. If there is one value system or way of life (or a finite number) that is (are) correct for all or most persons, we shall find this out by experimenting. We are not justified in assuming it is not so. Nor are we justified in assuming it is so. Similarly, we can make judgments according to S31 about the superiority or inferiority of one value system relative to another for ourselves, for other persons or for groups of persons. But these judgments will also be based on inductive evidence, and they will be more or less plausible judgments about what system of values is or is not more "worth trying" than others as a value experiment. I do not think value relativists are entitled to say more than this about value systems, but I think they are entitled to say at least this much. And that is why I said that value empiricism captures what is correct in the value relativist view.

We should add that value empiricism itself is a plausible, not a provable, view. The value empiricist view has a status similar to that of the more common form of empiricism with respect to factual knowledge, which, for purposes of contrast, may be called "fact empiricism." Fact empiricists can challenge their rationalist opponents to produce factual or synthetic propositions whose truth or falsity can be known *a priori*, and they can argue against any candidates that rationalists may produce. But they cannot claim to have examined every possible candidate for a synthetic *a priori* truth rationalists might offer, and cannot claim in this sense to have proven their view correct. Value empiricists are in much the same position. Without denying that we can have reliable evidence that certain value systems are superior or inferior to others for certain persons or groups, they can challenge any claim that such evidence and what it supports can be known *a priori*. But they cannot claim to have examined every possible candidate for a synthetic *a priori* truth about value systems that value rationalists might offer. Nevertheless, one can say of value empiricism what one can say of fact empiricism, that the burden of proof lies on the other (rationalist) side.

7.14 We can now return to the moral theory defined by S27-29 in the light of this discussion of value relativism and value empiricism. In S30, this moral theory was said to be a "potential relativism qualified by moral principle." It requires that we take a certain attitude to a restricted class of persons or groups (treating their reason sets as R-alternatives to our own) like the attitude some value relativists suggested we take toward all other persons or groups. The restriction is imposed by moral principle, or the moral point of view, as defined by S29 with the supporting definitions S27 and S28.

We are now ready to consider the question of why this restriction should be accepted. Why, in other words, should we accept such a limited relativism qualified by moral principle rather than an unrestricted value relativism or moral scepticism, or any other moral or anti-moral position? The question amounts to asking why one should take the moral point of view in the sense defined by S29, and it is thus a particular version of the question "Why be moral?"—that most difficult of questions in the theory of values, which has bedeviled and frustrated philosophers ever since Plato posed it in the *Republic* by telling the story of the ring of Gyges. We cannot avoid this question here, because as it turns out an answer to it is essential to a libertarian account of free moral choice.

One of the reasons, I believe, for the difficulties caused by the question "Why be moral?" over the centuries is that the kind of answer required has been misunderstood. It is a mistake I think to suppose that one can provide rationally convincing *a priori* arguments for the moral life, or the moral point of view. It is even a mistake, though a more subtle one, to think one can prove that it is necessarily irrational or illogical not to take the moral point of view, if you yourself want to be treated morally by others. I am not going to try to refute every theory that has defended these strong rationalist claims, a task that would take us too far afield. Some of these theories, like Alan Gewirth's recent moral theory (78), are impressive; and yet I think they all fall short of their goal. Instead, I want to explore alternative answers to the question "Why be moral?" that follow out the implications of S30 and S31. In other words, against such rationalist strategies, I want to suggest that answers to the question "Why be moral?"should be *value empiricist* answers. The moral life, like any other kind of life, is a value experiment. Or, we should more accurately say that moral *lives* are value experiments, for there may be many different incommensurable ways of life compatible with moral principle, according to S30, each requiring that other ways be treated with equal respect. Being a value experiment, a moral life like any other kind is not one whose worth can be proven *a priori*. What one can, and must, do is provide plausible arguments that moral lives are "worth trying" as experiments in living, more worth trying than non-moral lives.

Looked at in this manner, as ways of commending lives which take the moral point of view, many answers philosophers have given to the question "Why be moral?" make more sense. For these answers often provide reasons for being moral that may appeal to particular persons in particular cultural settings, without providing rational certainty. When one undertakes a moral life, there is risk involved, just as in any other experiment in living, and yet there may be good reasons to take the risk. Unfortunately, life does not allow us the *certainty* that moral struggle is worth the effort, and yet, for various reasons, it may *be* worth the effort.

I now want to illustrate this point of view by looking at some representative answers to the question "Why be moral?" that take this line. A discussion of the advantages and disadvantages of such answers will provide us with a further step in our theory. Value empiricist answers to the question "Why be moral?" may generally be divided into two kinds, "this-worldly" (or "secular") answers and "transcendent" (or "religious") ones. The former point to the alleged advantages in this world of the moral life, or of lives lived in a moral community; the latter find the ultimate ground for moral action in other-worldly or transcendent goals, beatitude, Nirvana, avoidance of eternal punishment, etc. One might argue that this-worldly, or secular, answers to the question "Why be moral?" may in fact take the value empiricist form, but transcendent, or religious, answers do not seem to fit the value empiricist pattern. For religious answers to the question "Why be moral?" generally provide, or purport to provide, the desired certainty that moral lives are worth trying. But I shall argue that both kinds of answers, transcendent and this-worldly, are value empiricist answers. In any case, we shall look at this-worldly answers first.

7.15 Many this-worldly answers to the question "Why be moral?" focus on the advantages of living in a moral community, a moral sphere in which persons treat one another with respect, in contrast to a life lived outside such a community. There are numerous variations on this theme. Plato's *Republic* itself provides one such variation, though it is marred from our point of view by a class structure which confines the true community of equal (maximal) respect to a ruling class. One of the clearest, and most uncompromising, examples of a this-worldly answer of this kind in recent philosophy is provided by Kurt Baier in his influential book, *The Moral Point of View* (66). Baier's answer is worth looking at first for what it tells us in general about this-worldly answers to the question "Why be moral?"

Baier's starting point is Hobbesian, but he departs from Hobbes at a crucial juncture. He wants to demonstrate the advantages of living in a moral community (in which persons "follow rules overriding self interest whenever [following self interest would be] to the detriment of others") over living outside all such communities, in a

Hobbesian "state of nature." He argues as follows: "To live in a state of nature is to live . . . in conditions in which there are . . . no reliable expectations about other people's behavior other than that they will follow their inclination or their interest. . . . In such a state reason will be the enemy of co-operation and mutual trust . . . reason will counsel everyone to avoid . . . risks by preventive action. But this leads to war," and hence, for most persons, to lives which in Hobbes' terms are "poor, nasty, brutish and short." Persons who would suffer in such a state of nature, Baier continues, would find it desirable to be part of a moral community in which persons follow rules overriding self interest when following self interest would be to the detriment of others. But following the rules of morality is not reasonable if others cannot be expected to do so as well. He concludes:

> The situation can change, reason can support morality, only when the assumption about other people's behavior is reversed. Hobbes thought that this could be achieved only by the creation of an absolute ruler with absolute power to enforce his laws. We have already seen that this is not true and that it can also be achieved if people live in a society, that is, if they have common ways of life, which are taught to all members and somehow enforced by the group. Its members have reason to expect their fellows generally to obey its rules, even when doing so is not, on certain occasions, in their interest. Hence they too have reason to follow these rules (p. 152).

In short, the peace and security necessary (though not sufficient) for leading the good life, which Hobbes' sovereign was supposed to provide, can be better provided without the dangers of absolute sovereignty by persons themselves mutually agreeing to live in a moral community and to be bound by rules of behavior curbing self interest when it is to the detriment of others.

There are a number of obvious objections to this argument. I shall mention the four important ones, together with Baier's attempted answers, and then bring out the value empiricist features of his argument in terms of these objections and answers. First, it may seem contradictory to say that it is in a person's interest to do what is sometimes contrary to his interests (i.e. to act morally). Baier answers this objection by distinguishing enlightened long term interest and narrow short term interest. Mutual trust and respect for others in a moral community, he says (p. 155), is in the long term interest of the agent, but may not always be in his or her short term interest.

But this answer leads to three other objections that Baier cannot so easily answer. First, what is to be said to persons who deny that life in a moral community is in *their* long term self interest? Some persons might argue, in the manner of Nietzsche, that the moral life is all right for the weak, but the strong will prosper in a state of nature. The state of nature may lead to lives that are poor, nasty, brutish, and short "for most persons," but for the powerful and resourceful it may not be so. Second, other persons might concede the advantages of peace and security that life in a moral community would afford, but see no reason not to act from self interest within the moral community whenever they can get away with it. Third, Baier's argument does not tell us how large a moral community must be. Why could not a community that was large enough to be self sufficient refuse to include or try to dominate other smaller communities rather than treat them with equal respect? Or, in general, why could a "moral" community not be limited or exclusive, if it could provide the necessary peace and security to its members?

Let us call these problems the "self-sufficiency," the "freeloader," and the "exclusivity" problems, respectively. They present the main problems for every this-worldly answer to the question "Why be moral?" which focusses on the moral community. Baier seems to be arguing (pp. 157ff.) that freeloaders (who would break the rules when they think they can get away with it) are being unreasonable. But his defense of this claim is not entirely convincing. Undoubtedly freeloaders take risks of being exposed and losing credibility. But the risks are greater or less in different situations. And in some situations they may rationally judge that the risks are minimal or worth taking, given the rewards. Thus, while freeloading may be immoral, it is not always irrational according to the canons of self interested rationality, short or long run. As for the self-sufficient types, while there may be those who overestimate their powers and self-sufficiency, there may also be some quasi-Nietzschean types who *would* flourish better in a state of nature, despite the risks. Baier's argument certainly does not solve the problem posed by the ring of Gyges story in the *Republic*. Gyges had a ring that would make him invisible, allowing him to do whatever he pleased without detection and thus making him more self sufficient. The argument from long term self interest need not appeal to Gyges.

Regarding the exclusivity problem, Baier has a valuable point to make. His argument implies that the same considerations inducing individuals to form communities of mutual trust and respect rather than live in a state of nature, should apply to communities themselves, to nations, societies, etc. (pp. 152-4). They too should recognize the long term advantages of a moral community of communities over a state of perpetual fear and readiness for war which is the common lot of the community of nations in our world. This is a good point, and no one could fail to see its appeal in a world where a state of nature generally tends to prevail among nations. But once again, at this level Baier's argument is likely to appeal more to the weak nations than to the strong, and is not likely to provide convincing arguments to dissuade freeloaders. So the self sufficiency and freeloader problems reinstate themselves at the level of relations between communities.

Baier has one other point to add, however, regarding the self-sufficiency and freeloader problems. The moral community, he says, can always protect itself, by force if necessary, from those who chose to live outside it, and by punitive action against those who violate its rules from within (pp. 129-32). This point is important from the perspective of the moral theory defined by S27-29. For the principle of equal respect not only allows, but requires, that members of the moral community (or community of communities) protect themselves and others from those who do not treat others with equal respect. Thus, if all persons cannot be persuaded to take the moral point of view, the moral community can protect itself against those who do not.

7.16 Now I think Baier's answer to the question "Why be moral?", like other this-worldly answers, is best viewed as a value empiricist answer. Viewing it this way, we shall not demand too much of it, nor credit it with too little. From a value empiricist perspective, what Baier is doing is commending moral lives, or lives lived according to the rules of moral communities, as more worth trying as value experiments, than non-moral ones. Any such argument may appeal to certain persons in certain circumstances, but need not appeal to all. We should not dismiss such arguments as failures because some Nietzschean or similar type will never agree to them, or because they do not catch the determined freeloader in some sort of logical muddle. As long as some persons are persuaded from their value perspectives that a way of life is worth trying, then the argument has significance. Others may be persuaded by different sorts of arguments. And a moral community once formed can protect itself, as just explained, from the threats of those who are not persuaded.

These remarks, as I suggested, apply to other this-worldly arguments for the moral life, as well as to Baier's. His view was discussed at length because it exemplifies most clearly the value empiricist themes. Other moral thinkers would regard Baier's emphasis on the Hobbesian values of protection and security as too narrowly based. There are other advantages to life in moral communities. The state of nature is not conducive to the development of many human talents, to the undertaking of many satisfying pursuits (e.g. in the arts and sciences), to the best marshalling of natural resources, and other conditions necessary for a flourishing culture. Thus, a number of moral philosophers have taken an approach similar to Baier's, but have stressed other positive values of communities of mutual respect besides those of protection and security.[14] (These views may be thought to find their point of departure in Hume rather than Hobbes, since Hume takes a similar approach.) As Peter French (80) puts it, summing up this approach, which he favors, "The *raison d'être* of" morality, "the flourishing community, is the condition of anyone's achievement of the good life" (p. 160).

Such views do not provide conclusive reasons for the correctness of the moral life, any more than does Baier's view. But they may persuade many to undertake that life as a value experiment. They do not solve the self-sufficiency and freeloader problems. But the moral community can protect itself from those not persuaded. Moreover, once a moral community is formed, there are at least three other factors that tend to provide an in-built resistance to freeloading. One is the moral education of the young to take pride in their way of life, including its traditions of mutual respect. The other is the fact that such communities are based on trust (recall the requirement of fair bargaining in 7.7) and any evidence that one is not to be trusted tends to erode the trust of others. Thus, the freeloader must play fair or be exceedingly cautious. Irreparable distrust may be spawned by one or a few instances of deceptive behavior unmasked. Third, there is the matter of love. For those bred on the moral point of view, the loss of respect that comes from deceptive behavior unmasked tends to undermine love. Thus parents are not necessarily being hypocritical when they tell their children to be honest, fair, etc. or the children will not be loved by others in adulthood. They are not being hypocritical, that is, if the children are growing up in a moral community.

7.17 Those who take an other-worldly or religious approach to the question "Why be moral?" are likely to think that all this-worldly arguments are weak. Indeed, religions often seem to provide the conclusive reasons for taking the moral point of view that secular theories cannot provide. Thus, it is often said that the only fully satisfactory answer to the question "Why be moral?" must be a transcendent or religious one. This attitude is expressed in a general way by S. Radhakrishnan (74):

> Any ethical theory must be grounded in . . . a philosophical conception of the relation between human conduct and ultimate reality. . . . We need to be fortified by the conviction that the service of the ideals is what the cosmic scheme demands of us, that our loyalty or disloyalty to them is a matter of the deepest moment, not only to ourselves, or to society, or even to the human species, but to the nature of things. If ethical thought is profound, it will give a cosmic motive to morality. (pp. 80,82)

This "cosmic motive" has taken many forms. It may be the fear of eternal damnation and the promise of eternal reward in an afterlife, as in many of the world's religions. It may be associated with the belief in a Karmic law that good and evil actions here and now will be reflected in future reincarnated lives. It may involve the belief that moral action is part of a larger program, or way, leading to the goal of Nirvana, and so on. But it will always be associated with the belief that moral action matters beyond the here and now of this life.

There is little question that transcendent or religious answers to the question "Why be moral?" provide more powerful motives than secular answers, for those persons who can accept the transcendent or religious beliefs involved. If eternal reward or damnation do indeed depend upon moral actions here and now, then the best of prudential reasons lie on the side of being moral. In this manner. transcendent and religious answers purport to provide a certainty that moral lives are worth living which is lacking in secular answers; and for this reason also they do not seem to fit the value empiricist pattern.

But I would nevertheless argue that transcendent or religious answers to the question "Why be moral?" *do* fit the value empiricist pattern, because the uncertainty and risk in the moral life is transferred to the transcendent or religious beliefs themselves. Accepting and living in accordance with a religious faith is itself a value experiment which carries its own risks. A religion is a Path or Way ("the Eight-fold Way," "the Way, the Life, and the Truth," "the Way and its Power (*Tao Te Ching*)") whose ultimate test must be that it does in fact lead to the goal proposed (Nirvana, beatitude, etc.). Thus, the only conclusive test for religious belief can be, in John Hick's expression, an "eschatological verification," the attainment of an ultimate end.[15] This is the case, not only because religions are paths or ways leading to certain goals but also because the goals themselves are transcendent ones that we only see *in medias res*, through a glass darkly, if at all. As a consequence, while there is a sense in which transcendent or religious answers to the question "Why be moral?" provide stronger reasons for being moral to those who accept the religious faith, the uncertainty and risk are not removed, but are transferred to the uncertainty and risk of the religious faith and the religious life itself.

We may now summarize as follows:

S32. In line with the general approach to values of S30-31, we postulate that answers to the question "Why be moral?" in general (and, in particular, to the question "Why be moral, or take the moral point of view, in the sense of S27-29?") should be value empiricist answers. The moral life, like any other kind of life, is a value experiment. Or, we should more accurately say that moral lives are value experiments; for there may be many different incommensurable ways of life compatible with moral principle, according to S30, each requiring that other ways be treated with equal respect.

The value empiricist pattern (of providing persuasive, though not conclusive, arguments that moral lives are more "worth trying" as value experiments than non-moral lives) is characteristic of both this-worldly, or secular, and of transcendent, or religious, answers to the question "Why be moral?" While the transcendent or religious answers provide more powerful motives for being moral to those who can accept the transcendent or religious beliefs involved, the uncertainty and risk that accompany secular answers are not removed by transcendent answers, but are transferred to the transcendent or religious commitments involved. Religions themselves, with their accompanying moral commitments, are paths, or ways, or value experiments, whose ultimate verification is eschatological, lying in the attainment of certain transcendent goals. In either case, undertaking a moral life involves risk. Moral lives may be worth the effort, but life does not allow us the rational certainty that they are.

This step, together with the other steps of the chapter, is critical to the account of libertarian moral choice to be given in the next chapter.

7.18 It may have been noted, with some head-shaking, that answers to the question "Why be moral?" according to S32, whether this-worldly or transcendent, involve an element of self interest. Several points must be made about this. First, self interest in a certain sense—the sense of self respect or self love—*is* an essential ingredient of the moral point of view, since this view requires treating all persons, including oneself, with respect. But self interest in this sense is compatible with altruism, or love of others, as many philosophers have pointed out. The distinction between self love and selfishness remains. Selfishness is acting in accordance with self interest *when* self interest comes in conflict with the principle of equal respect, and this is prohibited by the moral point of view.

It is therefore confusing and misleading to say that a value empiricist defense of the moral point of view is ultimately an appeal to self interest, if selfishness is meant. What would it mean to take the moral point of view for selfish reasons? It might mean acting with respect toward others in the hope of *someday* being in the position of a Gyges who can act selfishly toward others with immunity. Or, it might mean taking the position of a freeloader and acting with respect at some times so that one can act selfishly at other times (when one can get away with it). But neither of these policies expresses the moral point of view because each requires acting with respect toward others at some times in order to be able to act selfishly at other times. The moral point of view commends action in accordance with the principle of equal respect at all times.

Thus, if we keep in mind the distinction between self love and selfishness, the presence of an element of self interest (as self love) in answers to the question "Why be moral?" should not trouble us. For the message of the moral point of view is that self interest and an interest in the welfare of others, self love and altruism, are divergent in the short run, but convergent in the long run. Even transcendent answers to the question "Why be moral?" find it difficult to ignore this point. Kant argues, more forcefully than any other philosopher, that moral actions are good in themselves independently of reward. But his comprehensive answer to the question "Why be moral?" includes an appeal to a divine power capable of merging virtue and happiness in the long run.[16] In Plato's *Republic*, Adeimantus raises the objection that even religious answers to the question "Why lead a just life?" appeal to an afterlife of reward or punishment. One gets the impression that Plato disapproves of such an appeal to self interest as much as his older brother does. But, in the end, the *Republic* answers the question "Why lead a just life?" by appealing to the self's interest in attaining an inner harmony (justice in the soul) and relates this interest in turn to living in a community with others.[17]

Such positions will appear fraudulent only if one forgets the distinction between self love and selfishness, or fails to perceive the message of the moral point of view, which is that self love and love of others, though divergent in the short run, are convergent in the long run. It is a message of uncertain truth value, as S32 suggests, but it is a clear message nonetheless.

7.19 To conclude, let us return to the general themes of the first two steps of this chapter. They describe a connection between free will and certain features of a relativist view of values. Free will in its various manifestations requires the existence of relativistic alternative purposes, plans, and ways of life, defined for *practical* choice with respect to subsets of the reason set of a single agent, and for *moral* choice with respect to the reason sets of different agents. The resulting analogy between relativistic alternative reason sets *in foro interno* and relativist alternative reason sets *in foro externo* provides the connection between the libertarian theories of practical and moral choice. The moral side of this analogy was the subject of the remainder of the chapter.

In both cases, practical and moral, the R-alternative reason sets are limited to select groups in different choice situations. For practical choice the limiting factor is the "Reason" of the agent, or as we have often put it, the agent's total reason set. It provides the objective perspective in the internal environment, narrowing the class of potential alternatives to a restricted class of R-alternatives. But the objective perspective *in foro interno* need not always narrow the options to one best.

In moral choice, the analogous limiting factor is moral principle. or the moral point of view. The class of R-alternative reason sets is restricted by moral principle to the reason sets of those persons or groups who are treating the reason sets of others as R-alternatives to their own. The result of this limitation *in foro externo* is the "potential relativism (or pluralism) qualified by moral principle" of S30. It is important to recognize that the limitation on the moral side is not an *ad hoc* addition to this theory, but a natural consequence of taking seriously the ideal of equal respect for all persons by departing as little as possible from this ideal when one must depart from it.

An important corollary of the theory on the practical side is (i) that there may be more than one incommensurably good way of life consistent with a person's own total reason set, and on the moral side, (ii) that there may be more than one incommensurably good way of life (of persons, societies, or cultures) consistent with the dictates of morality. The first of these corollaries makes it possible to give a coherent libertarian account of practical choice; the second, as we shall see, makes it possible to give a choerent libertarian account of moral choice. When spelled out, the second corollary also provides the link, perceived by Kant, but differently described by him, between human autonomy (free will) and the moral law.

Notes

1. The classic formulation of such a respect for persons moral view is, of course. in Kant (56 and 59). More recent statements are in Downie and Telfer (70), Cranor (75), Donagan (77) and Dworkin (77). Similar views, somewhat differently defended can be found in Hare (65). Rawls (71) and Gewirth (78). Haksar (79) is a critique of some of these views.

2. This qualification is necessary because the view does not tell us how to behave toward animals and other living non-persons, a topic of considerable interest among philosophers since the publication of P. Singer (75). As a consequence, a respect for persons principle could not be said to define all of our moral obligations. But a case can nevertheless be made for saying that it defines our moral obligations *toward persons*. Thus, when I use the expression "moral point of view" throughout this and subsequent chapters, this qualification will always be assumed. We shall be talking about the "moral point of view toward persons."

3. Persuasion is allowed because it respects the free choices of the person involved. What is not allowed is coercion, when attempts to persuade fail. This remark on coercion, however, will be qualified in 7.4.

4. I am employing Kant's language of "ends" and "means" here because it is useful. But I am not going to try to explicate, or follow, his exact meaning. What I shall mean by treating a person as an end (=treating the person with respect as a person) is defined by S27. A person is treated as a means when that person is not treated as an end, i.e. not allowed to pursue his or her chosen experiment in living without interference.

5. Once again this is a familiar Kantian expression (Kant (59, p. 52) and it is used here to mean something similar to what Kant had in mind. He speaks of it as "only an ideal."

6. The idea of restoring the moral sphere "in a manner that shows greatest respect for the ideal . . ." is important here. For if restoring the moral sphere means only bringing peace back into the situation so that the assault or rape ends, this might sometimes be brought about more quickly by letting the assailant or rapist have his way and get it over with, rather than by interfering and

causing more violence. (The pacificist sometimes makes his case in this way, noting that violence breeds more violence.) One should be able to explain why stopping the guilty by force if necessary is the right move in such a situation rather than letting the guilty proceed, even when the latter would be a more effective or quicker way of bringing the violence to an end. It is not just the effectiveness of the action that counts, but the *statement* it makes about respect for the ideal.

7. See 7.6 and 10.9 on this.

8. Second best strategies for resolving conflict situations have been a major concern of social choice theorists. A good general discussion is Sen (70), which contains references to other works. A more recent discussion in a philosophical context is B. Ackerman (80, ch. 9).

9. I have in mind here the well known result of K.O. May (52), who proved that majority vote is the required procedure for solving conflicts if certain conditions of equality and maximal responsiveness to the input of each individual are to be satisfied.

10. Cf. 5.12 on these points.

11. See Quine (69 and 70).

12. Keeping in mind that the value system of a person contains all valuations (=evaluative propositions) believed to be true or whose truth is presupposed by the person's reason set (cf. 5.5), the value system will contain the propositions that boredom is bad, that joy is good, that disappointment is bad, etc.

13. Quine points this out in his Dewey lecture (69).

14. Prominent examples are Grice (67), Warnock (71), Mackie (77), and French (80).

15. Hick (73, p. 90).

16. Kant (56, 28ff., 115ff.).

17. Plato (74, 109ff.).

Moral And Prudential Choice

8.1 This chapter presents a libertarian account of free moral choice (8.1-10) based on the steps of the previous chapter, followed by an account of prudential choice (8.11-13) and a discussion of some general features of the theory (8.14-16).

We begin by singling out a certain kind of moral choice:

S33. On the theory of chapter 7, one makes a moral choice from duty when one chooses to act on the basis of the principle of equal respect (S28) in opposition to one's self interested motives. To act on the basis of the principle of equal respect is to act on the belief that the reason sets of a restricted class of other persons are R-alternatives to one's own, or, more precisely, that the total reason sets of these other persons are R-alternatives to the subset of one's total reason set that contains all of one's motives except the motives of duty.

The motives of duty include the beliefs about how one ought to act in various situations according to the principle of equal respect, and the desire to act in accordance with these normative beliefs. In sum, the motives of duty are those that define the moral point of view of S29.

Not all choices that could be called "moral" are of this kind. Some moral choices may be "in accordance with" moral principle, like the principle of equal respect, without being in opposition to self interested motives. Kant's distinction between choices made "in accordance with" duty and choices made "from" duty is relevant here, the latter being choices made in opposition to (present prevailing) inclinations. Kant has been justly criticized for thinking only of the latter as genuinely moral choices. But he had good reasons for singling out choices made from duty in opposition to self interest because he was concerned among other things with relating his moral theory to his (libertarian) conception of free will. And, on this point, he saw deeply into the situation. For he saw that choices made from duty in opposition to self interest have a special role to play in a libertarian conception of free will. Hence, we have defined moral choices of this kind in S33; and when we speak of "moral choices" hereafter without qualifying the expression, we shall mean choices of this kind. This is a matter of convenience, to avoid repeating the qualification "of the kind that are made from duty in opposition to self interest." We need not assume that all moral choices are of this kind; but moral choices of this kind have a pivotal role to play in the theory.

S33 underscores the claim of S25 that libertarian moral choices and practical choices are alike in that they are both accounted for in terms of R-alternative reason sets, with moral choice being distinguished by the fact that the reason sets in question are those of different agents. But this step also requires that we distinguish, within the moral agent's total reason set, two non-overlapping and mutually exhaustive subsets, the motives of duty and all other motives. For convenience, we are going to refer to motives other than those of duty as self interested motives. But this means that self interest will be understood in a broad sense, contrasted with duty, but not identified with selfishness. Some self interested motives, in the sense intended, may involve the love of others—children, parents, friends—and the sacrifice of our needs to the needs of these others. But such motives are still distinct from the motives of duty, insofar as we make such sacrifices because we want or prefer to, rather than because we feel an obligation to do so against inclination.

The point of distinguishing between these two distinct subsets within the self— the motives of duty and all other motives—is to describe moral choice situations as conflicts within the self in which the motives of duty play a unique role, as the following step explains.

S34. The conflict in a moral choice situation is between the agent's self interested reasons or motives and the reasons of other persons. The motives of duty (the beliefs involved in the principle of equal respect and the desire to act on these beliefs) go *proxy* in the mind of the agent for the *reason sets of others*, giving them a competitive status in the inner arena they would not otherwise have, and creating an internal conflict within the agent's own reason set between two subsets of reasons or motives. In this way, the motives of duty are reasons of a special kind among the agent's other reasons, having a unique function to perform.

Note that the underlying moral conflict is between the agent's self interested reasons and the reasons of *other agents*. But the reason sets of other agents do not have a natural standing in the agent's reason set allowing them to compete with self interested motives. It is the motives of duty that give them such a standing by going "proxy in the mind" for the reason sets of others. Thus, the moral conflict between agents is internalized in a single agent and the motives of duty, which make this possible, are motives of a special kind.

8.2 S33-34 provide an account of moral choice in terms of the steps of chapter 7. But they do not provide an account of *free* moral choice in the libertarian sense. To take this further step we must explain how indeterminism is involved in moral choice as described in these two steps. Indeterminism cannot be involved in the same manner in which it is involved in R-choices and free practical choices. One cannot treat the motives of duty, on one side, and the agent's self interested motives, on the other, as R-alternatives to be selected randomly. Taking the moral point of view precludes an attitude of indifference toward the alternatives. By contrast, it creates a characteristic inner struggle between duty and inclination in which the agent believes he or she should make the motives of duty prevail over those of self interest.

Perhaps we can attack the problem by taking note of another danger. The libertarian also cannot allow the clash between the motives of duty and self interest to be resolved by a deterministic "strongest motive" strategy. Recall the objection of W. D. Ross to Kant's theory discussed in 4.12. Ross insists that one cannot view the moral choice situation simply as a conflict between reason, on the one side, and desire, on the other. Mere reasoned belief that the moral law ought to prevail will not move one to act, he argues, without a strong desire to make the moral law prevail. So the clash involves desires on both sides, albeit of different kinds, and the strongest desire will presumably win out. This is compatible, Ross adds, with the determinist assumption that the desire which turns out to be strongest was determined by past circumstances, even when the strongest desire turns out to be the desire to act from duty.

The situation could be as Ross suggests. But it could also be otherwise. Just as in the case of practical choice, there need not always be a strongest determining motive. It could be that the intensities or strengths of the competing motives are not precisely determined, so that the outcome of the moral choice situation is not predictable, either by the agent or another. If we were to pursue this idea of indeterminate intensity of the competing motives, it would be natural to look in the direction of the motives of duty. For they are unique among the agent's reasons, and one could imagine that their level of intensity of strength was fixed in a special way.

8.3 Pursuing this suggestion, let us first consider an overly simple model:

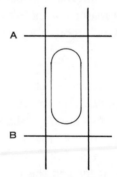

Figure 8.1

One might think of this as a picture of an air bubble in a glass tube filled with a liquid, with the lines A and B marked on the outside of the glass as on an ordinary carpenter's level. But this description is merely an aid to the imagination. We are going to give the bubble some extraordinary properties. The bubble may represent either the desire to choose to act from duty (out of equal respect) or the effort made to realize this desire in choice. The respective desire and effort are conceptually related because the desire is defined as the disposition to make the effort; and the intensity of the desire is measured by the intensity of the effort. The lines A and B in the figure represent choice thresholds. If the bubble passes above the line A, the choice is made to act from duty; if it passes below B, the choice is made to act on self interested motives. When the bubble is between the lines, as in the figure, no choice has yet been made.[1] A downward pull of gravity in the figure may be thought to represent the natural pull of one's self interested motives, which must be counteracted by an effort to resist temptation.

There is an ambiguity, essential to our problem, about what it means to say that the bubble "passes above" the line A, or "below" the line B. If the bubble passes above A, or below B, then the choice is made to act from duty, or from self interest, respectively. But does this mean that the bubble must be wholly, or only partly, above A, or below B? It is here that we give the bubble some extraordinary properties. We imagine that the bubble represents a probability space, so that, when it is partly above A, there is a corresponding probability, but not certainty, that the choice is made to act from duty, and when it is partly below B there is a corresponding probability, but not certainty, that the choice is made to act from self interest. When the bubble is wholly above A (or below B), it is certain that the choice is made to act from duty (or self interest). We then imagine a point particle in the probability space (the bubble) that moves around randomly, while always remaining within the space. That is, it has an equal probability of appearing in any one of a number of equal sized regions in the space. (There will be further comment on this partitioning and its significance in a moment.) If part of the bubble is above the line A for a certain time and the point particle is in regions all of which are wholly above the line for the same length of time, then the choice is made to act from duty (and similarly for line B).

To complicate matters further, we want to assume that the bubble or probability space does not have an exact position vis à vis the thresholds at any given time and that this inexactness of position is also due to the undetermined movement of the point particle in the regions. There are a number of ways to represent this in the diagram, but the simplest way is the following. Imagine, as in the following figure, that the choice thresholds A and B have indeterminate position so that they can be anywhere between (or on) the extremes A'-A" and B'-B" respectively:

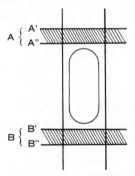

Figure 8.2

The distances between any two possible threshold positions for A (or any two for B) are equal and each possible threshold position corresponds to a region in the bubble such that, if the point particle is in that region, the threshold is at the corresponding position. But adjacent regions in the bubble need not correspond to adjacent positions of the thresholds and higher or lower regions of the bubble need not correspond to higher and lower threshold positions respectively.

What all this means is that the intensity of the effort to overcome temptation at any given time, which is a measure of the intensity of the desire to act from duty (represented by the position of the bubble vis à vis the thresholds and the position of the point particle within the bubble) is indeterminate. And, as a consequence, the outcome of the choice situation at a given time is undetermined and unpredictable as long as the bubble is not wholly above A' or wholly below B".

8.4 Let us now return to the account of moral choice in S34 to see what might be done with this picture. The motives of duty are reasons of a special kind among the agent's other reasons, having a unique function to perform, because they go proxy in the mind of the agent for the reason sets of others. We might therefore expect that the degree of intensity of the desire to act from duty (the volitional part of the motives of duty) would be specified or "determined" in a special way. If there is an indeterminacy to be found in moral choice at all, as the libertarian must believe, its source is likely to be found in the special nature of this desire to act from duty.

What makes this desire special is that it is a desire to act so that one treats the reason sets of others as R-alternatives to one's own (self interested) motives. Now the notion of R-alternative reason sets is something we are familiar with from the discussion of practical choice, though the reference to other persons' reason sets is a new twist. And in connection with practical choice, the notion of an R-alternative reason set is associated with an undetermined process in the brain that is activated to select between the R-alternatives. One might then suggest that introducing R-alternative reason sets in a new guise, under the rubric of the principle of equal respect, would activate this same undetermined process which then has an effect on the intensity of the desire to act out of respect for the values of others, thereby also influencing the intensity of one's desire to act from self interest. One might, in short, think of an undetermined process, the same one as involved in R-choice or an analogue, as determining the movement of the point particle in the probability space of the model, determining its position at any particular time in one or another of the equal sized regions of the bubble. The level of intensity of the desire to act from duty would not be determined exactly, because the intensity is influenced in part by an undetermined and unpredictable process; and this process is involved because the desire to act from duty is the desire to act on a belief of a unique kind, that other persons' value systems are R-alternatives to one's own.

On this account, the partitioning of the probability space (the bubble) into equal sized regions, and the equal probability for the point particle to be in any region at a given time, would correspond to the fact that the R-alternative reason sets are to be treated equally. But how many R-alternative reason sets, and hence how many regions, are involved? The answer is that no specific number is required. The principle of equal respect tells us to treat the reason sets of *all* persons satisfying certain conditions as R-alternatives to our own. We do not know how many persons *that* might be, though in ordinary circumstances it will be a large number. Thus, a large number of partitions will be involved, in the thousands, say, or tens of thousands, but the exact number will depend on the exigencies of neurological programming rather than on rational considerations, which provide no clue beyond "large." The number will be finite, but no specific finite number is required. Though a smaller number of other persons may actually be involved in a particular moral choice situation, the primary motive is always the desire to act in accordance with the principle of equal respect for all persons satisfying certain conditions, i.e. in accordance with "the Moral Law" generally.

Further, the appearance of the point particle in a particular region at a time is not to be regarded as a selection for favored treatment of a particular R-alternative reason set associated with that region, as in the case of R-choice. Favored treatment for one or another R-alternative is not the aim of moral choice. Rather, the succession of random selections among equiprobable alternatives (appearances of the point particle in different regions) is meant to be a continuing reminder (a mental or neurological representation) of the fact that the reason sets of other persons are to be treated equally. Having the motives of duty means having that continuing reminder; it means being disposed to be influenced by that mental or neurological representation.[2]

Needless to say, a basis for both the partitioning and the randomizing process must be found in the brain if this account is to have any factual standing. But I shall be discussing such factual or neurological matters in the next chapter. In like manner, if the theorizing of chapters 5 and 6 is to have any factual standing, neurological processes must exist corresponding to the randomizing activity of the spinning wheel *and* the partitioning of the wheel into equiprobable segments (red, blue, etc.) corresponding to the relevant R-alternatives. This too will be discussed in the next chapter. But our task here, as in chapters 5 and 6, is a conceptual one. We are asking what sense could be made of free will, as libertarians conceive it, *if* one could assume the existence of random processes (ambiguous possibilities, causal gaps) in the brain or elsewhere in nature as libertarians require.

We may summarize this section in

S35. Since the motives of duty are of a special kind, as explained in S34, we expect that the strength or intensity of these motives, in particular the desire to act from duty, will be fixed in a special way. And since the desire to act from duty is special because it is the desire to treat the reason sets of others as R-alternatives to one's own, we postulate that the intensity of this desire is influenced by an undetermined process selecting from among R-alternatives like the one involved in R-choice. The differences from R-choice are that (i) many more R-alternatives are involved corresponding to the many persons who must be treated with equal respect and (ii) the undetermined process does not select one of the alternatives for favored treatment. Instead, a succession of random selections from among equiprobable alternatives (corresponding to the movement of the point particle in the figures of 8.3) is a continuing reminder (a mental or neurological representation) of the fact that the reason sets of other persons are to be treated equally.

8.5 We are not to assume, however, that the outcome of the moral choice situation is entirely due to the undetermined process described in S35. Far from it. The agent's effort to overcome temptation has much to do with the outcome. The point of S35 is simply that the amount, degree, or intensity of the effort is not precisely determined. So the outcome is uncertain until one or another choice is made. This is meant to correspond to the intuition that in a moral choice situation, when one is trying to overcome temptation, the outcome is uncertain up to the last moment. The agent may overcome temptation and may not. And the libertarian wants to say that these "may"'s are to be taken in a strong sense. The outcome is genuinely undetermined. No one, including the agent, could predict it with certainty.

One may think, only slightly misleadingly, of the agent's effort to act from duty as moving the bubble upward toward the choice threshold A (or A'-A") against the downward drag of selfish desire. If the effort is sufficient to move the bubble wholly above the indeterminate threshold, i.e. wholly above A' in figure 8.2, then the indeterminateness is removed and the choice will certainly be made, because the point particle cannot but be above the choice threshold. In such a case, however, the *conflict* of the moral choice situation, the conflict between duty and inclination, is eliminated. This is moral choice "in accordance with" duty. Similarly, if the bubble falls entirely below the threshold B'-B", the conflict is eliminated in the other direction, and one chooses from self interest. It is when the bubble is between thresholds, or overlapping them, that one experiences the characteristic conflict between duty and inclination of the moral choice situation, and in such a conflict situation the outcome is uncertain.

But this image, while helpful, is not entirely accurate. For it suggests that the amount of effort to act from duty (moving the bubble toward the higher choice threshold) is wholly determinate, when in fact the movement of the point particle within the bubble makes the amount of effort at any given time indeterminate.[3] The bubble, after all, represents a probability space, a "wave packet," if you will, not a real space; and while we are to assume that it moves up and down, it never has an exact position vis à vis the choice thresholds. This peculiar feature is due to the special nature of the motives which it represents and which create the moral choice situation, namely, the motives of duty. They are unlike all other motives, insofar as they go proxy for the reason sets of others, requiring us to think of the reason sets of others as having equal claim to the sum of our other motives. This sort of motivation is abnormal, in the sense that it goes against the grain of normal self interested motivation, and it therefore operates in a different way, a way that has something to do with "equiprobable" outcomes.

We can now take note of another familiar feature of moral choice situations. Often when there is a conflict between duty and inclination, doubts and misgivings may persist *after* the choice has been made. A woman and her lover have decided to kill her husband. (This is the plot of a nineteenth-century soap opera by Zola recently dramatized by the BBC.) The two have in fact conceived a plan for doing it, a fake drowning accident, and are about to carry out the plan. But doubts persist even as they are getting into the rowboat, and one senses that the decision could be reversed at any moment before throwing the husband (who is a non-swimmer) overboard, and even after that, but before he has drowned. Clearly, such a situation of doubt after an intention has been formed can also exist in reverse. A man may decide to act from duty, for example, to return stolen property to its owner, and be tormented by doubts about the decision even as he is journeying to return the property.

Now these cases can be conceived in the following way. The choices were made when the bubble was partly below the lower threshold in the first (drowning) case (and partly above the higher threshold in the second (stolen property) case) and the point particle was simultaneously in regions wholly below (or above) the relevant threshold. But in these cases the bubble never does get wholly below or above the relevant thresholds even after the choice is made. It continues to move back and forth between thresholds, a process that corresponds to the ebb and flow of doubts, misgivings, pangs of conscience, etc. When the decision has been made to act from duty, as in the stolen property case, resolve may begin to crumble; there may be a backsliding between the time of choice and the completion of action, corresponding to a movement downward of the bubble. And as soon as the bubble begins to overlap the lower threshold there will be a possibility that the decision to act from duty will be reversed. The man returning the stolen property may decide to turn around and go home. Similarly, in the drowning case an effort of will to resist temptation may have moved the bubble above the higher threshold making a reversal of the decision possible. But the outcomes in either case are uncertain up to the moment they occur, just as the original decisions were. And the reversals must involve new *choices* or *decisions*. For it is assumed that the agents have formed the intentions (made the earlier decision) to kill the husband or to return the property, and these intentions must be changed. In this way, we can account for doubts, misgivings, backsliding, and diminishing resolve after moral choices have been made, but before the actions have been undertaken or completed.

We summarize this section in

S36. As a consequence of S35, the agent's effort of will to act from duty in moral conflict situations, which is a measure of the strength of the desire to act from duty, is indeterminate. If the agent does overcome temptation and act from duty, it will be because of his (her) effort, but the degree of effort prior to choice is an indeterminate variable. It is represented by a probability space or wave packet which has no exact position vis à vis the choice thresholds at a given time. Hence the outcome which depends on the effort is uncertain until the choice is made. This is meant to correspond to the intuition that in a moral choice situation, when one is trying to overcome temptation, the outcome is uncertain until the moment of choice. The agent may overcome temptation and may not. For libertarians these "may" 's are to be taken in the strong sense. The outcome is genuinely undetermined. Moral conflict can also persist after a choice is made but before the chosen action is undertaken or completed. The possibility of reversing moral decision in such cases, due to doubts, misgivings, backsliding, etc., can also be accounted for as an undetermined outcome, according to the theory, as explained in this section.

8.6 Many questions naturally arise about this account of moral choice, the most important having to do with the agent's rationality, control, and responsibility with respect to moral choices so described. We shall discuss these matters in connection with the following steps, which do for the account of moral choice what we did earlier for the accounts of R-choice and practical choice. That is, these steps relate the account of moral choice to the conditions of dual rational self control and sole or ultimate dominion.

S37. Moral choice as described in S35-36 satisfies the requirement of dual rational self control defined in 4.8. That is to say, though undetermined, the outcome either way (whether the agent chooses to act in accordance with duty or self interest) will be a rational choice with respect to the agent's prior reasons or motives. The reasons in question will be the motives of duty if the choice is made to act from duty, and self interested reasons if the choice is made to act from self interest—in short, one or another of the two disjoint sets of reasons of S34. To act from duty is to be rational in one sense, and to act from self interest is to be rational in an entirely different sense. The moral conflict situation is between what is believed to be the best move from the point of view of self interest, on the one hand, and what is believed to be the best move from the moral point of view, on the other. Whatever choice is made will thus be supported with reasons that are good reasons, though good in different ways, from different perspectives.

Now this step presents a problem concerning the case of acting from self interest. A person who holds the motives of duty, i.e. a person who takes the moral point of view, believes in some sense that it is more rational to do one's duty and is trying to make the motives of duty prevail over those of self interest. How then can it be rational at all for the person to act from self interest in such a situation?

To ask this question is to introduce the ancient puzzle about how weakness of will is possible as anything but irrational or compulsive behavior. The puzzle about weakness of will is associated with Socrates' contention in Plato's *Protagoras* that no person can *knowingly* and *non-compulsively* perform an action he or she believes to be wrong, or the lesser good.[4] In its general form, the puzzle concerns prudential as well as moral choice, but we are only concerned with the moral version at this point. Applied to moral behavior, the Socratic view implies that if the agent really knows what his duty is in a given situation, but does the opposite, he must be compelled by uncontrollable desires. Conversely, if his action is not compelled, he must be ignorant of what his duty is in the situation.[5] This view gives rise to a problem because many persons believe that at least some weak willed behavior should be explicable as the result of something other than ignorance or compulsion. But it is difficult to say how weak willed behavior in a rational agent can be explained in terms other than ignorance or compulsion.

The free will issue and the problem of weakness of will are often treated separately by philosophers. And some of these philosophers would no doubt argue that the two are entirely distinct and separable problems. But this is not the case. The two problems are related, and the link between them is the problem of dual rational self control. The Socratic puzzle about weakness of will has to do with one side of the problem of dual rational self control for moral and prudential choice; it has to do with the explanation of how choosing to act *from self interest* can be *rational* and *free* (which implies non-compulsive) when the agent believes he ought (morally or prudentially) to do otherwise. The other side of the problem of dual rational self control—explaining the rationality of acting from duty in such situations—does not present a similar difficulty.

8.7 To understand how I shall deal with the problem of weakness of will and thereby support S37, we must first add a step which takes us back to the discussion in chapter 7 of the question "Why be moral?":

S38. In S32 we postulated that answers to the question "Why be moral?" or "Why take the moral point of view?", whether this-worldly or transcendent, should be value empiricist answers. The moral life is undertaken as a value experiment with uncertain outcome. Taking the moral point of view is a commitment and a risky one. If a person taking the moral point of view *knew* that the motives of duty were the better, or more rational, ones in all circumstances, then it would be difficult indeed to explain weakness of will in moral conflict situations as anything other than irrational or compulsive behavior. But the person taking the moral point of view does not know that the motives of duty are the better ones. He or she believes it to be so, but this belief, as S32 makes clear, is a commitment to an experient in living which is constantly subject to challenge by the demands of self interest because its outcome is uncertain.

Ignorance of one's true good is then a necessary condition for weakness of will, as Socrates maintained, but it is not the sort of ignorance he had in mind. The relevant ignorance is not knowing that what one *believes* to be true (that the moral point of view is the best point of view, all things considered) *is* true. This sort of ignorance is the source of the ambiguous attitude one has toward the motives of duty in a moral conflict situation and the resulting indeterminateness in the strength of one's desire to act from duty.

But this step provides only a necessary condition for weakness of will as anything other than irrational behavior. How can an agent's acting from self interest in a moral conflict situation be rational when the agent believes, albeit on uncertain evidence, that the motives of duty ought to prevail and is trying to make them prevail? The answer is contained in the following step:

S39. If the reasons for thinking the motives of duty ought to prevail and for making the effort to make them prevail are value empiricist reasons, then this belief and related effort are based on uncertain evidence about the outcome of a long-range experiment. Weakness of will is therefore possible as something other than irrational or compulsive behavior in three ways. (a) The agent may have rationally grounded doubts that the goal of the experiment is attainable. In the face of such doubts about the attainment of a long range goal, desire and effort to act in certain ways to attain it can wane, making the attainment of some short range goal, with its own quite different rational attractions, seem temporarily more attractive. This is compatible with the agent's subsequently regretting his or her temporary "loss of faith." Or, (b) the temporary loss of faith described in (a) may sometimes be due to unconscious suppression of thoughts about the attractions of the distant goal. This suppression may be thought to be a natural tendency, more or less strong in different agents, associated with the drag of self interested motives. Part of what an agent is doing in making the effort to act from duty is overcoming this natural tendency toward suppression to which the distant goal is susceptible precisely because it is distant and uncertain. Or, (c) the agent may convince himself or herself that a temporary lapse from duty here and now does not rule out the attainment of the long range goal and hence the ultimate success of the experiment—in other words, that the means (acting from duty in all circumstances) is not a necessary means to the long range goal. The attainment of present pleasure plus attainment of the long range goal can seem more rationally desirable than attainment of the long range goal without present pleasure. ("All this and heaven, too.")

Case (c) is exemplified in a theistic context by a person who believes that a temporary lapse need not preclude salvation ("Sin now, repent later"), or by the Hindu who expects to make up for the lapse in a future life, or by the freeloader, in a this-worldly context, who believes that the moral community will survive his or her temporary lapse.

I think that all three cases of S39 correspond to recognizable failings in moral conflict situations. And all three depend upon the fact emphasized in S38 that the goal is distant and there is uncertainty both about its attainment and the necessary means for its attainment. Desire and effort to act on a normative belief can wax and wane when the belief is a commitment to a long range experiment whose outcome is uncertain. As a consequence, such a normative belief does not motivate with a fixed degree of strength. One can desire to and be trying to, make it prevail more or less at a given time and the more or less may not always be enough to overcome other motivating desires. If these other desires are supported by reasons of their own, then choosing in accordance with them can be rational in the sense that it can be explained by reasons which appeared to the agent to be stronger at the time of choice. Weak willed behavior can then be explained by reasons (self interested reasons), though it is not explained by, much less justified by, moral reasons.[6]

Finally, the choice from self interest need not be compulsive in the sense that the agent could not have resisted the temptation to act from self interest. The three cases of S39 are compatible with the assumption of S37 that the choice could have gone the other way, that the effort to act from duty could have prevailed. And these "could" 's may have the strong libertarian sense implying that the outcome was genuinely undetermined, without undermining dual rationality.

In this manner, the account of weakness of will in S38-39 can support the account of dual rational self control in S37, and in doing so it shows the connection between the traditional problems of weakness of will and free will for the case of moral choice. A similar connection will be shown later for prudential choice. And in its turn, the account of weakness of will in S38-39 is supported by themes of chapter 7, expressed in S31-32, having to do with the moral point of view.

8.8 We turn now to the requirement of sole or ultimate dominion. Recall that in connection with both R-choice and practical choice, the requirements of dual rational self control and sole or ultimate dominion were said to be satisfied with a qualification. The qualification was that the control of the agent's rational will over the outcome was only partial because the outcome was due to a combination of reason and chance. One should expect a similar result in connection with moral choice, and a similar result is what one gets from the account of moral choice given in S35-36. The moral choice outcome is partially due to the agent's rationally grounded effort of will (or weakness of will as the case may be) and partially due to chance. But just as in the cases of R-choice and practical choice, this partial control is compatible with the requirement of sole or ultimate dominion as defined in chapter 3.

> S40. The agent who makes a choice at a time t in a moral conflict situation as as described in S38-39, has sole or ultimate dominion over the choice in the sense that (i) the agent's making the choice at t rather than doing otherwise, or vice versa (i.e. choosing from duty or self interest), can be explained by saying that the agent "rationally willed at t to do so" in the sense of "endorsed reasons or motives at t for choosing as he or she did choose rather than doing otherwise" (the motives of duty or of self interest as the case may be), and (ii) no further explanation can be given for the agent's choosing rather than doing otherwise (or vice versa), or for the agent's endorsing the set of reasons he or she did endorse at t, that is an explanation in terms of conditions whose existence cannot be explained by the agent's choosing or rationally willing something at t.

It should be noted that this step is nearly a word for word transcription of S12, which says that R-choice satisfies the condition of sole or ultimate dominion. All differences merely reflect the substitution of references to moral choice for references to R-choice. And, as in the case of R-choice, condition (i) of the requirement of sole dominion is satisfied, given that the requirement of dual rational self control is satisfied. Condition (ii) is satisfied because the outcome, whether the agent "endorses" the motives of duty (or self interest) at the moment of choice rather than not, is undetermined. There is no causal or deterministic explanation of the outcome, and, while there may be a statistical explanation, the statistical explanation would not explain the occurrence of one outcome rather than another in the particular case. As noted in connection with S12, the peculiarity of reason-explanations in this regard is that they can answer a "Why this *rather than* that?" question for the particular case, even when the particular case is undetermined.

8.9 Now steps 37 and 40 have some rather disconcerting implications concerning the agent's responsibility in moral choice situations. The requirements of dual rational self control (S37) and sole or ultimate dominion (S40) are satisfied with the qualification that the agent's control over the outcome is only partial. If control is partial, then responsibility is partial as well. It seems to me that libertarians should face up to this implication of their view and bring it out into the open rather than try to obscure it in the mists of transempirical egos and non-occurrent causes. The fact is that in moral choice situations, on their view, human beings are vulnerable. The outcome really *is* uncertain and tragedy is an ever present possibility. To think otherwise for libertarians is a form of *hubris* or pride (a tragic flaw or prevailing sin, depending on whether one thinks in Hellenic or Hebraic terms). It is to labor under the illusion that you can be free in an undetermined sense *and* have total rational control over your situation. The present theory, from step 7 onward, has tried to expose this as an illusion, by showing the connection between the libertarian view of freedom, on the one hand, and the limitations of reason and consequent finitude of free beings, on the other. Among libertarians, William James is almost alone in recognizing this implication of the libertarian view and refusing to compromise it. His essay "The Dilemma of Determinism" is a paean to the vulnerability, and also the nobility, of free beings in an open universe, whose choices, moral and otherwise, are risky. Similarly, if God were to give human beings free will in this libertarian sense, then in response to their efforts God's justice would rightly be tempered with mercy.

But let us not mistake partial control and partial responsibility for no control and responsibility. It would be a mistake for the free agent to reason that since his effort does not determine the outcome his effort does not matter. In one sense, the sense of S40, one's effort or lack of it is the only thing that matters. The degree of effort is indeed indeterminate. Yet *if* it is enough, then *I* make enough effort, and if it is not enough, then I do not make enough effort. I can kick myself for not having made more. In this respect the indeterminism of moral choice is more intimately related to the contribution of the rational will than indeterminism is so related in either R-choice or practical choice. For the indeterminism is built into the definition of the degree of effort of will because of certain features of the motives of duty. As a consequence, I cannot say that I made a certain (determinate) amount of effort and then it was a matter of luck as to whether *that* amount of effort was enough. One cannot say this because the amount of effort made was itself indeterminate. Similarly, one could not say of two persons in exactly the same situation, that they made the same amount of effort and, by chance or luck, one of them managed to overcome temptation while the other did not. Such claims are meaningless on the theory of S35-36. The effort and the chance cannot be separated and viewed as independent variables. The chance is simply the indeterminateness of the effort. This is why it is never possible to absolve oneself from responsibility in moral choice situations on grounds of bad luck, even though the outcome is not determined.

8.10 Despite all this, one still may have misgivings about the partial control and responsibility implied here by indeterminism, similar to the misgivings one may have had earlier in connection with R-choice and practical choice. I appreciate these misgivings. I share them. It is just that I do not think libertarians can allay them short of appeals to two level strategies or non-occurrent cause strategies: and I have already made clear what I think of these strategies. If you are going to reconcile the common intuitions that one controls one's free choices *and* that they are not determined, then you are going to have to talk about partial control. You cannot have it both ways. The task for the libertarian is to grab hold of this deviant child (partial control) and drag it back as close *as possible* to the norms of common sense. One cannot get all the way back, but no view on the free will issue fully satisfies common sense. Whatever may be said for the compatibilist view (the best of bad alternatives?), it also does not have the unambiguous support of common sense intuitions, at least not for most people.

It is true that we all have the idea that free will means being "master of my fate," "captain of my soul," and we perhaps believe vaguely that this involves total rational control. Libertarians may try to reconcile this captaincy of the soul with the indeterminist condition by postulating a transempirical ego or non-occurrent cause. Let there be causal gaps or ambiguous possibilities in the brain, they may say. The transempirical ego or non-occurrent cause nevertheless fills the gaps determining the matter one way or the other; and it is in total control. But why did the transempirical ego or non-occurrent cause determine the outcome in this way rather than that? The transempirical ego or non-occurrent cause, you see, was not determined to go one way rather than the other, even by its own reasons. So either one says that the "rather than" question (concerning dual rational self control) cannot be answered for a transempirical ego or non-occurrent cause ("It's a mystery"), or one tries to answer it along the lines of S37. I do not think libertarians *can* answer the "rather than" question any better than S37 does even if they introduce a transempirical ego or non-occurrent cause (if they try to answer it at all). In like manner, if the action of the transempirical ego or non-occurrent cause, one way or the other, is not determined, then I do not think that they can explain its sole or ultimate dominion any better than S40 does (if they try to explain it at all). But if one must take the route of S37 and S40 to account for dual rational self control and sole or ultimate dominion in any case, then why not take this route at the empirical level and not multiply entities without necessity. If appeals to a transempirical ego or non-occurrent cause serve any further purpose, it must be as mechanisms of defense, i.e. as ways of saying that the questions about dual rational self control and sole or ultimate dominion do not have answers within a libertarian view.

8.11 More will be said about the implications of S37 and S40 later in this chapter and in chapter 9. But we must now complete the theory by turning to prudential choice, and eventually to practical choice once again. Like moral choice, prudential choice involves a conflict between present inclination and what the agent believes he or she ought to do, but the prudential "ought" involves choices and actions thought to be necessary for the attainment of some future or long term personal goal. Unfortunately, this familiar characterization is too general to distinguish prudential from moral choice as we have described the latter. One must add that the motives of duty do not play an essential role in a prudential conflict situation. This added condition may be spelled out by saying that a prudential conflict situation is one that could in principle arise for a person who did not take the moral point of view. An athlete who wants to win a future race believes he ought to run ten miles today, though he does not now want to run the ten miles. A student with a strong desire to sleep believes she must study all night for an exam if she is to improve her chances of being accepted by a law school. These are conflicts between what an agent wants to do and what the agent believes he or she ought to do in order to attain some future goal that can in principle arise for persons who do not take the moral point of view. They are thus prudential conflict situations according to our criterion. On this account, prudential conflict situations can arise for persons who do take the moral point of view as well as for those who do not, but moral conflict situations can arise only for those who take the moral point of view.

I said that the libertarian view of moral choice in this chapter would suggest an analogous account of prudential choice. The analogy we want to pursue is clear enough in broad outline. The agent's own interests are to the interests of other persons in moral choice, as present inclination is to long term self interest in prudential choice. But the relation of self interest to the interests of others in moral choice was spelled out in terms of R-alternative reason sets and these became an integral part of the theory of moral choice. Is there something to play a role similar to that of R-alternative reason sets for prudential choice?

An answer to this question is suggested by the following remarks of Thomas Nagel (70), who has written perceptively about prudential choice. (It should be noted that Nagel's accounts of prudential and moral choice differ from mine on matters not the subject of these quotes.) "The metaphysics to which I shall appeal," says Nagel of his account of prudential choice, "is the metaphysics of a person," which interprets the constraints of prudential choice as "the practical expression of an awareness that one persists over time" (p. 58). He continues:

> The ideal of a temporally persistent human being is an exceedingly complex one and many philosophical problems can be raised about it. . . . What will concern us, however, is an extremely abstract feature of the conception. . . . It is the condition that a person be equally real at all stages of his life; specifically the fact that a particular stage is *present* cannot be regarded as conferring on it any special status. This is a truism, for every stage of one's life is present sooner or later; so all times are on an equal footing in that regard (p. 60).

Nagel goes on to say that the imprudent person tends to accord to the present stage of his life (the present moment and the immediate future) a privileged status, viewing the present as more real in the sense of more important than the distant future and consequently viewing the satisfactions of the present as more worthy of being realized.

Following Nagel, we may think of "the prudential point of view" (an analogue of the moral point of view) as a view which forbids our regarding present or near present satisfactions as superior to future one's merely because of their temporal location, i.e. because they are closer to the present (where, by "satisfactions" we mean states or changes viewed as good). In this sense the prudential point of view, like the moral point of view, can often be opposed to natural inclinations. Just as in moral cases, where we are naturally inclined to give special status to our own interests, thinking of them as more worthy of being realized than the more remote interests of others, so in the prudential case we are naturally inclined to give special status to present or imminent satisfactions, thinking of them as nearer, more palpable, and in that sense more real than distantly future satisfactions. The prudential point of view resists this natural tendency to favor the present, just as the moral point of view resists the natural tendency to favor one's own interests.

Yet this cannot be the whole story. For the prudential point of view seems to require that we favor future satisfactions over present ones rather than according them equal status. It obliges us to sacrifice present satisfactions for the attainment of future states or changes viewed as good. This is true enough. But the implication of the previous paragraph is that, in prudential conflict situations, future satisfactions are not to be favored merely *as future* (just as present satisfactions are not to be favored merely *as present*). To illustrate, let the student in our earlier example imagine that she will find a law school acceptance letter on her desk after a long night of study. And let her ask herself whether, in such circumstances, she would prefer to study all night or sleep and wake well rested without such a letter on her desk. If the answer is that she would prefer to study all night in such circumstances, this will tell her that the future satisfaction is preferred to the competing present one, not because it is future, but because it is believed to be better by her, independently of temporal considerations. It is the distorting aura of presentness that makes the present satisfaction seem so tempting and the prudential point of view is meant to counteract this distortion. It counsels us first to place present and future satisfactions on an equal footing for purposes of comparison, independent of the distortions of temporal distance, and *then* to compare their merits in the light of our overall preferences.

8.12 We now have the necessary information to say what might play a role for prudential choice analogous to role of R-alternative reason sets for moral choice. From the prudential point of view, present (or imminent) and future satisfactions (states or changes viewed as good) are to be treated as *time-relativistic* (or *tR-)alternatives* in the following sense: Present and future satisfactions are to be judged and compared on an equal footing with respect to the overall preferences of the agent, independent of their temporal location with respect to (or temporal distance from) the present. Such tR-alternatives need not turn out to be R-alternatives for the agent in the sense of S4. But they are to be treated as equal in a certain sense. No one of them is to be regarded as superior or inferior to others because of its temporal location (and this because, as Nagel says, a person is equally real at all stages of his life). In this sense, they are to be treated as time-relativistic alternatives.

According to this conception, different moments of time in the agent's life history correspond to the relativistic "frames of reference" (which in moral choice are provided by the perspectives of the different agents). The prudential point of view counsels us to give equal weight to these frames of reference, or temporal perspectives, thus allowing us to make "objective" judgments about the comparative merits of the expected satisfactions at different times. It guarantees equal treatment against a certain kind of temporal bias, but it does not guarantee that the expected satisfactions will be judged to have equal worth once this temporal bias is removed. Similarly, the moral point of view guarantees equal treatment to the value experiments of different individuals, but it does not guarantee that the value systems once tested will turn out to be equally worthy. The theme is the same in practical choice as well, where an "equal hearing" for considered options prior to a final decision (indifferent receptiveness to considerations that might favor any one of them) does not mean that in the end the options will be judged to have equal worth.

8.13 With the prudential analogues of moral choice in hand, we can now proceed to a parallel account of prudential choice.

S41. To take the prudential point of view is to have (i) the belief that present and future satisfactions (states or changes viewed as good) ought to be treated as time-relativistic (or tR-) alternatives in the sense defined in 8.12. In addition, it is to have (ii) the belief that one should fulfill obligations required to attain future satisfactions when the future satisfactions would be preferred to present ones in a time independent comparison that results from treating present and future satisfactions as tR-alternatives. And it is to have (iii) the desire to act in accordance with the beliefs (i) and (ii).

The normative beliefs and the desire described by (i) to (iii) are to be referred to collectively as the motives of prudence and the desire described by (iii) as the desire to act from prudence.

S42. The motives of prudence, like the motives of duty, are of a special kind, since they require the equal treatment of certain items in a certain way that we might not normally be inclined to treat as equal in just that way (present and future satisfactions treated as tR-alternatives in the one case, the reason sets of other persons as R-alternatives in the other). We therefore postulate that the intensity or strength of the motives of prudence (like those of duty), and, in particular, the intensity of the desire to act from prudence, will be fixed in a special way. It will be influenced by an undetermined process selecting from among tR-alternatives like the process described for moral choice in S35, based on the model of the point particle moving in the probability space described in 8.3.

Further comments about moral choice in S35 and S36 can then be made, *mutatis mutandis*, about prudential choice. In particular, (i) a large, but not specific, number of tR-alternatives is required by the prudential point of view, corresponding to the satisfactions associated with possible moments of one's life that are to be treated equally. (ii) The undetermined process does not select one of the alternatives as superior, as in R-choice. Instead a succession of random selections from among equiprobable alternatives representing the moments of one's life is meant to be a continuing "reminder" of the fact that present and future satisfactions are to be viewed time independently. To take the prudential point of view is to be influenced by this continuing reminder. (iii) The effort of will required to act from prudence is therefore indeterminate, reflecting the ambiguous attitude one has toward placing distantly future satisfactions which may never be attained on an equal footing with satisfactions that would more assuredly come about by pursuing present inclinations.

Just as the indeterminateness in the desire and effort to act from duty was connected to the "unnaturalness" of placing the reason sets of others on an equal footing as one's own, so the indeterminateness in the desire and effort to act from prudence is here connected with the "unnaturalness" of thinking that future satisfactions are just as real as present or imminent ones. The "unnaturalness" in both cases is reflected in the special way that the intensity of these motives is fixed and in the ambiguous attitude one has toward sacrificing the present to distant and perhaps unattainable goals.

This leads to a parallel treatment of dual rational self control and weakness of will in prudential choice situations.

S43. Prudential choice situations as described in S42 can satisfy the condition of dual rational self control *if* the problem of weakness of will can be solved, that is, if weakness of will is possible in prudential choice situations as anything other than irrational or compulsive behavior. But weakness of will *is* so possible in three ways similar to those described for moral choice situations in S39. (a) The agent may have rationally grounded doubts that the future satisfaction will ever be attained, and this temporary "loss of faith" may make the present satisfaction appear more attractive. (b) The temporary loss of faith described in (a) may sometimes be due to unconscious suppression of thoughts about the attractions of the distant goal, which are possible precisely because it is distant and uncertain. And (c) the agent may convince himself or herself that a temporary lapse from prudence here and now will not rule out the attainment of the future satisfaction.

The athlete may doubt that he will ever become a great runner and these doubts may weaken his resolve in difficult prudential contexts (a). Persons who know they must diet to preserve their health often suppress thoughts (in the manner of (b)) about painful long range consequences, or, they may convince themselves (in the manner of (c)) that one extra dessert will not do them in. The fear that there may not *be* a future, that one may not live long enough to attain a future satisfaction can also play a significant role in weakening prudential resolve. Future moments can be given equal treatment only if it is believed that they will be "moments of one's life."

In general, the normative beliefs that define the prudential point of view, like those that define the moral point of view, do not motivate with a fixed degree of strength. Desire and effort to act can wax and wane when commitment is to a long range and uncertain goal. It is this that makes it possible to explain weakness of will as something other than ignorance or compulsion.

Finally,

S44. One who makes a choice in a prudential conflict situation such as described in S42 has sole or ultimate dominion over the choice in a manner that parallels the agent's sole or ultimate dominion over a moral choice in the sense of S40 and over an R-choice in the sense of S12.

Just as S40 was a transcription of S12 with the references to R-choice changed to references to moral choice, so this step could be written out in full as a transcription of S12 for prudential choice.

8.14 I shall now complete the theory with three synoptic steps. The first relates the account of moral choice to evolutionary themes in chapters 5 and 6. The second relates the discussion of moral and prudential choice in this chapter to the earlier discussion of practical choice, adding a new dimension to the latter. The third provides an overview of the theory.

Step 14 (of 6.3) states an evolutionary theme associated with the discussions of R-choice and practical choice in chapters 5 and 6. We can now extend that theme to moral choice. It was said that practical human freedom is a natural extension of the evolutionary process, allowing analogues of genetic mutations to occur in the minds of individual agents which are then subjected to rational rather than natural selection in an inner arena. These mutations suggest new cultural options which individuals are empowered to test, first through thought experimentation (vicarious value experiments) and then, in fact, by experiments in living. The result is that cultural evolution involves a leap forward, indefinitely multiplying the possibilities for experimentation with diverse forms of life within a single species; and the role and importance of individuals of the species who choose to engage in diverse experiments is enhanced by comparison with natural evolution. Even when experimentation takes place in groups, the identity of the group does not eliminate diversity or individual experimentation, especially as cultural evolution advances, and the persistence of group experimentation depends upon the commitments of individuals to live in certain kinds of communities.

To this we can now add

S45. Though moral imperatives expressing the ideal of equal respect were not consciously designed by human beings for an evolutionary purpose, they can be viewed as having an important role to play in the process of cultural evolution described in S14. If the aim of cultural evolution, as suggested by S14, is the creation and testing of diverse forms of life within a given species, the aim is best fulfilled if the different value experiments are allowed to run their course without interference. If new and different forms of life were to be destroyed or suppressed by existing and established ones, the aim of cultural experimentation would to that degree be thwarted. Moral imperatives therefore counteract our natural xenophobic tendencies to destroy or suppress the different and the unusual—tendencies that are a by product of our *natural* evolutionary past, not altogether well suited to cultural evolution. These xenophobic tendencies remain powerful in the human species and moral impera- tives only control them imperfectly. We remain creatures of nature as well as of culture. Moreover, too much diversity at any one time can lead to conflict and chaos threatening the survival of communities and even of the species. But the principle of equal respect has built in checks for this. It imposes limits to "allowing individual value experiments to run their course without interference."

Just as cultural evolution thereby enhances the role of individuals of a spe- cies in evolutionary experimentation, so the moral point of view endorses and protects this enhanced role by according dignity to the individual experimenters. It introduces a new kind of motivation that is often opposed to natural inclina- tions and is, as most religions have viewed it, a necessary step in transcending the natural order. This new kind of motivation is related to a fundamental pre- supposition of free practical choice and value experimentation, that there may be many incommensurably good ways of life, R-alternatives to one another, for the members of a single species.

Sophocles' Antigone says of moral imperatives: "They were not born today or yesterday. They die not and no one knoweth whence they spring." This step—S45— may provide some clue to why they "die not" and "whence they spring."

8.15 The steps of this chapter also allow us to add something about practical choice that would not have been understood earlier. There is a sense in which an indeterminate effort of will can be involved in practical choice, just as such an indeterminate effort is involved in moral and prudential choice. One cannot deny, I think, that practical decision making can also involve considerable effort of will. We symbolized this in chapter 5 by describing Everyman's arduous journeys to Careen and Baltar and his subsequent struggles to decide between alternatives. Even when confronted with the potential R-choice, he insisted on making further efforts to resolve the dilemma on his own. In our ordinary practical decision making, we do not often journey to check out the alternatives (though sometimes we do), but we do always journey in our minds, searching out reasons to prefer one to the other; and this search often involves an effort of will. We may be tempted at any time to give in and simply decide on the material available. There is no natural end to the consideration of possible options and consequences in deliberation, as explained; the termination of the process at a given time is up to us. One may want to terminate, out of exhaustion or impulsiveness or to get on with something else. But one may resist this temptation, saying "I cannot make a too hasty, or snap, decision on this matter. It is important, and I want to do it right, give it my best." This aspect of the effort is prudential. Indeed, prudential choice and effort are often intertwined with practical decision making because of the long range importance we may place on making the right decision.

But there is another kind of effort of will involved in practical decision making that is peculiar to it. As in prudential and moral choice, this kind of effort is based upon a unique kind of motivation. To advance in practical decision making, we have to be receptive and open to new and possibly relevant considerations that have not yet entered consciously into deliberation (cf. S24). We do not seek out and assess the relevance of these considerations one by one, as if we knew in advance which ones we were looking for. We do not know this, and therefore we allow them to come to consciousness as chance selected considerations, before assessing their relevance. But this means being guided by a "Taoist" motivation—making an effort "not to make an effort," to let the considerations come unforced. Rather than go down into hell like Orpheus, we play our music outside the gates to see what will come out. These thoughts suggest the following step.

S46. The steps of this chapter allow us to say that an indeterminate effort of will, beyond prudential effort, is also involved in practical decision making. In order to allow chance selected considerations to arise from the unconscious, we must place ourselves in a receptive frame of mind, as described in S24. The motivation to do this goes against the natural grain in a certain sense, as do the motives of duty and prudence. We want to retain rational control over the search for relevant reasons, but we are required to allow chance selected considerations to well up uncontrolled. We know chance selected considerations are not equal with respect to deliberation. Some will be seen as relevant, once they occur, others as irrelevant; and of the relevant ones, some will be judged more important than others. But, in allowing them to be chance selected, we are *antecedently* treating them as equally worthy of consideration, that is, antecedently treating them as R-alternatives (cf. S18).

This suggests that we may interpret the effort to be receptive to chance selected considerations in practical deliberation—the "unnatural" effort not-to-make-an-effort—in the way in which we interpreted the "unnatural" efforts of moral and prudential decision making. This effort, which is an effort to antecedently treat potential chance selected considerations as equally worthy, will be fixed by the movement of the point particle of the probability space, in accordance with the model for moral and prudential choice of 8.3 (the equi-probable regions now standing for the potential chance selected considerations). This means that in practical decision making the movement of the point particle will have a dual role to play. It will be making the chance selections of the potential considerations and, at the same time, rendering indeterminate the effort of will required to proceed in this way, to go on making this special effort to be receptive.

In this manner, there would be two different sources of indeterminateness of effort in practical decision making. One would be the indeterminateness of prudential effort (to go on searching for the best *end*) as described in this section, the other, the unique indeterminateness of practical effort, which has to do with the receptive *means* by which one carries out the search for the best end. (We might add that, given the analogies between practical decision making and creative problem solving described throughout chapter 6, this same dual indeterminateness would be involved in the effort of will that creative problem solving also involves.)

8.16 The final step provides an overview of the theory:

S47. The theory of chapters 5-8 was developed in three stages. The first stage was the discussion of R-choice, which introduced some important themes in a mythical fashion. But R-choice itself was regarded as an extraordinary kind of choice, an idealization. It was brought closer to ordinary intuitions by the discussion of practical choice in chapter 6. This was the second stage. R-choice was viewed at this stage as a limiting case of practical choice, by virtue of the macro-analogy, which viewed practical choice as an R-choice analogue stretched out over time. Practical choice represented something of an antithesis to R-choice in another sense, however, in that the indeterminism of R-choice had to be displaced in practical choice from the willing (the choice itself) to the willing to will to will (the having of a reason to endorse reasons for choice). In this manner, the regress of willings to will, discussed in chapter 2, came to play a role in the theory, but it was not an infinite regress.

The discussion of moral and prudential choice represented a third stage of the argument. Moral and prudential choice were described in a way that synthesized important features of both R-choice and practical choice, while eliminating certain deficiencies. Like practical choices, and unlike R-choices, moral and prudential choices were described as ordinary, everyday choices, not idealizations. But as in R-choice, and not in practical choice, the indeterminism of moral and prudential choice was located in the choice itself and not in a higher order willing. The indeterminacy was returned to the moment of choice itself and was fused with the effort of will as an indeterminacy *of* the effort. Finally, in S46, we returned to practical choice, showing how this fusion of effort and indeterminacy (reason and chance) plays a role in practical decision making as well.

There is some justification for viewing these three stages as a Hegelian triad— thesis, antithesis, and synthesis. The first stage, on R-choice, though revealing, is abstract and to that degree false. The second stage, on practical choice, is more concrete, but still does not tell the whole story, even about practical choice. And the third stage represents a genuine synthesis of the first two. This synthesis suggests that libertarians like Kant and C.A. Campbell, who saw the highest expression of libertarian freedom in moral choice, saw something of importance. But they should not have neglected prudential choice, nor denied that libertarian freedom can be manifested in practical choice as well.

Notes

1. This claim will be modified in 8.5 to allow for situations in which moral conflict persists after a choice has been made.

2. The term "representation" may be misleading here, since it suggests conscious imagery. What I mean to imply is only the existence of a patterned neurological process that disposes the agent to act in certain ways. It need not involve conscious imagery.

3. To be more accurate, greater amount of effort to act from duty corresponds to a higher position of the bubble relative to the choice thresholds. But since the position of the thresholds at any given time varies in accordance with an undetermined process, the position of the bubble *relative* to the thresholds is not determinate.

4. See Plato (37, pp. 121ff.). Mortimore (71) is an excellent collection of readings on the subject from both ancient and modern sources. In addition to the essays in Mortimore, the following have especially influenced my thinking: Hare (65, ch. 5), Davidson (69), Watson (77), Bratman (79), A.O. Rorty (80).

5. The ignorance could have two sources. It might be ignorance of the moral principles or ignorance about certain features of the situation that are morally relevant. Aristotle, for example, rejected the simplistic view that the weak willed person must be ignorant of moral principle. But he nevertheless tried to explain weak willed, or incontinent, behavior in terms of a kind of ignorance— ignorance of particular features of the situation that are morally relevant (08, vol. 9, bk. 1, ch. 3).

6. Many writers on weakness of will have made the correct point that what is wanted is a psychological explanation of weak willed behavior, not a justification of it, moral or otherwise. Cf. Davidson (69).

Factual Issues and Incompatibility Revisited

9.1 At the beginning of chapter 5, I said (i) that an adequate libertarian account of free will was not something we were likely to find somewhere already embodied in a familiar language or conceptual scheme, (ii) that its development would be a theoretical construction, not merely an analysis of ordinary language, involving a step by step use of traditional and new materials, (iii) that the construction would amount to a possibility argument answering a question about the conceivability, not the actuality, of libertarian freedom, and (iv) that it would involve the doctrine of value relativism in an essential way.

I added that any construction which escaped confusion and emptiness was likely to fall short of some libertarian aspirations—aspirations that I believe cannot ultimately be fulfilled. I have no illusions about this failure to capture everything libertarians have wanted. Many will think it a fatal flaw, including well intentioned libertarians who share my aspirations but not what they may view as my self destructive tendencies to avoid mystery at all costs. From the moment we followed Everyman and the Chief Elder into the game room after Step 4, we were in for a rough time of it. Like Baron von Münchhausen, we have been trying to pull ourselves from the ditch by our bootstraps ever since. I quoted Wiggins in chapter 1 as saying that progress on the free will issue is hindered by the lack of an intelligible account of the libertarian view. Perhaps this theory is not it. But, if not, let it be a challenge to those who think that libertarians can do better, while avoiding appeals to mysterious forms of agency. The theory allows us to connect many diverse and recurrent themes in the history of debates about free will and I suspect, for this reason, that any better theory will incorporate many of its insights.

In this chapter, I have two aims. The first is to discuss factual issues relating to the theory, the second to discuss normative issues. If such a freedom as the theory describes is possible, (a) what are the chances that it exists in fact, and (b) why should anyone want to possess it? The first of these questions leads to a discussion of possible neural mechanisms underlying the theory (9.2-6). The second question returns us to the arguments of chapter 3 concerning the compatibility of free will and determinism. We shall pick up the arguments for the libertarian view where chapter 3 left off (9.7-15). The compatibility issue is all the more pressing now that a libertarian theory is clearly before us and its limitations apparent.

Finally, after discussing these matters in the present chapter, we shall turn in the final chapter to the theory of values presupposed by the theory of free will. Discussion of that theory of values will speak to another demand made by Wiggins in the quotation of chapter 1, that the libertarian say "how his conception of metaphysical freedom is connected with political and social freedom."

165

9.2 Of major importance is the question whether humans actually possess a libertarian freedom of the kind we have described, or of any kind. This is a question
ultimately for scientific study and not for armchair speculation; but some things can
be said about it and I would be remiss if I did not address it. Most libertarian
theories, not merely my own, are vulnerable to certain kinds of scientific evidence,
more so than some other philosophical theories. For libertarians must insist that the
causal gaps or ambiguous possibilities they require in nature actually be there, even
if they postulate transempirical egos or agent causes to fill those gaps. Moreover,
they cannot simply postulate indeterminism anywhere in nature. It is of no help to
them if undetermined processes take place in distant galaxies or in interstellar space,
but nowhere near or within the human organism. The indeterminism must be where
the action is, where it can serve the purposes of free agents and be amplified to have
macroscopic effects. This suggests that libertarians look to the brain for its location—
not a new or surprising suggestion by any means. The suggestion is already embodied in the very first step of our theory, Bramhall's thesis, which places the indeterminism in the will of the agent, between reasons and choice.

But when we look at current research on the brain, things get complicated; and
they do not look altogether promising for libertarians.[1] Information is transmitted
in the brain by means of the firing or non-firing of individual neural cells or neurons.
Many millions of neurons are, of course, involved in the functioning of the nervous
system, but each individual neuron is confined to an all or nothing, yes or no,
response. If the electrical stimulation it receives from other firing cells reaches a
certain critical level, the neuron will fire, otherwise it will not. The electrical charges
delivered by other firing neurons must all be delivered within a certain interval of
time, or charges received earlier will have dissipated by the time later ones arrive.

Though such transmission of charge from one neuron to another is the elementary process by which information is transmitted in the brain, this process itself is
quite complex biochemically. And therein lies the first of many problems facing one
who would look for non-negligible indeterminacies in the activities of the brain.
The transmission of charge between neurons takes place across a synaptic cleft or
space between the membranes of the two cells. The sending neuron releases a chemical
transmitter substance which crosses the cleft transmitting the charge. But the transmitter substance consists of such an enormously large number of molecules that quantum indeterminacy would seem to be negligible with regard to predicting when and
if an individual neuron will fire. And if quantum indeterminacy is negligible at the
level of individual neuron firing, it may be argued, then it will be negligible in the
overall information processing of the nervous system, which involves the firing of
large numbers of neurons.

Sir John Eccles, who has thought about these matters as much as any working
scientist, has made a suggestion as to how quantum uncertainty might play a less
than negligible role in the firing of individual neurons, the effects then being amplified by other parts of the nervous system.[2] To take a hypothetical example, assume
that a particular neuron must receive charges from twenty others within a certain
time in order to fire, and suppose that it has received nineteen of these charges. The

twentieth charge must be received within a very small fraction of a second or the neuron will not fire. If there is an indeterminacy as to when the twentieth charge is delivered, this indeterminacy will be reflected in whether the neuron fires at all. Eccles calls such a neuron "critically poised." The transmitter substance is packaged in small vesicles situated near the membrane walls of the transmitting neuron. When the vesicle is stimulated it moves to the wall of the membrane and releases its molecules. Eccles has calculated that there is an indeterminacy in the position of such a vesicle carrying transmitter molecules of about fifty angstroms in one millisecond. But if the position of the vesicle is indeterminate then the time at which it will reach the membrane and release its molecules is also indeterminate. Eccles shows further that the firing or not firing of a critically poised neuron is no minor matter; it can have substantial effects in various parts of the brain in a very short time.

We are in no position to pass judgment on Eccles' suggestion or others that have been made along similar lines.[3] But it does allow us to bring out several points of general importance. First, if one is to look for indeterminacies at the neuronal level in the brain, a most likely place to look is the timing of neural firing and delivering of charges to other neurons. Anything that could create an indeterminacy in the time at which neurons fire or deliver their charges, even of milliseconds or less, could make an enormous difference. Second, indeterminacy at the neuronal level is of no value to the libertarian unless its effects can be amplified within the nervous system.

9.3 Regarding this second point, most scientists and philosophers who have speculated about the possible effects of indeterminism in the brain upon human decision making have postulated what Popper (72) calls a "master-switch-*cum*-amplifier model" (p. 233), hereafter called an MSA model. In such a model, microscopic indeterminacy affects neural firing (the master switch) and is thereby amplified within the nervous system, influencing choice or decision, and is then amplified further to have an effect on physical motions of the organism. (Popper, it should be noted, is critical of MSA models and has suggested an alternative that we shall consider later.) The general idea behind MSA models goes back to the beginnings of quantum physics. Erwin Schrödinger suggested a well known thought experiment for another purpose in which a small energy undetermined process (an example might be the emission of a single alpha particle from a radioactive nucleus, though this was not Schrödinger's example) would be recorded and electronically amplified, so that if emitted within a specified time interval, a cat would be electrocuted. Thus, a macroscopic occurrence of no small importance, especially to the cat, would be as undetermined and as unpredictable as the microscopic process that generated it.

This general idea of a master switch plus amplifier has particular relevance to the functioning of organisms, which are well suited to play the role of amplifier systems. The idea has a number of interesting biological applications independent of brain research, as the following quotes will show. Molecular biophysicisit H. J. Morowitz (80) has this to say about a master switch plus amplifier process in biological evolution:

Before the coming of genetic life . . . fluctuations in temperature or noise were averaged out, giving rise to precise laws of planetary evolution. Afterward, however, a single molecular event at the level of thermal noise could lead to macroscopic consequences. For if the event were a mutation in a self replicating system, then the entire course of biological evolution could be altered. A single molecular event could kill a whale by inducing a cancer or destroy an ecosystem by generating a virulent virus. . . . The origin of life does not abrogate the underlying laws of physics, but it adds a new feature: large scale consequences of molecular events. This rule change makes evolutionary history indeterminate and so constitutes a clear cut discontinuity (p. 17).

Morowitz suggests that a similar rule changing discontinuity may be involved in the origin of reflective thought in primate evolution.

The second quote is from biologist J. Z. Young (77), writing on recent developments in immunology:

Developments that Peter Medawar started in immunology have had much wider repercussions than this. The body has the most astonishing capacity to produce antibodies against almost anything, including for instance synthetic organic chemicals that have not yet been invented. The mechanism for recognizing each foreign body cannot therefore have been evolved by natural selection in the past, but it may depend upon a sort of natural selection going on within the body. According to the theory of Nils Jerne, the lymphocytes, which are the cells that produce the antibodies, are formed in a special organ dedicated to producing a variety of random mutations. This Generator of Diversity (GOD to the profane) continually provides new varieties of lymphocytes out of which some can be selected for multiplication if needed to make antibodies to a new antigen, such as a substance that the chemists have thought up (p. 29).

If such a process of generating diversity or random mutations can be seriously entertained for the immunological system, then why not for the brain as well? Such a process would have useful functions in the brain, generating new ideas and associations and thereby playing a significant role in creative thinking (and practical deliberation) as we argued in chapter 6. One might therefore make a case for the evolutionary advantage it would confer. Human beings have to invent solutions to newly created problems with few hereditary clues, just as the immunological system has to invent new antibodies against newly created chemical substances with few hereditary clues.

Both the above quotes suggest the existence of master switch plus amplifier processes within living organisms. We do not know if something similar goes on in the brain of cortically developed creatures like ourselves, but I suspect it must if libertarian theories are to succeed. The main problem is the one addressed by Eccles of locating the master switch and the mechanisms of amplification. We have no substantial empirical evidence on these matters (especially regarding the master switch), merely speculation, and libertarian theories may fail dismally at this juncture. But there is much to be learned yet about the brain; and research exists as the above quotes indicate suggesting that master switch plus amplifier processes play more roles in the functioning of organisms than was previously supposed. What I would like to do in the next two sections, then, is to show how an MSA model, using Eccles' notion of critically poised neurons as a working hypothesis, might be adapted to the theory of practical, moral and prudential decision making of chapters 5-8.

9.4 The role of indeterminism in practical, moral, and prudential decision making, according to this theory, involves large numbers of equiprobable alternatives, represented at various times as places on a spinning wheel or regions of a probability space. In practical choice situations, these options are related to potential chance selected considerations (occurrent thoughts, images, associations, memories, etc.) of which there are an indefinite number that might be relevant to any given deliberation. In the cases of moral and prudential choice, the options are related respectively to the reason sets of different agents deserving equal respect and to potential present and future satisfactions, of which there are also large numbers. R-choice is a special case in which a small number, say, two, three, or four such equiprobable alternatives are involved. Thus, R-choice, which is known to be special in ordinary terms, would turn out to be special in neural terms as well, if it ever actually occurred.

Keeping these points in mind, let us now suppose that there are neurons in the brain, critically poised in Eccles' sense, whose probability of firing within a small interval of time is .5. (We shall tamper with this simplifying assumption in a moment.) For every n such neurons, there are 2^n possible ordered combinations of firings and non-firings, which may be represented by sequences, such as (101...), (01101...), where the "1" 's indicate firings, the "0" 's non-firings, and the dots indicate that the sequences are continued with "0" 's up to n figures. A reasonably small number of such neurons, say a dozen, would yield ordered combinations.in the thousands, enough for the purposes of the theory. As indicated in 8.4, the exact number of possible alternatives or partitionings does not matter so long as it is large; it would likely depend on the exigencies of neurological programming rather than the demands of the theory.

For practical choice, these ordered combinations of firings and non-firings of critically poised neurons would correspond to places on a spinning wheel, most of which would give rise to chance selected considerations, opening doors to consciousness of possibly relevant memories, triggering associations of ideas and/or images, focussing attention in various ways, etc. Some combinations of firings and non-firings might draw a blank. But the wheel would keep spinning until it hit something worth considering, so long as the practical reasoner or creative thinker were in a receptive, yet reflective, state of mind. Then the relevance of the consideration to deliberation would have to be assessed and the consideration either accepted or rejected.

In the cases of moral and prudential choice, the combinations of firings and non-firings would correspond to regions of the probability space (the bubble) in the figures of section 8.3, and consequently also to different possible positions of the indeterminate choice thresholds A and B. Each combination of firings or non-firings of the n critically poised neurons would fix the point particle in a particular region and the thresholds at a given level for a small interval of time, thereby contributing to the indeterminacy at that time of the motives of duty or of prudence. Thus, the process would function differently for practical choice, on the one hand, and for moral and prudential choice, on the other, corresponding to the different ways that R-alternatives (or tR-alternatives) function in the different kinds of choices, but it could be the same neurological process in all cases.

One might further imagine that such a process originated for practical choice, because of its selective advantages in practical reasoning and creative thinking (S14) and was later adapted to moral and prudential decision making, as suggested in S45. In the case of moral choice, this adaptation would correspond to an extension of the notion of R-alternative possibilities, already operative at the practical level, to the purposes and ways of life of other individuals.

9.5 Several questions immediately arise about these suggestions. First, how would the nervous system recognize different *ordered* combinations of firings and non-firings of critically poised neurons? In line with Eccles' remarks about the effects of the firing of a critically poised neuron on other parts of the nervous system, it can be assumed that the firing of each of the n neurons making up the ordered combinations is associated with a distinctive pattern of firings of other neurons in the brain. Thus the sequence (100...) would give rise to a pattern of firings of other neurons we may call pattern 1, (001...) to a pattern 3, (101...) to a pattern consisting of pattern 1 plus pattern 3, and so on. The different patterns of firings in other parts of the brain would constitute recognition by the nervous system of the different ordered sequences.

A second problem concerns the assumption that the probability of firing of each of the critically poised neurons is .5. This is required if the sequences are to be equiprobable, something in turn required by the assumptions of R-alternativeness in the theory.[4] But is this requirement realistic? It may not be, but the defect is easily remedied within an MSA model. Suppose that the probability of firing of critically poised neurons from a given stimulus at a given time, is very high, so that the probability of not firing is, say, only one in ten million (.0000001). This indeterminacy, or any similarly minute indeterminacy, can be amplified to produce the situation described in the previous section, given sufficient complexity in the nervous system.

Let the critically poised neurons, whose probability of not firing is .0000001, be members of set V. Then consider a set W of neurons, each member of which is connected with 5 neurons in V, such that each member of W fails to fire if and only if any one of the five neurons in V connected to it fails to fire. The probability that a neuron in W will not fire is then .0000005. Now consider a set X of neurons, each of which is connected to a hundred neurons in W, such that a neuron in X will fail to fire if and only if at least one of the neurons in W connected to it fails to fire. The probability that a neuron in X will not fire in the circumstances is .00005. We can then imagine a set Y of neurons connected to a hundred neurons of X, as the neurons of X are connected to those of W, and a set Z of neurons, each of which is connected to those in Y, as those in Y are to those in X. The probability of not firing for each of the neurons in Y would then be .005, and for each of the neurons in Z, .5. The neurons in Z could then play the role of the critically poised neurons forming the ordered sequences of the previous section.

What is going on here? We have taken a small indeterminacy in the non-firing of certain neurons (in the set V) and amplified it within the system to produce the kinds of equiprobable sequences desired. The MSA, or master switch plus amplifier, system is being used to produce randomness, or equiprobable alternatives, out of minute quantum indeterminacies. There would be further amplification involved, of course, as the sequences are involved in practical, moral and prudential decision making, and the decisions are transformed into large scale bodily actions. But it is noteworthy that the system can increase uncertainty as well as imposing greater control over quantum indeterminacies. The complexity of the nervous system plays a crucial role in all of this. Thousands of neurons are involved in the process just imagined; and we may have underestimated the numbers involved. In principle, probabilities much lower than one in ten million, one in billions or trillions, could be amplified, given sufficient neural complexity.

One might argue that the indeterminacy in such circumstances would really be down in the original neurons of set V (not in those of set Z); and the probability of non-firing for neurons in V is not .5. Technically, as soon as one knew how the neurons of V had fired, one could predict how the neurons of the other sets would fire and which combinations ((01101...), etc.) of firings and non-firings of neurons in Z would occur. This is true. But it is not a fatal objection, as one can see by returning to the situation of Everyman in the game room. After the wheel has spun and landed on blue for Baltar, it takes a small, but finite, time for Everyman and the others to perceive the outcome and to process the information received in their brains. One might say that, for a fraction of a second, when the wheel has landed on blue, the selection has been made, but Everyman does not yet know what it is. Similarly, when the neurons of set V have fired or failed to fire, as the case may be, the selection of a combination, (01101...) for example, has been made, but the nervous system has not yet recorded what the selection is. (Remember that only milliseconds need be involved between firings of neurons in the different sets.) One can think of the amplification as a processing of the information already contained in the firings of V, a processing which involves a *partitioning* of firings and non-firings of neurons in V into equiprobable combinations. It remains the case that before the neurons of V have fired (or not fired) the outcome is indeterminate. The rest is a process of interpreting the results in a certain way. Undetermined processes and outcomes mean nothing, as emphasized in earlier chapters, without the surrounding rational interpretation, which includes an imposed partitioning and the assumption of certain meanings to the partitions.[5]

We can now see why R-choice is special. The above process is designed for ordinary practical, moral, and prudential choices involving many partitions, or ordered sequences of firings and non-firings. R-choice, if it were to take place, would involve a further partitioning superimposed upon the set of possible sequences ((01011...), etc.) depending upon the number of R-alternatives involved, two, three, or whatever. The simplest way to get this special partitioning would be as follows. Assuming three R-alternatives, assign the combination (100...) to the first alternative, (010...) to the second, (001...) to the third; all other combinations would draw a blank (as if the wheel of the game room in Everyman's case had many more options than red and blue). Then let the process proceed until one or another of the designated combinations turns up. The first to turn up is the selection. Clearly, this would be an extraordinary use of an existing neural mechanism; and learning how to make use of it, by some sort of biofeedback training, would constitute a further evolutionary development. Other intelligent beings in the universe may have such capacities. We could only do it now by using some physical randomizing process for R-choice to play the role of the neural mechanism.

9.6 In the previous two sections, I tried to explain how an MSA, or master switch plus amplifier, neurological model might be adapted to the theory of chapters 5-8. We should now note that MSA models have sometimes been criticized as inadequate to the needs of libertarian theories of freedom. One prominent critic is Popper. His lecture "Of Clouds and Clocks" is in honor of the noted physicist, A. H. Compton, who himself wrote a good deal about the free will issue, trying to defend a libertarian position.[6] Compton at one time suggested an MSA model to explain how indeterminism could be involved in human decision making, arguing that undetermined processes, like quantum jumps, could be amplified in human decision making so that they would affect large scale behavior. Popper objects that decisions conceived in this way would have no similarity to anything we could call rational decisions (p. 228). Such a model, he says, would reduce all decisions to arbitrary, snap decisions and would thereby "lend support to the thesis of Hume and Schlick that perfect chance is the only alternative to perfect determinism" (p. 228).

We first encountered an objection of this kind in chapter 1. If libertarians had their causal gaps or quantum jumps in the brain, what could they do with them that was not arbitrary? I have been laboring long and hard since then to answer this question. What is needed, and what is missing in Compton's proposal, is a theory of free decision, like the theory of chapters 5-8, that would allow one to make sense of undetermined decisions as rational decisions, and, indeed, as dual rational decisions. Given such a theory, MSA models like that of 9.4-5 can be adapted to it, without being subject to Popper's criticism.

Popper himself attacks the problem of physical modeling for the libertarian view in a different way, in terms of the metaphors of clouds and clocks. By clouds, he means physical systems that are "highly irregular, disorderly, and more or less unpredictable" (p. 207). His favored examples of clouds are gases in which the individual molecules move about irregularly, or a cluster of flies or gnats which keeps together despite the fact that each individual gnat is moving about in an irregular and disorderly fashion. By clocks, on the other hand, Popper means "physical systems which are regular, orderly and highly predictable in their behavior" (p. 207). His favored example, from which the name is taken, is "a very regular pendulum clock."

In order to make sense of a libertarian freedom, Popper argues, we must imagine a clock-like orderly (meta-)control being imposed upon a cloud-like system, whose individual parts are not determined. He is not specific about certain aspects of this suggestion, including what would constitute the cloud-like, undetermined processes in neurological terms. This is perhaps because, on his view, all physical systems, including the brain, are clouds, more or less. Clocks are simply less cloudy clouds. Thus, he speaks of clock-*like* and cloud-*like* processes, meaning to refer to processes that are nearer to one or the other of the extremes of perfect order or perfect randomness. He has more to say about the clock-like meta-control that is to be superimposed on the cloud-like processes of the brain. This meta-control, he says, must be a *rational* control, and to understand it we must "try to understand how men . . . can be 'influenced' or 'controlled' by such things as aims, or purposes, or rules, or agreements" (p. 230), in short, by a "universe of abstract meanings." At this point, in other words, Popper introduces his "content theory," discussed and criticized in chapter 4, in order to explain how rational meta-control can be imposed upon physical cloud-like, undetermined systems.

Now Popper's clock and cloud metaphors are suggestive. But they are not necessarily opposed to MSA models. A master switch plus amplifier system can be viewed as imposing a clock-like meta-control (the amplifier) over cloud-like, undetermined processes. The proposal of 9.4 can be viewed in this way, for example, with the undetermined neural firings at the lowest level, in the set V, representing the underlying cloud which is then structured and given meaning by the process of amplification. Thus, Popper's view is not opposed to MSA models *per se*. What he seems to oppose is the idea of master switches, or randomness, playing a non-negligible role *at* the level of rational meta-control. For this seems to be opposed to our ordinary understanding of rational decision making.

But this requirement, that randomness be non-negligible at the level of rational meta-control, points to the main difficulty with Popper's view. In all of his sometimes vague, but always suggestive, talk about clouds and clocks, Popper never really comes to grips with the problem of dual rational self control.[7] When rational meta-control is imposed in decision making, why is it imposed in this way *rather than* otherwise? Popper does not provide an answer to this question in a way that would account for two way rationality; and failing this, he fails to answer compatibilist critics of the indeterminist condition. His "content theory," with its appeals to abstract entities, is meant to provide the required account of rational meta-control. But, as argued in chapter 4, content theories cannot solve the problem of dual rational self control unless they are supplemented by two level theories; and two level theories cannot solve the problem unless they are supplemented by non-occurrent cause theories. Popper's proposals push him inexorably in the direction of postulating a transempirical ego, like Eccles', or some other kind of non-occurrent cause, to account for rational meta-control.

The only alternative, I think, is to solve the problem of dual rational self control in the manner I have proposed. But the lesson of my theory is that the problem of dual rational self control cannot be solved *if* randomness is rendered negligible at the level of rational meta-control, at least up to the point of choice or decision.

After choice or decision randomness can become negligible. Talk of systems of meta-control in the brain is all right. In fact, it is necessary, if we are to understand freedom.[8] But if randomness is smoothed out, rendered negligible, before one gets to the meta-level of rational choice or decision, the problem of dual rational self control will not yield to a solution. Thus, the model of 9.5 first amplifies to equi-probable outcomes, before imposing a more rigid control of choice over action. The alternatives are either to fall prey to compatibilist objections or to take refuge in obscure forms of agency or causation.

If Popper had come to grips with the problem of dual rational self control and solved it in the manner I proposed, his criticism of all master switch plus amplifier systems would have lost its force. MSA systems are simply the most plausible ways of accounting for the clock-like control over cloud-like processes that the libertarian theory demands.

In conclusion, these remarks about neural models necessarily leave the important factual questions unanswered. If libertarians are right, the master switches, or cloud-like processes, and the amplifier systems must be present in the brain; and there is no solid evidence to date that they are there. I myself believe, contrary to Popper, that the existence of the cloud-like processes in a suitable form is the main stumbling block. It helps to know that minute indeterminacies in neural firings could be amplified in the way described in 9.5. But this in itself does not guarantee the existence of master switches in the brain. The issue, in any case, is not one to be ultimately settled by philosophical speculation.

9.7 We now take up the second task of this chapter, which requires a return to the compatibilist-incompatibilist debate of chapter 3. Why, if at all, should we accept a libertarian theory and consequently an incompatibilist account of free will over compatibilist alternatives? This question is all the more pressing now that a libertarian theory is on hand and its limitations apparent. If we place a premium on avoiding confusion and emptiness, then libertarian theories will have certain limitations, or so I have argued. How do these limitations affect the case for the libertarian view?

This question will be addressed by considering in order the following six themes: (I) CNC control (II) Sole or Ultimate Dominion, (III) Formation of Character and Motives, (IV) Resentment and Gratitude, (V) The Reactive Attitude, and (VI) Openness, Creativity, and Causal Chains. Each theme is related in one way or another to arguments for incompatibilism. Theme (I) summarizes points that are implicit in the arguments of chapter 3, while the other themes pick up the argument where chapter 3 leaves off.

A preliminary point about methodology is necessary. As argued in chapter 3, if the dispute between compatibilists and incompatibilists remains at the level of analysis of ordinary concepts, it tends to stalemate, because the relevant concepts, like "power," are not clear enough. If, in addition, factual evidence is not decisive, how does one resolve the issue? It seems to me that William James had the right idea about this aspect of the free will debate. Over and above conceptual analysis and factual evidence (and I am certainly not denying the importance of these to the debate) is the matter of the value or importance that different individuals attach to viewing themselves and their place in the cosmos in certain ways.[9] James called such considerations "pragmatic." I call them "value empiricist." The main point, as we learned when discussing value empiricist answers to the question "Why be moral?", is that different answers and arguments may appeal to some persons but not to others, depending upon the commitments they may have and the value or importance they attach to certain things. In the case of major issues, like the free will issue, the matters of importance attach to our ways of viewing ourselves and our place in the universe. We can expect that the attractions of incompatibilism, such as they are, will come down to this.

9.8 Theme (I): *CNC Control*. The discussion of chapter 3 faltered over the move from (3) "CNC control (covert non-constraining control of the will by another intelligent agent) takes away freedom in a significant sense," to (4) "mere determination (without control by another intelligent agent) takes away freedom in the same sense." Those who accept (3) believe that while CNC controlled agents may have control over and responsibility for their actions in some senses, they lack a certain ultimate control and responsibility which belongs to the agent who has covertly controlled them (assuming that agent is not being controlled in turn). In Bramhall's words, the controlled agent is a "staff in another's hands." We argued that many persons, including many compatibilists, would accept such a conclusion about CNC control. But the compatibilists, at least, would reject a similar conclusion with regard to mere determination by non-intelligent causes.

Before taking up the difficult move from (3) to (4), we should note that the acceptance of (3), together with the claims supporting it, already provides a reason for some persons to take an incompatibilist view of freedom. I have in mind religious persons who are concerned about theodicy, or justifying the ways of God to man. A theist, who accepts (3) for the reasons given in chapter 3, cannot consistently believe that a good and just God could create any kind of world. If, for example, God were to create a determined world, or a world in which all of the choices and decisions of human and other intelligent agents were determined, then God would be a CNC controller of those agents in that world (like the controller of Ishmael's world 1) and would be ultimately responsible for the good and evil they created. The only way to avoid this result, if you accept (3), is to say that God does not create a world in which free choices of intelligent agents are determined. In short, one must ascribe an incompatibilist freedom to those agents.

To ascribe such a freedom is not necessarily to deny that God is omnipotent. One merely has to say that, in creating the world, a good God would have voluntarily limited the exercise of omnipotence by choosing not to determine how free agents would choose to act. Many theists have, in fact, said this.[10] But to say even this much is to say that intelligent agents in a world God creates must possess an incompatibilist freedom. Their free choices are not determined.

The only way to avoid this conclusion, I believe, is to take the hard compatibilist, or predestinationist, line of Hobbes and Edwards and deny the claims about CNC control supporting (3). Hobbes and Edwards argue that while God created our natures, or characters and motives, we and not God are nevertheless responsible for the actions determined by these natures, or characters and motives, because they are *ours*. I argued against this view in 3.9, showing why it is regarded as counterintuitive by most persons, and need not repeat the argument here. Its counterintuitiveness is the reason why many have agreed with Bramhall that an incompatibilist view of free will was necessary to quiet "the outcry against divine justice," as Milton puts it in his *De Doctrina* (36, p. 202).

I do not think that considerations of divine *omniscience* and *foreknowledge* alter this conclusion in any substantial way, though issues about divine knowledge are, in some ways, more subtle than issues about divine power and control. The critical question to ask is whether or not divine omniscience implies that God must create a causally determined world. Many theists answer no. Some base a negative answer on the belief that God's knowledge is timeless. Since God does not literally *fore*know all occurrences in a temporal sense, they say that divine omniscience is compatible with a causally undetermined world.[11] Others have said that God can temporally foreknow all occurrences in a causally undetermined world, and have suggested some unusual senses of foreknowledge to account for this.[12] I have my suspicions about views such as these.[13] But the main point here is that even if one of them was true it would not alter the earlier conclusion of this section. For if divine omniscience does not imply a causally determined world, then divine omniscience would not rule out an incompatibilist view of freedom. Indeed, such doctrines about divine knowledge are usually put forward to preserve the causal indeterminism thought to be necessary to salvage divine justice.[14]

If, on the other hand, divine omniscience does imply that God must create a causally determined world, then, if one accepts (3) the problem about justice stated earlier arises once again. If God knowingly and willingly creates a determined world, then God is a CNC controller of the choices and actions of intelligent agents in that world and is ultimately responsible for the good and evil they create. Thus, whatever position one takes on the question of whether or not divine omniscience implies that God must create a causally determined world, the earlier conclusion remains: *if* one accepts (3), the only way to "quiet the outcry against divine justice" is to accept an incompatibilist view of freedom.

This first of our six themes provides a good example of what I meant in 9.7 by saying that different reasons for accepting an incompatibilist view of freedom would appeal to some persons, not to others, depending upon the commitments the persons have and the importance they attach to certain things. Persons with theistic beliefs already have reasons to hold an incompatibilist view of freedom, if they accept the claims made about CNC control in chapter 3. Others will want further arguments.

9.9 Theme (II): *Sole or Ultimate Dominion*. Near the end of chapter 3, I argued that the transition from (3) "CNC control takes away freedom . . ." to (4) "Mere determination takes away freedom . . ." was not reasonable unless one could identify an *important* kind of freedom that both CNC control and mere determination take away. Libertarians believe there is such a freedom, which they variously describe as the "power to determine oneself," "dominion over one's own will," "control over the springs of one's action," and so on. The problem, as discussed in 3.14, is that attempts to explain such expressions in other than compatibilist terms give rise to Hobbesian charges of "confusion or emptiness." Libertarians seem to want a control over original character and motives, or something else equally unattainable. My response in chapter 3 was to describe a kind of freedom that libertarians have in mind when they use the above quoted expressions. It is an unconstrained freedom of choice which satisfies the condition of sole or ultimate dominion defined by D3. We have arrived at the point where we can pick up the argument of chapter 3 and ask why this condition is thought to be important.

According to D3, an agent's power over choice satisfies the condition of sole or ultimate dominion, if and only if, (i) the agent's making the choice at a time t rather than doing otherwise, or vice versa, can be explained by saying that the agent rationally willed at t to do so and (ii) no further explanation can be given for the agent's choosing rather than doing otherwise (or vice versa), or for the agent's rationally willing at t to do so, which is an explanation in terms of conditions whose existence cannot be explained by the agent's choosing or rationally willing something at t.

The first thing to be said about this condition is that it does seem to capture what libertarians like Bramhall have meant by having the "power to determine oneself," or "dominion over one's own will," or "control over the springs of one's own action." For what they had in mind was that the genesis of one's own choices or actions could be traced back to one's rational will and no further. The agent's choosing or doing otherwise could be explained by what the agent rationally willed to do, and by nothing else. Second, the condition implies that not all of the agent's willings (choosings, endorsements of reasons) can be determined by earlier occurrences. Some willings might be determined, but these would not satisfy the condition of sole or ultimate dominion. They might be based upon intentions or other reasons whose genesis was traceable to earlier choices which did satisfy the condition of sole or ultimate dominion, and were not determined. At these earlier.choices, the chain of explanation would terminate in the agent's rational will. By contrast, if all willings were determined, the chain of explanations would continue backwards, producing the muddle of how the agent could have determined his or her original character and motives. Third, the condition of sole or ultimate dominion can be associated with what libertarians have meant by the agent's ultimate responsibility for choices as explained in 3.15, since choices which satisfy the condition can be explained by the agent's will and by nothing else.

These remarks suggest why many have been attracted to the condition of a sole or ultimate dominion. But what is the source of this attraction? I think that Ted Honderich has the right idea at this point. He has written perceptively in defense of an incompatibilist view of freedom, though ultimately to defend a hard determinist, rather than a libertarian, position. Honderich (73a) says that if all of our decisions and actions were determined, something important would be lost, something which he refers to as the sense of "individuality." He says: "What I have in mind is only this," that if a person's choices or actions were determined, then "what [the person] did is *explained* by something that is not individual to, or peculiar to, [the person]" (pp. 210-11). While I think this is the right idea, I would not speak simply of the loss of "individuality," since that term can be given enough meanings to keep compatibilists happy. I would rather say that what determinism takes away is a certain sense of the importance of oneself as an individual. If I am ultimately responsible for certain occurrences in the universe, if the only explanation for their occurring rather than not is to be found in my rational will, then my choices and my life take on an importance that is missing if I do not have such responsibility. This responsibility is in turn connected with the enhanced importance of the individual in cultural evolution, emphasized at various places in chapters 5-8, and with the idea of individual dignity or respect. Persons are to be treated as ends, rather than as means, because they are the *ultimate* originators of their own ends. It is worth noting here that these themes—an enhanced role for the individual in cultural evolution and equal respect for the individual—were essential to the demonstrations that practical and moral decision making could satisfy the condition of sole or ultimate dominion.

9.10 Now compatibilists will say that this is all very nice, but it ignores the main problem. The condition of sole or ultimate dominion looked attractive when first encountered in chapter 3. But when one follows the account of it through chapters 5-8, the original attractions tend to wear off. Compatibilists probably entertained the suspicion in chapter 3 that the condition, though superficially attractive, was confused or empty. Attempts to explain it would result in the dilemmas of chapters 2 and 4. My attempt to explain it avoided the dilemmas, but at a price: one can have sole or ultimate dominion in practical, moral, and prudential decision making, provided that the control over one's own will is partial. The outcome will be the result of reason and chance, effort and indeterminism. It is true that in all three cases (practical, moral, and prudential) one can show how the reason and chance, effort and indeterminism, are intertwined, the effort itself being indeterminate. But it remains true that agents can have sole or ultimate dominion only if their rational control over the outcome of choice is limited. And this seems to undermine the attractions of possessing sole or ultimate dominion. The *causa sui* is partly at the mercy of circumstances he or she cannot control.

This objection is central and should be answered straightforwardly by libertarians. They must insist that, despite the limitations of partial control, sole or ultimate dominion remains attractive because of its implications concerning the importance we attach to ourselves as individuals. Knowing that the control of one's rational will and effort is partial or limited does not undermine the importance of knowing that one's rational will and effort (limited though they may be) provide the only explanations for one's choices. I do not have to feel omnipotent with regard to what I will, in order to feel important as an individual because my choices cannot be explained by anything other than my will.

Consider, by way of analogy, the attribution of creativity to an agent. The discoverer of a new theory may grant you that her discovery was the result of a lot of hard work and some luck. The admission that elements of chance and uncontrolled inspiration played a role does not undermine her sense of worth or merit. But she is likely to resist the suggestion that the discovery could be completely explained by causes outside of herself, intelligent or otherwise. Even the idea that others could have predicted the outcome before it occurred is demeaning, suggesting the superiority of those others and the dispensability of herself. In other words, *partial* responsibility is acceptable to her sense of worth or merit, but the denial of *ultimate* responsibility is not. Libertarians must look at free actions in the same light. They can and should argue that, since sole or ultimate dominion is important to one's sense of worth or merit, it is better to have it under conditions of partial or limited control than not to have it at all.

One might object that the above argument depends upon the claim that sole or ultimate dominion precludes determinism. Since a compatibilist need not be a determinist, the argument does not therefore meet the compatibilist head on. But the argument can be directed more specifically against compatibilists, if slightly rephrased. Compatibilists must be committed to the view that satisfaction of the condition of sole or ultimate dominion (which requires indeterminism) is irrelevant to one's conception (or conceptions) of freedom. Satisfaction of such a condition, for compatibilists, is either *unattainable* or *unimportant*. Libertarians, I am claiming, must reject both of these alternatives. The above argument is designed to show that sole or ultimate dominion is both attainable and important.

9.11 Theme (III): *Formation of Character and Motives*. The case for the importance of sole or ultimate dominion, with partial control, can be strengthened by focussing on another problem discussed in chapter 3—the problem of formation of character and motives. To explain how we can have "control over the springs of our own actions," libertarians who accept a theory such as mine need not assume we have some primordial control over our earliest formed character traits and motives in childhood, or that we form original character. They can admit that character traits and motives formed in childhood were not freely made by us and that original character and motives could not in principle be formed by us. Yet they may say that, as time goes by, we form and reform our character and motives by practical decision making, by undertaking novel value experiments, by making moral and prudential choices; and each of these may involve, or be influenced by, undetermined processes along the way, as described by the theory. In this way, we make our character and motives as we go along, and yet do so by constantly transcending, or "rising above," prior character and motives, as libertarians from Bramhall to Campbell say we must. Each step, involving free practical, moral, and prudential decision making, is a new beginning, undetermined by past character and motives. Yet it is consistent with past character and motives and can be explained in terms of the agent's rational will. The influence of past character and motives is "loose" in the sense that it allows for different pathways, each of which is rational in its own way.

These considerations allow us to broaden our conception of sole or ultimate dominion. We have been thinking of the agent's sole or ultimate dominion over a given choice in terms of the contribution made by the agent's effort of will to the choice itself. But *past* choices and efforts contribute as well, to the degree that they have influenced the formation of present character and motives. Keeping this in mind, and thinking along the lines of the previous paragraph, we can view the present character and motives of an agent at any given time as the cumulative effect of many free practical, moral, and prudential choices, each of which was an undetermined new beginning, and over each of which the agent had partial, but nevertheless sole or ultimate, dominion. In this respect the agent is partially, but ultimately, responsible, not only for the outcome of the present choice, but *for the character and motives* influencing that choice. Free agents can think of themselves as having gradually formed their characters and motives by a series of free choices (and consequent experiments in living) over which they had a limited, but nevertheless, ultimate control.

If I view my own past in this way, I can say that I was "making myself" by incremental steps. I struggled, made uncertain or *indeterminate* efforts of will, and took risks or *chances* all along the way. But the efforts were mine, the risks were mine, and the resulting character and motives were ultimately of my making. This ultimacy means that my present character and motives could not have been the result of another's control, nor could they have been explained by or predicted from knowledge of my original character and motives or any other facts about my past. If partial control at each step is the necessary price for this kind of cumulative influence over the formation of one's character and motives, libertarians may argue, then it is a price worth paying. In sum, sole or ultimate dominion with partial control looks more attractive when we view its cumulative effects in the life histories of free agents.

9.12 Theme (IV): *Resentment and Gratitude.* This theme is a continuation of themes (II) and (III). Incompatibilists, including Bramhall, have often argued that a certain class of emotions and attitudes directed at the choices or actions of persons, including gratitude, resentment, admiration, and regret, would be inappropriate, if we believed the choices or actions prompting them were determined. This theme has been the subject of some recent discussions about freedom.[15] It is a subtle theme, not easily argued on either side because the relevant terms, like "gratitude" and "resentment," are vague in ways that parallel the vagueness of terms like "power" and "responsibility." But I think there are meanings of these emotion terms associated with incompatibilist notions of ultimate dominion and responsibility; and the burden of proof ought to be on compatibilists to show why these (incompatibilist) meanings are inappropriate.

The following example concerns resentment and is suggested by a recent trial in our city of a nineteen year old boy who had raped and murdered a sixteen year old girl. The girl's father attended the trial on a daily basis and his presence gave rise to the example. I imagine myself to be the father of a murdered girl attending such a trial. I am filled with a great deal of anger and resentment directed at the boy. But as I sit in the courtroom listening to the testimony about the boy's past, a surprising thing happens. My resentment against the boy decreases as I learn more about the environmental factors influencing his character and motives. He is a mean and calculating young man, to be sure, and there is no doubt in my mind that the rape and murder were premeditated. He planned it carefully in order to increase his influence over the members of his gang by showing that he was capable of a fearless and ruthless act. The motivations were perverse to me, but, in his own narrow world, they had a rationale. What decreases my resentment, however, is the story of how he came to have the mean character and perverse motives he did have, a story of poverty, parental neglect, bad role models, and so on.

To the extent that I come to believe the young man's character and motives were determined by his heredity and environment, my resentment against him as a responsible individual decreases. At first, my feelings are directed toward the parents, then toward the society which created such a cultural environment. But if I believe the characters and motives of everyone involved were determined, these feelings might shift to God, or the universe, or Fate. Now, it will be argued that anger and resentment can be transferred to the parents, or to God, because these emotions are person directed emotions. But they cannot be transferred to non-personal objects like the universe or Fate. This may be true, but it does not affect the main point. If my resentment cannot be transferred to some other persons, then it will be *transformed* into something else, call it bitterness, sadness, frustration, or a combination of these and other feelings or emotions. The main point is that the resentment I initially had toward the young man when I first entered the courtroom is now being directed *away from* him as an individual toward other things, and may be undergoing transformation into other emotions in the process.

I do not want to say that this "transformation of my resentment" comes about easily. I would resist it all along, wanting to hold onto my original assumption that he was ultimately responsible for the act in a sense that presupposes sole or ultimate dominion. But determination, whether by the actions of other intelligent causes, or by non-intelligent causes, is incompatible with this kind of ultimate responsibility. So the belief that his character and motives were determined by something other than his own will must erode this original conviction.

Compatibilists must argue that such a transformation of my resentment to something else and into something else is either unjustified or is based on something other than evidence of mere determination. If there is no evidence of CNC control, then there must be evidence of coercion, compulsion, or some other form of constraint to justify the transformation. But the young man's choices and actions were not coerced in any ordinary sense of the term. He never chose or acted in this matter against his will. Nor did he act under threat of coercion. The only operative threat of coercion opposed the action. He took great care to perform the act where there would be no witnesses and little chance of apprehension.

Compulsion is the most subtle form of constraint, and the most difficult to detect. It is possible that the young man acted compulsively and I did not know it. But the point is that I do not have to *believe* he acted compulsively or under any other form of constraint in order to justify the transformation of my resentment. His action was compulsive, according to the account of 3.8, if he acted on some desire or motive that he would not have resisted acting on, even if he had wanted to resist acting on it. And I do not have to believe *this* of any of the desires or motives he acted on, in order to have a justification for the transformation of my resentment.

My resentment can justifiably be transformed to something else and into something else simply if I believe he was not ultimately responsible for *not wanting* to resist acting on any of the desires he acted upon. And this ultimate responsibility, which presupposes sole or ultimate dominion, is lacking if his character, motives, choices, and actions are determined.

By contrast, my resentment may be mitigated, but will not be transformed, if I view the life history of the young man in the manner of the previous section. The mean character and perverse motives that led to his act were not determined by heredity and environment. They were brought about by free choices in practical, moral, and prudential contexts that satisfied the condition of sole or ultimate dominion. Each of these choices was a new beginning, influenced by past character and motives but not determined by past character and motives. He did not create his original character and motives, but he was constantly reforming them, "rising above" them, by decision making whose outcomes could not be imputed wholly to other persons or to circumstances wholly beyond his control.

To say these things coherently, I must assume that his own control and responsibility were partial. They were partial in two senses. First, his heredity and environment surely limited his options to some degree, though the options were not limited or "determined to one." Libertarians can recognize and accommodate mitigating circumstances of this sort in their theory. But, given my theory, they at least have the means for explaining how persons can be said to be partially but ultimately responsible for their present character, motives and choices.

Second, these free choices involve partial control and responsibility in another sense. Since the agent's effort is indeterminate, the outcome is not determined and is not completely within the control of the agent's rational will. This second limitation, as I see it, is an inherent feature of all genuinely free choices on the libertarian view. One might say that the human condition (of free beings) on this view is a mitigating circumstance. Recognizing this, libertarians ought to be ready to recognize mitigating circumstances of other kinds. I said in chapter 8 that a just God who made a libertarian universe would be merciful; and we should be no less merciful. But we should not be so merciful that we absolve all persons at all times from ultimate responsibility because they have no ultimate dominion. What the libertarian wants is mercy with *respect*, the respect that comes from having ultimate, albeit partial, dominion over the creation of one's own ends. Wiggins (73) says something that is relevant in this connection: "Perhaps it is the most distinctive mark of the rational man that he falls into barbarism if he takes the notion of autonomous agency, whether mythical or not, either too seriously or too lightly" (p. 56).

In sum, there is a sense of ultimate responsibility for present character, motives, and choice that will support incompatibilist senses of resentment, gratitude, admiration, and regret. This sense of responsibility presupposes sole or ultimate dominion, which in turn is incompatible with determination. If I come to believe, as I did in the courtroom, that a person's character, motives, choices, and actions were determined, these emotions will be transferred to something else and/or transformed into something else.

9.13 Theme (V): *The Reactive Attitude*.[16] One takes a reactive attitude toward other persons when one reacts to their actions without knowing or attempting to know in advance how they will act and without controlling or attempting to control their behavior, coercively or non-coercively. The reactive attitude is opposed to coercive, manipulative, and predictive attitudes toward the behavior of others. Taking the reactive attitude, one waits to see how persons will act on their own rather than trying to coerce certain responses from them, or to manipulate them (i.e. to exercise covert non-constraining control), or to predict with certainty how they will act before they do act.

The reactive attitude is associated with an attitude of respect for other persons as autonomous agents. Most persons, compatibilists included, would agree that coercively controlling, or attempting to coercively control, others is not acting in accordance with such an attitude of respect. Libertarians agree, of course, but they are typically more concerned with the manipulative and predictive attitudes toward the behavior of others. They want to affirm of themselves (and others) a freedom of will such that manipulative and predictive attitudes toward their free choices by other persons would be inappropriate *in principle*. They want this to be true as a consequence of features intrinsic to their free choices and their powers as free agents, rather than merely as consequences of the limitations of the others (e.g. how intelligent those others are or how much they know).

Just as one gets little debate about whether constraining control is opposed to an attitude of respect for others as autonomous agents, one gets little debate about whether the *manipulative* attitude (CNC controlling or attempting to CNC control others) is opposed to such an attitude of respect. Only the hard compatibilists, like Hobbes and Edwards, would demur. It is the *predictive* attitude that raises the central issue here, an issue related to the move from proposition (3) in chapter 3 (about CNC control) to proposition (4) (about mere determination). Why is the predictive attitude toward the behavior of others—knowing or attempting to know in advance how they will choose and act, rather than merely reacting to their choices and actions after these choices and actions have been made—opposed to an attitude of respect for others as autonomous agents, *if* the predictive attitude is not accompanied by attempts to manipulate or coerce? This is a central question in the compatibility debate, and I think that libertarians must answer it in the following way: to take the predictive attitude toward a person is to treat that person as a *type*, subsuming his or her behavior under general laws, rather than treating the person as a unique individual.[17]

This uniqueness, or "individuality" in an honorific sense, is something libertarians have always cherished, though they have often described it improperly. Many have regarded it as inconsistent with the subsumption of their own behavior or the behavior of other free agents under *any* general laws whatever, whether physical, physiological or psychological, whether deterministic or statistical. (This is undoubtedly one motivation for postulating transempirical egos, noumenal selves, and other such agents outside the order of natural laws.) But the uniqueness in question is consistent with the assumption that the behavior of free persons is part of nature, subject to physical and physiological laws, as long as those laws allow some room for chance in nature, as do quantum laws, and the chance can be amplified in appropriate ways. The uniqueness in question is also consistent with statistical psychological and social laws which do not allow prediction in the particular case. In other words, the uniqueness in question can be realized by creatures in the natural order *if* the indeterminist condition is satisfied. Moreover, it can only be realized by creatures *in* the natural order if the indeterminist condition is satisfied. For only then would manipulative and predictive attitudes toward the behavior of persons be inappropriate in principle. *Satisfaction of the indeterminist condition is a device for thwarting manipulative and predictive intentions toward one's behavior in principle*. It is a screen placed between ourselves and others to enforce the injunctions: "Do not *manipulate* me" and "Do not *type* me." "Pay attention to *me* rather than to your physiological and psychological formulae, your machine programs, your laws of nature, because I will surprise you, no matter how comprehensive your knowledge is," "Look at me and wait to see what I am going to do; then react accordingly."

Persons with libertarian intuitions are obviously troubled by the deterministic presuppositions and implications of psychological, historical, and social scientific research. Sir Isaiah Berlin's controversial essay "Historical Inevitability" (69), referred to in chapter 1, is a clear expression of libertarian fears in this regard. Such fears are often misunderstood by the psychologists, historians, and other social scientists at whom they are directed. These students of human affairs insist that they have no desire to use their knowledge to coerce or manipulate others. They merely want to know how and why humans behave as they do. And it may turn out that the knowledge they gain can greatly benefit humanity, if and when persons voluntarily make use of it.

While there is merit in this response, what is missing in it is the realization that a predictive attitude toward the behavior of others *supported by deterministic presuppositions* is itself demeaning to persons who want others to take a reactive attitude toward them, even if the predictors foreswear any intent to coerce or manipulate. Libertarians are claiming that most humans want to possess a uniqueness that would make it impossible for others to treat them as types, subsuming all of their behavior under deterministic laws. There is nothing wrong with psychological, historical, and social research, therefore, as long as it is consistent with this assumption, i.e. as long as it is not supported by deterministic presuppositions.

9.14 Theme (VI): *Openness, Creativity, and Causal Chains*. The reactive attitude, like the other themes after (I), is an elaboration of the theme of sole or ultimate dominion. Whereas (II) and (III) focus on the ultimate responsibility of free agents for their choices and the formation of their character and motives, (IV) and (V) focus on the responses *other* persons must make to agents possessing such responsibility. This final theme is a set of further variations on both these self- and other-regarding perspectives.

In a contemporary symposium on freedom and determinism, William Barrett (58) makes the following point. Critics of indeterminist theories of freedom, he says, often omit "one of the main motives in the rebellion against determinism, not only on the part of ordinary people but also of those modern philosophers who have been most vigorously opposed to the determinist position: namely, the desire for freshness, novelty, genuine creation—in short, an open rather than a closed universe" (p. 46). Such assertions can easily lead to fruitless debate in which compatibilists and incompatibilists talk at cross purposes. Compatibilists will insist that novelty and genuine creation are not incompatible with a determined universe. The first use of the steam engine or explosion of an atomic bomb would be novel events in a determined universe, in the ordinary sense that events of these kinds had never occurred before. Newton and Einstein would be creators in a determined universe in the ordinary sense that they created new theories previously unknown. Clearly, persons like Barrett have something else in mind when they talk about "genuine" novelty and creation; and what they have in mind is, of course, "undetermined" novelty and creation. But then their statements merely inform us that many persons prefer an open or non-deterministic universe, without telling us why.

Though the appeal of statements like Barrett's is elusive, I think it can be understood if related to sole or ultimate dominion and the reactive attitude. William James strikes a similar note in a passage near the end of "The Dilemma of Determinism." "The great point" in the libertarian view, he says, "is that the possibilities are really *here*." "At those soul-trying moments when fate's scales seem to quiver," we acknowledge "that the issue is decided nowhere else that *here* and *now*. *That* is what gives the palpitating reality to our moral life and makes it tingle, as Mr. Mallock says, with so strange and elaborate an excitement" (56, p. 183). It is easy to ridicule James' assertion that a "zest" or "excitement" would be taken out of choice situations if we knew that their outcomes were determined, though many ordinary persons and some philosophers, like myself, would agree that it is true. Behind such assertions, however, lies the connection with ultimate dominion and the reactive attitude. The undetermined character of my choice is a necessary condition for my having ultimate (though partial) responsibility for the outcome; and this gives a significance to the present moment and my present effort of will they would not have if I did not have such an ultimate responsibility. Similarly, others cannot take either a manipulative or predictive attitude toward the outcome. They cannot know it until the moment of choice arrives; and this also gives added significance to the moment of choice. James pictures the whole universe "waiting to see" which of several open pathways will be taken at this moment as a result of my effort—a fanciful picture to be sure, but one that captures the intuitive appeal of the reactive attitude. My point is that statements like those of Barrett and James *do* have appeal, but the appeal is inseparable from the appeal of sole or ultimate dominion, the reactive attitude, and associated beliefs about ultimate responsibility and individual uniqueness.

Similar remarks apply to Barrett's comments about "creativity" or "genuine creation." Analogies between creative thinking and practical decision making were developed in chapter 6, with regard to the role of inspiration, the unconscious, receptivity, etc. Many persons would agree with Barrett that determinism undermines genuine creativity. For example, Popper says that determinism would "destroy . . .

the idea of creativity," reducing to "a complete illusion the idea" that the creative act produces "*something new*" (p. 222). Such statements require qualification, as we saw earlier. But there is a point underlying them. Why do many persons find it repugnant to think that the creative acts of themselves and others are determined? They want to believe they have ultimate dominion over such acts and ultimate responsibility over their products. And this desire is not diminished by the thought that creativity involves some uncontrolled elements of inspiration, luck, and chance. The woman who discovered a new theory in the example of 9.10 was willing to grant that her discovery was the result of hard work and some luck, while resisting the suggestion that it could be completely explained by causes outside herself. She could live with partial control, but not with the denial of ultimate control. She could live with the thought that the discovery might not be wholly her doing, but not with the thought that it could be explained as the inevitable result of states and changes over which she had no control.

The physicist Alfred Landé (58) compares two cosmological images that have relevance to the libertarian position regarding creativity and freedom. The image of classical statistical mechanics, according to Landé, is one in which the randomness in the universe "was set up *once*, a long or infinite time ago, and random distributions observed at present are but the deterministic effects of that one initial 'shuffling of the cards' " (p. 85). The other image, that of quantum mechanics, is one in which "mini-shufflings" and reshufflings of the cards are taking place at all times in the history of the universe at the level of microphysical processes. Each new shuffling is a new beginning in the sense that its outcome is not determined by earlier conditions of the universe, including the primordial "initial" conditions. To explain creativity and freedom, in their sense, libertarians must make use of this second image. Creative and free beings must somehow be able to take hold of these pockets of randomness occurring at the present time, amplifying them so that they "break through" to the macroscopic order, and making them serve the needs of creative problem solving and rational decision making. In this way, their creative and free acts will be new beginnings, explicable only in terms of their rational wills. This is not an unintelligible view, as the theory of this books shows, and there are reasons to believe that our intuitive ideas about ultimate responsibility for free and creative acts conform more closely to Landé's second cosmological model. He himself thinks they do.

The idea underlying this use of Landé's second model, and the idea underlying libertarian conceptions of sole or ultimate dominion, is the idea that some *causal chains*, when traced backwards in time, must *terminate in the creation of purposes by intelligent beings*. Therein lies the *ultimacy* of dominion and responsibility that libertarians want. Landé's "pockets of randomness" make such ultimacy possible (to a limited extent at least) for finite creatures who do not have the luxury of creating the universe and themselves *ab initio*. Libertarians who postulate non-occurrent causes to explain their view have a clear notion that this is what they are after. In a passage cited in 4.16, Richard Taylor expressed the assumption behind non-occurrent cause theories by saying that "some . . . causal chains . . . have beginnings and they begin with the agents themselves." The problem with non-occurrent cause theories is that they cannot explain these beginnings in terms of causes or reasons. In my theory, the beginnings can be explained by reasons, though they are not caused; and this is possible because of the existence of incommensurably good reasons for alternative pathways. What makes it all work, however, is the indeterminist condition. Any dominion that can be said to be ultimate must be a dominion whose exercise is undetermined.

9.15 Discussion of the six incompatibilist themes is now complete. All of them, after (I), have been elaborations of the theme of sole or ultimate dominion. This is as we should have expected from chapter 3. For chapter 3 suggests that the two main themes in the case for incompatibilism are CNC control and sole or ultimate dominion. The discussion of the latter in (II)-(VI) related it to ultimate (though partial) responsibility for choices (II), to the gradual formation of character and motives (III), to the implications of beliefs about ultimate responsibility for our emotional responses to others (IV), to the uniqueness of the individual which precludes in principle both manipulative and predictive attitudes by others (V), and to the desire to live in an open universe in which one's creations cannot be entirely explained by causes outside of oneself (VI).

The bottom line of all this is the respect due to individuals capable of creating their own purposes in ways that cannot be completely explained by causes outside of their rational wills. Or, to put it another way, the bottom line is the "dignity of the individual," the worthiness to be treated as an end because one is *the ultimate originator of one's own ends*.

Notes

1. For the elementary information that follows, I have relied on Eccles (53 and 70), C. Smith (72), and Rose (76).

2. First, in Eccles (53).

3. Meehl (58 and 78) and Thorp (80) take the Eccles suggestion seriously, though they deal with it in different ways.

4. It is possible to depart somewhat from the ideal of equiprobability or randomness, but it remains an ideal because it means maximal unpredictability and uncontrollability. Libertarians have been customarily embarrassed by the idea of randomness in choice, but according to the present theory randomness, which we associate with R-alternativeness, is precisely what is wanted. See 9.6 for more on this.

5. Cf. ch. 5 note 14; also 6.6 and 8.4.

6. Compton (35). MSA models are mentioned in this work.

7. This objection against Popper is also made by O'Connor (71, p. 96-7), who thinks that Popper's approach is otherwise promising.

8. Cf. Hofstadter (80, 710ff.).

9. See James (56).

10. E.g. Aquinas (45, Vol. I, *Summa Theologiae*, I, question 19, article 80; Bramhall (44, p. 157); Milton (36, pp. 927ff.).

11. Cf. Boethius (62), Aquinas (45, Vol. I, *Summa Theologiae*, I question 14, art. 13); Bramhall (44, p. 153).

12. Cf. Ockham (69); Rowe (78).

13. The timeless view of divine knowledge is criticized by Hartshorne (62), Kretzmann (66), and Pike (70).

14. This is true of any thinker putting forward such a doctrine who holds that divine fore*ordination* is incompatible with human freedom, but that divine fore*knowledge* and/or omniscience is compatible with human freedom.

15. Strawson (74); Honderich (73a); L. Davis (79, ch. 6).

16. The expression "reactive attitude" is Strawson's (74). But I am using it here in a distinctive way related to the discussion of chapter 3.

17. Honderich (73a, p. 211), also makes this point about types and uniqueness. He adds however that the uniqueness requirement would rule out subsumption of free behavior under statistical as well as deterministic laws. The libertarian cannot say this, I contend, without rendering his view unintelligible. (Honderich, not being a libertarian, has no worry on that score.)

Values, Relativity, Ethics, Politics

10.1 David Wiggins was quoted in chapter 1 as saying that "the free will dispute has reached a point where real progress depends . . . upon a more precise and . . . sympathetic examination of what the libertarian wants, of why he wants it and of how his conception of metaphysical freedom is connected with political and social freedom." We are going to deal with the connection to political and social freedom in this chapter by way of a discussion of the theory of values underlying the theory of freedom in chapters 5-8, and (beginning in 10.4) by way of a discussion of some contemporary social and political thinkers, including Berlin, Skinner, Dworkin, Rawls, Nozick, and others.

To review that theory of values, let us return to the analogy with physical theories of relativity introduced in chapters 5 and 7. The first half of this century saw both a relativistic revolution in the physical sciences and an abortive relativistic revolution in anthropology. Historical connections between the two revolutions were tenuous, though some thinkers thought they saw some conceptual connections.[1] Yet it is safe to say that attempts to draw analogies between physical theories of relativity and doctrines of value relativism were generally regarded as superficial at best, confusing and pernicious at worst. I do not think such analogies are superficial; and they are confusing and pernicious only if one fails to note the differences between physical and normative laws.

Theories of relativity in physics and doctrines of value relativism are alike in form, though concerned with different subject matter. The physical theories imply (I) that measurements of certain physical quantities may differ in different physical frames of reference of a certain class, and (II) that no one of these frames of reference is privileged or superior to any of the others in the sense that it gives the absolute, uniquely true or correct, measurement. Each frame provides a correct measurement from its perspective and the perspectives are equally valid. The value theories imply (I') that valuations (evaluative and normative propositions) whose truth is presupposed by different persons (societies, cultures) may differ, and (II') that no one person's (or group's) valuations are privileged or superior in the sense that they are absolute, or uniquely true, valuations. Each is correct from its perspective and the perspectives are equally valid.

The number and kinds of relativistic "frames of reference" can be limited in both physical and value theories. Einstein's Special Theory of Relativity limits the class of relativitic frames to inertial frames—those standing in a certain relation (moving with constant velocity relative) to one another. The moral theory of chapter 7 limits the class of relativistic frames to the reason sets of different persons (or cultures) standing in a certain relation—of mutual respect—to one another. Other frames are deviant and need not be treated equally. What marks off the relativistic (non-deviant) frames in the physical theory is the fact that the *laws of nature* are invariant, or have the same in form, in all of them. This is the respect in which they have equal validity. Corresponding to the invariant laws of nature in the physical theory, we have in the moral theory, an invariant *moral law*, or principle of equal respect, which is accepted in all non-deviant frames. In both cases the relativity and equal validity of frames is related to the invariance of laws. But in the physical theory, laws of nature are *true* in all non-deviant frames. In the moral case, the moral law is *accepted* in all non-deviant frames. This difference is connected with the fact that the relativistic frames in the moral case are the reason sets of beings possessing free choice.

10.2 Free choice is thereby related to the difference between physical and normative laws, which is associated with most of the significant differences between physical and value theories of relativity. Normative laws, including the moral law, can be *violated* by the actions of free beings in a way that has no parallel in the relation of physical objects to the laws of nature; and normative laws must be *accepted* if they are to have an influence upon the actions of such beings and on the world at large. This means that in the moral world there may be departures from "invariant" law. Some persons or groups may not accept the moral law as a guide to their actions, and others, who accept it, may sometimes violate it thorugh weakness of will. Thus the moral world is subject to imperfections that have no analogues in the physical world. Situations can arise in the moral world in which it is impossible in principle to treat every person with equal respect. (The assault and rape examples of 7.3 are cases in point.) Some value systems must then be treated unequally, and some frames as deviant. The result of this line of reasoning was the "potential relativism or pluralism qualified by moral principle" of chapter 7.

Such a restricted theory of value relativity seemed to pose a problem for the physical analogy; but in fact it did not. Limited physical theories of relativity, like Einstein's Special Theory, are deficient in generality. One seeks a more general theory that will remove the restrictions on non-deviant frames, those in which the laws of nature are invariant. Since relativity theories in physics are a by product of the search for invariance, the move to greater generality is to be expected. But a similar move in moral theory would produce the unrestricted value relativism of traditional relativists—presumably not a better, but a worse, moral theory than the qualified relativism of chapter 7.

The problem was dealt with in chapter 7 by noting that if we lived in an ideal world, or a "kingdom of ends" in which everyone was treating everyone else with equal respect, a General Theory of moral relativity would hold. The moral law would be accepted in all frames and none would be deviant. So a General Theory is also the ideal in moral theory and would be preferred to a Special Theory in an ideal world. But because of violations of the moral law that are possible for free beings, this is not an ideal moral world. There are situations in which the general injunction to treat all persons as ends and not means cannot in principle be followed. A limited or special theory is therefore required which "departs as little as possible" from the general principle in situations in which one must depart from it.

10.3 Thus, those twentiety-century relativists, like Benedict and Herskovits, who pleaded for tolerance, respect, and understanding toward all cultures had to assume an ideal world which did not exist. This is one reason why the relativistic revolution in anthropology during the first half of this century was abortive. Yet these relativists were saying something important, even about our non-ideal world, or so I contend. Suitably restricted, their idea of R-alternative value systems is necessary for understanding free will, the moral point of view, and some of our most important social and political ideals.

Could these relativists have come to accept the potential relativism qualified by moral principle of chapter 7? The answer is affirmative if three conditions had been satisfied. First, they would have had to see that their arguments did not satisfy an unrestricted value relativism, but the weaker doctrine of value empiricism defined by S31. What value relativism and value empiricism have in common is the belief that judgments of value must be justified *internally*, i.e. relative to, or from the perspective of, some value theory which is held by, or could be held by, some person or culture. The common element is the pragmatic-coherence theory or values discussed in 7.12-13. But such a view does not of itself imply that certain value systems could not be superior or inferior to others in the long run for some persons or groups, or even for all persons or groups. We cannot have certainty about the superiority or inferiority of value systems, but we are free to formulate more or less plausible judgments about their comparative merits on inductive grounds. And some of these judgments may be justified by experiment in the long run. Thus the limitation imposed by the value empiricist view does not imply total scepticism, or nihilism, or unrestricted relativism.

Second, having opened this door, these relativists would have had to accept one, or a combination, of the reasons for taking the moral point of view in 7.15-17. One can guess that twentiety-century relativists like Benedict and Herskovits would have satisfied this condition. For they argued that if all persons would learn to understand others (persons and cultures) as these others understand themselves, and practice tolerance toward them, this would be a better world to live in for all.[2]

Third, being sufficiently motivated to take the moral point of view and actually to treat others' value systems as R-alternatives to their own, these relativists would have had to realize that the injunction to so treat the reason sets of all others cannot be followed in every situation in an imperfect world. Then, reasoning as we did in 7.4-5, they would have come to the principle of equal respect (S28) and the limited relativism qualified by moral principle of S30. In this manner, they could, at least theoretically, have kept the Hitlers and Stalins at bay.

Now it is my contention that the failure of relativists to satisfy the first and third of these conditions was due simply to philosophical error or oversight. Thus, only an absence of motivating reasons (this-worldly or transcendent) to practice the qualified tolerance their view suggested would have justified their not accepting the potential relativism qualified by moral principle of chapter 7.

In the Introduction, I said that many persons become relativists by default, because of a failure to find convincing arguments for any particular objective or absolute standards of value (i.e. standards that are not internal to the value system of some actual or potential person or group). Their position was said to be like that of the physicists at the beginning of this century who, after numerous disappointing attempts to establish the existence of an ether, decided that the more reasonable course of action was to endorse some theory of motion that did not assume the existence of an ether. (The theory these physicists eventually endorsed was, of course, Einstein's Special Theory of Relativity.)

Similarly, after numerous disappointing attempts to find an objective standpoint from which to make value judgments, relativists make an abductive leap and postulate that all judgments of value must be internal to some non-unique system of values. This gets them, however, only to value empiricism, not to an unrestricted value relativism as they may mistakenly suppose. Moreover, it is an abductive leap, beyond the evidence, but one that can be justified on a provisional basis until someone shows them how value judgments may be justified from some objective perspective. Similarly, as argued in 7.13, the fact empiricist view is a response to failure to find synthetic *a priori* factual truths and may be held until someone shows how such truths can be found. Value empiricism, the kernal of truth in relativism, is recommended by the same sorts of arguments in the practical sphere as fact empiricism in the theoretical sphere.[3]

It is with all this in mind that I said in the Introduction that "relativism is partly true and partly false, true with certain qualifications, false otherwise. Postulating its qualified truth [provisionally] is not a prelude to moral anarchy, but a first step toward moral insight."

10.4 If the doctrine of free will requires a value theory of the kind just described, then it has obvious implications concerning social and political freedom. We are now going to consider these implications by way of a discussion of some contemporary social and political thinkers whose works are widely read. The first of these is a figure quoted on the side of the libertarian view in chapter 1, Sir Isaiah Berlin.

In two influential lectures on history and politics given in the 1950s,[4] Berlin deals with the two central themes of this book, free will and the relativity of values, tying them together, though not quite as closely as I have done. In his Comte lecture, "Historical Inevitability," he defends a libertarian conception of free will against the tendencies of historians, political theorists, and other students of the sciences of man to interpret human affairs deterministically. In the Inaugural Lecture at Oxford, "Two Concepts of Political Liberty," he invokes a second theme of "value pluralism" in opposition to utopian and totalitarian political ideals. "Pluralism," he says, "seems to me a truer and more human ideal . . . because it does, at least, recognize the fact that human goals are many, not all of them commensurable and in perpetual rivalry with one another" (p. 171). Berlin invokes this pluralist ideal against authoritarian and utopian thinkers who prefer to believe they have found the ideal scheme of values and have the right to impose it on others. These thinkers, he argues, systematically ignore the fact that the legitimate "ends of men are many, and not all of them are in principle compatible with one another" (p. 169).

Berlin's value pluralism is close to the potential relativism qualified by moral principle that has just been described as the value theory of chapters 5-8. And the anti-authoritarian, anti-utopian implications of such a theory are among its most important implications. These implications were first noted in chapter 5 when we were discussing value experimentation and the Many Goods principle. Now it is true that Berlin is very critical in his lectures of relativist theories of values (as well as of deterministic and utopian theories of man). But what he fears in relativist views is what any sane person would fear, the implication that the totalitarian views of a Hitler or Stalin or their ilk must be regarded as equally valid, no better nor worse, then other views of the good life and other social and political ideals.

Such a fear is not justified by the present theory. On the contrary, as argued in chapter 7, the relativist ideal itself imposes definite restrictions on the tolerance and respect due other value systems in an imperfect world. Berlin's pluralism assumes such restrictions, but he does not spell them out or derive them in a systematic way from his assumptions. By contrast, the argument of chapter 7 showed how one can get the restrictions Berlin and other pluralists seem to require (excluding the Hitlers, Stalins, aggressors, rapists, thieves, and the like) by trying to depart as little as possible from the ideal of respect for persons, when you must do so.

At the same time, Berlin fails to say that the value pluralism he advocates is relativistic in a qualified sense. For, once the deviant frames are excluded, the remaining ones are to be treated as incommensurably good, no one intrinsically superior or inferior to others. In short, they are to be treated as *R-alternatives* in our sense. No doubt, Berlin wants to keep his distance from the term "relativism," tainted as it is in the minds of most persons. But if one wants to understand the intellectual currents of the twentieth century, one does well to note the connections between (i) pluralist theories of value, of the kind advocated by Berlin and other modern thinkers, (ii) doctrines of value relativism and (iii) theories of relativity in physics. That is why I have spoken of a potential "relativism" qualified by moral principle, despite the tainted associations of the term "relativism." "Pluralism" is also an accurate description, but it does not reveal the conceptual roots of such a theory, or suggest its historical connections. It is important to make clear that value pluralists like Berlin are advocating the same attitude of tolerance and respect toward persons and cultures as certain relativists like Benedict advocated toward all, and that *this attitude is rooted in the relation of relativity to invariant law.*

10.5 While the notions of free will and value pluralism are central to many of Berlin's philosophical writings, in the two lectures mentioned he invokes them separately against different targets, free will against determinist views in history and social science, on the one hand, and value pluralism against utopian and totalitarian social views, on the other. He recognizes a connection between the two (free will and pluralism), but I think, if anything, he underestimates the importance of the connection. For in a later work, commenting on his two earlier lectures, he concedes that there is a problem involving his (libertarian) conception of free will that remains unsolved.

The notion of an uncaused choice as something out of the blue is certainly not satisfactory. But (I need not argue this again), the only alternative permitted by [determinists]—a caused choice held to entail responsibility, desert, etc.—is equally untenable. This dilemma has now divided thinkers for more than two thousand years. . . . It may be that it stems, at least in part, from the use of a mechanical model applied to human actions; in one case, choices are conceived as links in a kind of causal sequence . . . in the other, as a break in the sequence. . .

Neither image seems to fit the case at all well. We seem to need a new model, a schema that will rescue the evidence . . . from the beds of Procrustes provided by the obsessive frameworks of the traditional discussions. All efforts to break away from the old obstructive analogies . . . have so far proved abortive (p. xxxvi).

It is clear that I have tried to provide a schema that would do what Berlin thinks is required to resolve this age-old dilemma. What is interesting, however, is the way in which this schema makes use of that other central idea of irreducible value pluralism which Berlin invokes against utopian and totalitarian social schemes in his Inaugural Lecture. The idea of value pluralism, or qualified value relativism, is just what is needed by a libertarian account of free will, if such an account is to escape the Hobbesian charges of confusion and emptiness.

Aside from its intrinsic interest, this result sheds light on some other themes in Berlin's lectures. For example, he suggests that the desire for "positive" political liberty (the desire to be master of one's own decisions and purposes) has often been perverted in history into authoritative and totalitarian justifications for repression (69, pp. 131ff.). Now if we make the reasonable assumption that Berlin's conception of positive political liberty presupposes a libertarian conception of free will, then we can make the argument against such perversions of positive liberty even stronger than he makes it. For it turns out that free will, correctly conceived (without confusion or emptiness), and hence positive political liberty also, *presupposes* the very idea that is opposed to authoritarian and totalitarian political schemes, namely, the idea that there is no one single conception of the good life, but instead, many incommensurably good alternatives. Thus, the libertarian idea of free will would be opposed to authoritarian and totalitarian political schemes by virtue of its conceptual foundations. To oppose Hobbes' compatibilist view of freedom (as Bramhall does) would be *ipso facto* to oppose Hobbes' totalitarian political views (as Bramhall also does).[5]

But such a result follows in this way only if the libertarian idea espoused is that of chapters 5-8. If, in order to secure the libertarian position on free will, one appeals instead to obscure or mysterious forms of agency such as those discussed in chapter 4, the anti-totalitarian result will not automatically follow. In fact, the authoritarian and totalitarian perversions of positive liberty that Berlin opposes generally appeal to obscure conceptions of agency.[6] Fortunately, appeals to mysterious forms of agency to secure the libertarian position can be rejected on other grounds. They are empty of explanatory content, as we argued, and therefore do not escape the Hobbesian charge of confusion or emptiness.

10.6 Berlin's anti-utopian and anti-authoritarian themes deserve further treatment, and there could be no better medium for providing it than discussion of the views of a modern utopian also mentioned in Part I, namely, B. F. Skinner.[7] I said in 3.5 that Skinner is the kind of figure libertarians would have had to invent if he did not already exist. For he advocates as social policy the very thing they most oppose, namely covert non-constraining control of the wills of other agents. To be sure, Skinner advocates behavioral engineering of the wants and purposes of human agents for their own good, so they will be able to have and do whatever they want and choose. If we have an effective science of human behavior at our disposal, he argues, it would be foolish not to use it to make men happy, to bring about the good life for all.[8]

Skinner is probably overly optimistic about the present and future possibilities for behavioral engineering. But that is not the most serious problem with his proposals. What is the good life and who shall decide what the good life is for human beings? These are the questions that bedevil his and all similar utopian projects. His behavioral engineering is a technology that may provide a means to an end, but it does not tell us what the end should be.

Skinner has not failed to address these questions about ends and the good life, and has done so most clearly in his fictional work *Walden Two* (62), in which an ideal social order is described in some detail. The answer he gives in that work is quite revealing for our purposes. At a certain point in the work, Frazier, the fictional founder of Walden Two, is expounding on the value scheme that informs the work. In response to questions of the philosopher Castle, he summarizes his vision of the good life in the following five points (p. 159). The good life consists, first, in physical and psychological health, second, in an absolute minimum of unpleasant labor, third, in a chance to exercise talents and abilities, fourth, in intimate and satisfying personal contacts, and fifth, in relaxation and rest. He then adds: "And that's it, Mr. Castle—absolutely all. I can't give you a rational justification for any of it. I can't reduce it to any principle of 'the greatest good.' This is the Good Life. We know it. It's a fact, not a theory. It has an experimental justification, not a rational one" (p. 161). "The "experimental justification" Frazier speaks of is just the community of Walden Two itself which, as he never tires of telling his guests, actually works. As for Skinner, he has never deviated far from this account of the good life in other works. Throughout his writings, he stresses the evolutionary values of health and survival in the design of cultures, and views the other values listed by Frazier as contributing to health, and ultimately to survival.[9]

Now Frazier has *not* defined the good life for his audience. I say this, not because his guests, or some other human beings, might disagree with his list of values or order them differently. There is a problem, even if we assume for the sake of argument that most or all human beings would agree that Frazier's five values are ingredients in any good life. The problem is that the values, as described, do not define a particular life or way of life at all. They are too general. They could be satisfied in an indefinite number of ways, by different cultural arrangements, that might compete and conflict with one another if they existed in the same, or a proximate, environment. When we become more concrete about the actual ways in which these values will be realized, say in a particular society like Walden Two, then the possibilities for disagreement increase. It becomes possible for someone to say "I can think of other ways in which these general values can be realized, some of which suit my temperament, interests, and abilities better. And I would like to try one of these other ways."

10.7 To put the matter concretely, consider a young man growing up in Walden Two who is particularly imaginative and creative. (Life in Walden Two inspires such traits, we are told.) He frequents the Walden Two library, reads a great deal about history and other cultures, sees films, etc. (Reading, lifelong study and pursuit of the arts is encouraged in Walden Two, we are also told, and there is time for it because of the abundant leisure.) Well, our young man is intrigued by some of the things he reads. He wants to explore the world and engage in adventurous and sometimes dangerous journeys; and he wants to do this, not just occasionally, but as a way of life. Or, to take an extreme contrast, he is intrigued by his study of Buddhism, and becomes obsessed with the idea of reaching Nirvana in a community of persons pursuing the eight-fold way. He wishes to join such a community or perhaps found one, if he can persuade like-minded persons to join him. Parents are regretfully aware that imaginative young persons sometimes get these "crazy" ideas, even in the "best" of home environments. You might say it could not happen in Walden Two, because the behavioral engineering would prevent its happening. But we shall return to that possibility in a moment.

Meanwhile, let us suppose for the sake of argument, that this particularly creative young man, an alpha plus, slips through the engineer's net and does get such ideas. Suppose further that he cannot pursue his goals in the community and chooses to leave. What could the members of Walden Two say to dissuade him? They might try to persuade him that, after all, Walden Two provides the best and most satisfying way of life. But he might reply: "I agree that Walden Two provides a good life. I have been reasonably happy here. It may even be the best way of life for you and for me. But I, for one, do not know that it is the best way of life for me. And how can I tell if I haven't tried any other ways of life?" Now such a reply places Frazier and Skinner in a difficult position because, on their view, finding the good life is an experimental matter. And the curious fact about value experiments emphasized in chapters 5 and 7 is that the success of a value experiment does not show that you have found the (one and only) good life, even for yourself; it proves only that you have found *a* good life for you. To refute Skinner and other utopians who want to impose their ideal on all, one does not have to prove their ideal is bad; one merely has to show it is not the *only* good.

The general problem illustrated by the example is that, while Skinner emphasizes experimentation with values throughout his works, he does not take it seriously enough to investigate both its similarities to and its differences from scientific experimentation. (Cf. 5.11-12.) The young man's challenge brings out some of the issues. Have Frazier and Skinner actually tested the Buddhist eight-fold way by experiment? Do they have sufficient evidence from the experiments of others to say that Nirvana is not a worthy goal, or is not in principle attainable? How then can they say authoritatively that the Walden Two way is better for the young man? And how can they say it is better for all persons? Undoubtedly Skinner is sceptical about traditional religions. Perhaps he thinks they lead to psychological ill health and thwart human talents. History tells us that many persons have been harmed by excessive religious convictions. But have all religions been bad for all persons? Would they be harmful to all future persons? Might there be new religions that would not be harmful? Suppose the young man had announced that he was going to found a new religion rather than follow the Buddhist eight-fold way. How would Frazier or Skinner know in advance of experimentation that it would not make the young man happy? They might have suspicions based on past experience. But to claim to know such things in advance is to take an anti-experimental, anti-scientific, authoritarian attitude. Why take such an attitude toward value theories when you do not take it toward factual theories? If you are a fact empiricist, why not be a value empiricist as well?

We can now return to the objection that no young man would get such ideas in Walden Two because the behavioral engineering would prevent its happening. If the childhood conditioning advocated by Skinner were successful, presumably the young man would never be tempted to pursue an alternative lifestyle. This presents a dilemma for Walden Two. Either so condition all persons, including the young, that they lack curiosity and creativity of the kind the young man manifested, or limit the kinds of books and films available to them in the Walden Two libraries. Frazier and Skinner would undoubtedly reject the second (censorship) alternative as being coercive. But, on either alternative, the founders of Walden Two would be choosing a way of life and imposing it on all the members. On the first alternative, they would merely be choosing a different means to attain a similar end, engaging in covert non-constraining control of the wills of others, rather than allowing those others to design their own ways of life. And the justification for doing so would be that they have discovered *the* good life. If one has discovered the good life, then why not bring it about that people live it? But our argument shows that there can be no such justification for controlling others. For the good is to be found by experiment and by experiment one cannot definitely discover *the* good life. The story of the imaginative young man is therefore unfair to Skinner, but only because Skinner's program is unfair to the young man. The program is based on a false premise about what the good is for him or any other person.

It is now evident that the anti-utopian and anti-authoritarian implications of the theory of chapters 5-8 flow from the empirical or experimental conception of values, called "value empiricism" in S31—a conception presupposed by our libertarian conception of free will. Skinner's failure to extend his empiricist attitude with sufficient care to value theories is a stunning oversight, though he is surely not the only scientifically inspired utopian guilty of this oversight. And the oversight is connected with his rejection of free will.

10.8 These remarks, first on Berlin, then on Skinner, lead naturally to current debates in political philosophy. Something like the value theory of chapters 5-8, pluralist on the one hand, empiricist on the other, seems to lie behind some recent attempts by political philosophers to rethink the foundations of classical liberalism. A case in point is an essay by Ronald Dworkin (78) in which he asks whether there is a core belief, or set of beliefs, distinguishing liberal from other political philosophies. After dismissing some common answers, Dworkin settles on an answer framed in terms of the following distinction between two theories of political equality.

> The first theory of equality supposes that political decisions must be, so far as possible, independent of any particular conception of the good life, or of what gives value to life. Since the citizens of a society differ in their conceptions, the government does not treat them as equals if it prefers one conception to another, either because the officials believe that one is intrinsically superior, or because one is held by the more numerous or more powerful group. The second theory argues, on the contrary, that the content of equal treatment cannot be independent of some theory of the good for man or the good life because treating a person as an equal means treating him in the way the good and wise person would wish to be treated (p. 127).

Dworkin argues that the first theory of equality is the distinguishing feature of political philosophies adhering to the classical liberal ideal of minimal government intrusion into the decision making of individual citizens (p. 127). If this is so—and it is certainly a plausible claim in the light of Dworkin's arguments and those of other recent writers (Berlin included)[10]—then there is a connection between the classical liberal ideal and the value theory we have been discussing. For a philosophical foundation for Dworkin's first theory of political equality can be found, I believe, in a pluralist and empiricist theory of values like that of chapters 5-8. If there is a plurality of incommensurably good ways of life, and if the superiority and inferiority of these ways of life for particular persons or groups must be established by experiments in living, then a government that imposes an official version, or versions, of the good life on all would be in the same position as the leaders of Walden Two when faced with a person who wished to try a non-official way. Theoretically, there could be no adequate justification for imposing an official way on all, even if it was a good way of life for some or many. In practice, an official way would be one thought to be superior, or simply favored, by the more numerous, the more influential, or the more powerful group.

This conclusion has an interesting corollary. It supplies at least a general answer to Wiggins' question about the implications of the libertarian conception of metaphysical freedom for political and social freedom: libertarian metaphysical freedom and liberal political freedom have their roots in the same theory of values. The theory of values presupposed by a libertarian theory of free will provides theoretical foundations for classical liberal ideals of freedom and equality. Such a result is not entirely unexpected. Some humanists assumed a connection between a libertarian view of freedom and the tolerant attitude of liberal political thought.[11] The result is remarkable for the way in which the elaborated theory supports this intuition.

Nevertheless, the implication is one way. The metaphysical theory of freedom implies the political one and not the other way around. It is conceivable, in the first place, that liberal political views might be grounded on theories of value (e.g. utilitarian) other than that of chapters 5-8, though I do not think they would be as well grounded.[12] In the second place, the pluralist and empiricist theory of values of chapters 5-8 might be held independently of a libertarian theory of freedom. The theory of free will in chapters 5-8 implies the theory of values, but the converse does not hold. I wish this were not so, for then another argument for the libertarian theory would be available (one directed at those who hold the value theory). But philosophical reasoning does not always support wishful thinking. The case for the libertarian view of free will must rest on the arguments of chapter 9 regarding CNC control, sole or ultimate dominion and responsibility, the reactive attitude, uniqueness of the individual, and so on. Yet these arguments are connected to matters of political and social freedom. The arguments of chapter 9 may be viewed as attempts to provide metaphysical grounds for the respect due to individual value experiments from governments as well as from other individuals. Our political and social freedoms, from a libertarian perspective, are supported by a cosmic vision of ourselves as beings with ultimate dominion and responsibility. In religious terms, political and social freedoms are an extension of the gift of freedom from divine sovereignty, which God can give to creatures only by placing them in a certain kind of (undetermined) universe. This is Bramhall's view and it is connected with his rejection of Hobbes' view of political sovereignty.[13]

10.9 It should be added that the value theory of chapters 5-8 does not support Dworkin's first theory of political equality without qualifications. The qualifications come from the principle of equal respect (S28). (They would therefore be qualifications Dworkin would be likely to accept, since he endorses a similar principle of "equal concern and respect" for all.) A government or state cannot treat *all* conceptions of the good life as equal, in the sense of not preferring one to another in every situation. The attempt to do so would be thwarted by the same impossible situations that arise for individuals when the moral sphere has broken down. When one person or group is treating another as a means rather than as an end, it is not possible in principle for third parties to treat both as ends. The reasoning of chapter 7 showed why, on the basis of the ideal of equal respect itself, the guilty party must be restrained, though with minimal force necessary to restore the moral sphere. Police, courts, and other instruments of law enforcement are therefore necessary to protect individuals from moral sphere breakdown within the society, and military force to protect against aggression from without. The result of this qualification to the principle of equal respect would be, *at least*, a night-watchman or minimal state of the kind favored by political libertarians like Nozick.[14]

But there is more to the principle of equal respect than the qualifications about one or more persons treating others as means. There are also the qualifications concerning conflicts of interest. As we saw, the ideal result in conflict of interest situations is a bargained compromise in which all parties agree and none is cheated or manipulated. But there are impediments to the realization of this ideal, even in situations involving only a few persons—impediments involving the good will of others, knowledge of other minds and the incommensurability of values. In the example of a dispute between husband and wife in 7.7, the problem was to determine whether a night out with friends was more important to him than his completing a chore was to her. The assessments were made in terms of standards internal to their respective value systems and their priorities differed. The point made about incommensurability of values was that an objective standpoint in such situations allowing one to say which set of priorities is the better one need not exist. When it does not exist, fair compromise can be an elusive goal, even where only two persons are involved and the level of trust and love is high.

This result has important implications for social and political situations in which the number of persons involved in conflicts of interest is often large and the levels of trust and love may be low. It is little wonder that in social and political contexts one must resort to the "second best" strategies mentioned in 7.8 for resolving conflicts of interest, e.g. to specifically appointed arbitrators, civil courts, majority vote, selection by lot, submission to the judgments of elected or appointed officials, or bureaucratic superiors, and so on. Such strategies almost always fall short of the ideal of fair compromise, but they are chosen (or should be chosen) because they *depart as little as possible from that ideal* in imperfect situations. Thus, they are called for by the principle of equal respect in certain circumstances. Regarding majority vote, for example, a well known theorem of social choice theory proved by K.O. May (52) shows that in certain conflict situations, majority vote is the only decision procedure that will satisfy conditions preserving equality of voters and maximizing responsiveness to each individual's input. In other words, such a procedure preserves as much respect for the views of individuals as certain kinds of imperfect situations allow. In a similar manner, the arguments of chapter 7 provide general guidelines for assessing all kinds of "second best" social and political strategies.

10.10   Difficulties in resolving conflicts of interest that call for second best strategies have wider implications for political theory. If the only qualification to the principle of equal respect had to do with clear cases in which some persons were treating others as means, then the interference of the liberal state in the value experiments of individuals could be confined to the policing and military functions favored by political libertarians like Nozick. But the possibilities for conflicts of interest stemming from the incommensurability of values and related factors create inevitable pressure for further government involvement. This is especially so when it comes to conflicts of interest involving the distribution of scarce resources or involving equality of opportunity. There is no way to insulate such conflicts from the influence of the principle of equal respect, if one is committed to that principle. For the abilities of persons to pursue their chosen experiments in living depend in large part on the material resources and opportunities, educational and otherwise, at their disposal.

As a consequence, the principle of equal respect does not specify a particular level of government involvement independent of circumstances. In an ideal society in which all persons were treated as ends and conflicts of interest were regularly resolved by fair bargaining, the anarchist dream of no government involvement at all could be realized. In societies in which material resources were comparatively abundant and accessible to all, something close to Nozick's minimal state might be realized. In actual present day societies, where competition for available resources is great, where power is unequally distributed, where proper management of the environment, of the societies' collective resources, and of their productive capacities. are necessary even for a semblance of equal respect for all, then government involvement must be greater. But the problem of determining the exact extent of this involvement has, I think, no abstract and general solution. The principle of equal respect provides general guidelines, but nothing more, a fact that is evident in personal conflict situations, like that of the husband and wife, and is more evident in political conflict situations.

This leads to a problem that every liberal theory must face. If the principle of equal respect does not dictate specific solutions in all conflict of interest situations, might it not be the case that some of these conflicts must be resolved by supposing that some conceptions of the good life are intrinsically superior to others (over and above the moral suppositions involved when some persons are treated as means)? In short, must concessions be made to Dworkin's second theory of political equality mentioned in 10.8?[15] When the state, or any individual or group, must be involved as third party arbitrator, through executive order, legislative decree, or judicial decision, can it (he, she) always act justly without making and supporting claims that some practices or ways of life are intrinsically superior or inferior to others?

I think it fair to say that third party arbitrators, governments included, must sometimes make such judgments. But, in conceding this, we must not forget the "value empiricist" aspect of the theory. Such judgments of superiority or inferiority, when they have to be made, are fallible judgments, made on inductive grounds, concerning what ways of life are more likely to lead to satisfaction for the individuals involved and are more likely to harmonize with other existing ways in society. And the policies suggested by such judgments must be tested by experiment on the same grounds. We must not suppose that because appointed officials and other third party arbitrators must sometimes make judgments of superiority and inferiority that they must have a privileged access to the true and the good, or that *a priori* knowledge of what ways of life are intrinsically superior is somehow a precondition for making such judgments. Political judgments are value experimental, not authoritative, and politics is the ultimate value experiment.

10.11   In summary, of the last three sections, I have suggested that the value theory of chapters 5-8, pluralist on the one hand, empiricist on the other, provides foundations for a view of political freedom and equality associated with the classical liberal tradition. This provides a general answer to Wiggins' question about the relation of the libertarian conception of free will to political and social freedoms.

The libertarian conception of free will implies a classical liberal conception of social and political freedoms. But the brief discussion of these sections necessarily leaves many questions unanswered and others not fully answered. Some of these questions concern the nature and limits of the classical liberal ideal itself and the relation of these limits to the theory of free will. Liberal societies have always had their critics on both the left and the right. Many of the common criticisms are old, and many were stated by Plato. Erosion of the social order, loss of common values, loss of respect for authority and of shared values between young and old, moral decay, increase in crime,[16] are all said to be inevitable results of societies in which governments refuse to endorse and promulgate perfectionist ideals—conceptions of the best life for all to follow—but instead leave such matters to individual choice.

That these tendencies constitute a danger for all liberal democratic societies is widely acknowledged. The critics of such societies, from Plato to Solzenitzyn, have a point. But until they tell us who is going to decide upon the perfectionist ideals we are all to follow and how these ideals are going to be enforced on all, we do well to remain sceptical. One may be convinced by these critics that the burdens of liberal societies are great and the risks many, without giving up the ideal. For my part, I have emphasized throughout this book that free will is not merely a blessing or a burden, it is both blessing and burden; and indeterminism is not merely a blessing or burden, it is both. (Cf. 3.7.) So it is natural to add that free societies are not merely blessings and burdens, they are both. Societies based on a theory of values required by the theory of free will should have all the potentialities of free wills themselves to produce good *and* evil.

10.12   This central theme of freedom as both blessing and burden, good and evil, is nicely illustrated in relation to the theory of this book by a scene in C.S. Lewis' novel of fantasy, *Perelandra* (62). Lewis describes the journey of a man named Ransom to the planet Venus, called "Perelandra" in the novel. Unlike its real counterpart, Perelandra is an idyllic world of islands floating on water and covered with exotic foliage. Ransom finds only one human-like creature there, a green skinned woman who tells him of her God, Maleldil, and her search for a man of her own kind who also inhabits the world. Their conversation is interrupted one day when Ransom says that the floating islands make him uneasy and suggests that they move over to the fixed land. She is appalled by this suggestion and tells him that it is the command of Maleldil that one should never set foot on the fixed land. Ransom's response puzzles and confuses her, for he tells her that in his world everyone lives on the fixed land and no one believes it to be wrong. Is it possible that there are other right ways to live and that Maleldil allows some people to live in one way, others in other ways? In her confusion she is sorely tempted to go with him to the fixed land.

As the conversation proceeds, Ransom realizes that they are reenacting the Garden of Eden scene between Eve and the serpent, and he is playing the serpent. The "knowledge of good and evil" that confuses and tempts her is not the knowledge that there is good and evil, right and wrong, but the knowledge that there is more than one good or right way even in the eyes of God. Such knowledge brings an end to moral innocence—the secure feelings that the rights and wrongs learned in child-hood are definitive, unchallengeable and unambiguous. And it tempts one to think that, since no laws are unchallengeable and unambiguous, no laws are binding against the demands of inclination and desire. Moreover, such knowledge implies that con-flicts of interest are inevitable and difficult to resolve in a world in which the legitimate "ends of men are many and not all of them are compatible with one another." This is the bitter taste of the fruit of knowledge of good and evil. But the alternative to tasting it is not to *have* true knowledge of good and evil. Our litera-ture of tragedy continually reminds us of this fact; and in doing so it reminds us of the blessings and burdens of societies of beings possessing free will.

10.13   In conclusion, let us return to the analogy with which this chapter began and add a final twist to it. Relativity theories in physics and of values are connected with the search for invariance. Indeed, relativity and invariance are two sides of a single theoretical coin. In a physical theory like Einstein's Special Theory, variations in spatial and temporal measurements are conceptually related to the invariance of the speed of light *in vacuo* in all inertial frames of reference, and the invariance of this speed is in turn related to the invariance of electrodynamic laws. In other words, some quantities vary as a consequence of the fact that others, connected with invariant laws, remain the same.

A similar situation prevails in value theory. The invariant law in this case is an invariant moral law described in chapter 7. But this law has its source in certain other invariant properties that are shared in different frames of reference. These are the shared capacities that define different persons, or members of different cultures, *as persons*, the capacities to use *language*, to *reason*, to exercise *free choice* in the creation of one's own values or ends. These are the traditional capacities defining human nature, or better, personhood, and they underscore the morally relevant claim that, despite cultural differences, we are all equal as persons. We use different languages, but we all use language; we reason differently, but we all reason; we choose different ends, but we all choose ends.

Moreover, as in the physical case, these invariant capacities are conceptually related to the variations from frame to frame. We create different languages because we can all create language; we reason differently, because we can all reason, we choose different ends, because we can all choose ends. Species lacking these capacities can-not create different cultures and value systems at all, and are bound in their ways of acting by the constraints of nature. Use of conventional symbolism is the recog-nized watershed between nature and culture; and precisely because it is conventional, not natural, it gives rise to variations of culture and value.

In other words, the invariant capacities (for reason, language, and free choice) are *preconditions* for the variations of cultures and values. The invariance of certain human capacities and the variations in their expression are two sides of a single coin. Similarly, the invariance of the speed of light and related laws in the physical theory is a precondition for the variation in measurements of spatial intervals and temporal intervals, as the mathematics of the theory shows. The invariance of cer-tain quantities and the relativity of others are two sides of a single coin.

Recognition of the relativity of values, therefore, even in a qualified sense, is one side of a coin, the other side of which is the recognition of the shared (i.e. invariant) capacities (to reason, use language, and make free choices) that (i) are preconditions for the relativity and, at the same time, (ii) account for our equality *as persons* despite our differences. Recognition of the relativity of values is connected in this way to recognition of the dignity of persons as persons; and both are connected to free will, on the one hand, and to the invariance of (moral) law, on the other. According to that law, to respect persons as persons is to respect the differences by which they are likely to express their personhood. Here, the general relation between invariance and relativity takes on practical meaning. The resulting connection between the relativity of values and human dignity was never more clearly expressed than in the words of the Sioux Indian chief, Sitting Bull, spoken to U.S. government agents in 1883:

> If the great spirit had desired me to be a white man, he would have made me so in the first place. He put in your heart certain wishes and plans, in my heart he put other and different desires. Each man is good in his sight. It is not necessary for eagles to be crows.

Notes

1. See, for example, the essay by Ortega y Gasset in L. Williams (68, pp. 147-57).

2. See Ladd (73, Introduction), Benedict (46), and Herskovits (47).

3. Cf. 7.13. The comparison made there between fact and value empiricisms is critical to the argument and is meant to justify the claims made in the Introduction, and restated in this paragraph, concerning value relativism.

4. Both lectures are reprinted in Berlin (69) with several other essays and a long Introduction in which Berlin attempts to answer his critics.

5. The last section of Bramhall (44) is a critique of Hobbes' political theory.

6. Berlin (69, pp. 132-3).

7. I am using "utopia" as Berlin and others do, to mean an ideal society or way of life which is put forward as the best attainable for all persons. Nozick (74, Pt. III) describes a "framework of utopias" in which many different communities are experimenting with different ways of life and presumably not interfering with one another. Nozick's framework of utopias is not inconsistent with the value theory of this work; in fact it is very much in accord with that value theory. But none of his utopias claim to represent *the* best life for all in the manner of traditional utopias.

8. Among his many statements of this case, the clearest are Skinner (62, ch. 29, and 71, ch. 1).

9. In addition to (62, ch. 20), see especially (71, chs. 6-8).

10. In addition to the works of Berlin and Dworkin cited, there is Dworkin (77) and a recent book by B. Ackerman (80) which makes the case most forcefully. Popper (62) also belongs to this tradition, as does the work of political libertarians like Nozick, a fact which shows that persons who may espouse Dworkin's first theory of equality may differ widely about the extent of justified government interference in the lives of individuals. The moral theory of chapter 7 is not indifferent toward this issue, as we see in 10.10. Other thinkers, like J. S. Mill and John Rawls, who espouse liberal ideals on utilitarian or contractual grounds, are referred to later. (See note 12.)

11. E.g. Pico della Mirandola (56).

12. Two noteworthy alternatives are the utilitarian defense of liberal ideals by J.S. Mill (56) and the contractarian defense of Rawls (71). It would be interesting to compare these two theories to the value theory of this book, but the task goes well beyond what this chapter can achieve. An interesting contrast with utilitarianism is suggested by Bernard Williams' criticism of certain presuppositions of the utilitarian view (72, p. 97): Utilitarians "might say that they were not committed to the view that the common currency of happiness is money. But they are committed to something which in practice has this implication: that there are no ultimately incommensurable values. Nor is it an accidential feature of the utilitarian outlook that the presumption is in favor of the monetarily quantifiable . . . because quantification in money is only the obvious form of what utilitarians insist upon, the commensurability of values. . . . There is great pressure for research into techniques to make larger ranges of social value commensurable. Some of this effort should rather be devoted to learning . . . how to think intelligibly about conflicts of values which are incommensurable."

13. Bramhall (44, pp. 307-9).

14. Nozick (74, Pt. II).

15. This issue has been raised recently by Vinit Haksar (79). He argues that liberal theories must be supplemented by "perfectionist" principles asserting that certain forms of life are intrinsically superior to others.

16. All these points are either explicit or implicit in Plato's criticism of democratic societies and the democratic character in *The Republic* (74, 555b-569c).

Bibliography

References in the text and footnotes to works in this bibliography are by the author's name followed by the last two figures of the date of publication. The following abbreviations are used for frequently cited journals. *AJP: Australasian Journal of Philosophy; A: Analysis; APQ: American Philosophical Quarterly; JP: The Journal of Philosophy; M: Mind; N: Nous; PR: The Philosophical Review; PS: Philosophical Studies; P: Philosophy; R: Ratio: RM: Review of Metaphysics.*

Ackerman, Bruce. *Social Justice in the Liberal State.* New Haven: Yale University Press, 1980.

Adams, R. M. "Must God Create the Best?" *PR* 81 (1972):317-32.

Adler, Mortimer, ed. *The Idea of Freedom.* 2 vols. New York: Doubleday, vol. I (1958), vol. 2 (1961).

Allen, Diogenes. "Deliberation and the Regularity of Behavior." *APQ* 9 (1972):251-8.

Anscombe, G. E. M. *Intention.* Oxford: Basil Blackwell, 1958.

Aquinas, St.Thomas. *Basic Writings of St. Thomas Aquinas.* Ed. by A. C. Pegis. Vols. 1 and 2. New York: Random House, 1945.

_____. *De Malo.* In vol. 2, *Questiones Disputatae.* Turin-Rome, 1931.

Aristotle. *The Works of Aristotle Translated into English.* Ed. by W. D. Ross. Vols. 1-12. Oxford: Oxford University Press, 1908-1952.

Armstrong, David M. *A Materialist Theory of the Mind.* London: Routledge and Kegan Paul, 1968.

Ashby, Ross. *Introduction to Cybernetics.* New York: John Wiley & Sons, 1956.

Audi, Robert. "Intending." *JP* 70 (1973):387-403.

_____. "Moral Responsibility, Freedom and Compulsion." *APQ* 11 (1974): 1-14.

_____. "A Theory of Practical Reason." *APQ* 19 (1982):25-39.

Augustine, St. *On the Free Choice of the Will.* Indianapolis: Bobbs-Merrill, 1964.

Aune, Bruce. "Hypotheticals and 'Can'." *A* 27 (1967):191-5.

_____. "Pritchard, Action and Volition." *PS* 25 (1974):117-23.

_____. *Reason and Action.* Dordrecht: D. Reidel, 1977.

Austin, J.L. "Ifs and Cans." In Berofsky (1966):295-321.

_____. *Philosophical Papers.* Oxford: Oxford University Press, 1970.

Ayer, A. J. "Freedom and Necessity." In Ayer, A. J. *Philosophical Essays.* New York: St. Martin's Press, 1954.

Ayers, M. R. *The Refutation of Determinism.* London: Methuen, 1968.

Baier, Kurt. *The Moral Point of View.* New York: Random House, 1966.

Barrett, William. "Determinism and Novelty." In Hook (58):46-54.

Barry, Brian. *The Liberal Theory of Justice.* Oxford: Oxford University Press, 1973.

Bateson, Gregory. *Mind and Nature.* New York: Bantam Books, 1979.

Benedict, Ruth. *Patterns of Culture.* New York: Pelican Books, 1946.

Bennett, Daniel. "Action, Reason and Purpose." *JP* 62 (1965):85-95.

Bennett, Jonathan. *Rationality*. London: Routledge & Kegan Paul, 1964.

Bergson, Henri. *Creative Evolution*. Trans. by A. Mitchell. New York: Random House, 1944.

Bergmann, Frithjof. *On Being Free*. Notre Dame: University of Notre Dame Press, 1977.

Berlin, Isaiah. *Four Essays on Liberty*. Oxford: Oxford University Press, 1969.

Bernstein, Richard. *Praxis and Action*. Philadelphia: University of Pennsylvania Press, 1971.

Berofsky, Bernard. "Determinism and the Concept of a Person." *JP* 61 (1964): 461-75.

––––––. ed. *Free Will and Determinism*. New York: Harper & Row, 1966.

––––––. *Determinism*. Princeton: Princeton University Press, 1971.

Binkley, Robert. "A Theory of Practical Reasoning." *PR* 74 (1965): 423-48.

Blakney, R. B., editor and translator. *The Way of Life of Lao Tzu*. Translation of the *Tao Te Ching*. New York: New American Library, 1955.

Blumenfeld, David. "The Principle of Alternative Possibilities." *JP* 68 (1971): 339-45.

––––––. "Is the Best Possible World Possible?" *PR* 84 (1975):163-77.

Blumenfeld, Jean. "Is Acting Willing?" *N* 17 (1983):183-95.

Boethius. *The Consolation of Philosophy*. Indianapolis: Bobbs-Merrill, 1962.

Bonjour, Laurence. "Determinism, Libertarianism, and Agent Causation." *Southern Journal of Philosophy*. 14 (1976):145-56.

Borst, C. V. ed. *The Mind/Brain Identity Theory*. New York: St. Martin's Press, 1970.

Bourke, Vernon. *Will in Western Thought*. New York: Sheed & Ward, 1964.

Boutroux, Émile. *Contingency of the Laws of Nature*. Trans. by F. Rothwell. Chicago: Open Court, 1916.

Boyle, J., G. Grisez, and D. Tollefson. *Free Choice: A Self Referential Argument*. Notre Dame: University of Notre Dame Press, 1976.

Bradley, F. H. *Ethical Studies*. Oxford: Oxford University Press, 1959.

Bradley, M. C. "A Note on Mr. MacIntyre's 'Determinism.'" *AJP* 40 (1962): 146-58.

Bradley, R. D. " 'Ifs,' 'Cans,' and Determinism." *AJP* 40 (1962): 146-58.

Bramhall, John. *The Works of John Bramhall*. Vol. 4. Oxford: John Henry Parker, 1844.

Brand, Myles, ed. *The Nature of Human Action*. Glenview: Scott, Foresman and Company, 1970.

––––––. and Douglas Walton, eds. *Action Theory*. Dordrecht: D. Reidel, 1976.

Brandt, Richard. *Ethical Theory*. Englewood Cliffs: Prentice Hall, 1959.

Bratman, Michael. "Practical Reasoning and Weakness of Will." *N* 13 (1979): 153-72.

––––––. "Intention and Means-Ends Reasoning." *PR* 90 (1981):252-65.

Brentano, Franz. *The Foundations and Construction of Ethics*. New York: Humanities Press, 1973.

Broad, C. D. "Determinism, Indeterminism and Libertarianism." In Morgenbesser and Walsh (62):115-32.

Brown, D. G. *Action*. Toronto: University of Toronto Press, 1968.

Brown, James M. "The Appraisal of Value Judgments." *R* 18 (1976):56-71.

Browning, Douglas. "The Feeling of Freedom." In Enteman (67):216-39.

_____. *Act and Agent*. Coral Gables: University of Miami Press, 1964.

Campbell, C. A. "Is 'Free Will' a Pseudo-problem?" In Berofsky (1966a):112-34.

_____. "The Psychology of Effort of Will." In Berofsky (1966b):345-63.

_____. *In Defence of Free Will*. London: Allen & Unwin, 1967.

_____. "Has the Self Free Will?" In G. Dworkin (1970):98-110.

Campbell, Keith. *Body and Mind*. Garden City: Anchor, 1970.

Camus, Albert. *The Myth of Sisyphus*. Trans. by J. O'Brien. New York, 1955.

Canfield, J. "The Compatibility of Free Will and Determinism." *PR* 71 (1962): 352-68.

Care, Norman and Charles Landesman, eds. *Readings in Action Theory*. Bloomington: Indiana University Press, 1968.

Castaneda, H.N. *Thinking and Doing*. Dordrecht: D. Reidel, 1975.

Chisholm, R. M. "J. L. Austin's Philosophical Papers." In Berofsky (1966a): 339-45.

_____. "Freedom and Action." In Lehrer (1966b):11-44.

_____. "He Could Have Done Otherwise." *JP* 13 (1967):409-17.

_____. *Person and Object*. London: George Allen & Unwin, 1976a.

_____. "The Agent as Cause." In Brand and Walton (1976b):199-211.

Cicero. *De Oratore, De Fato, et al.* Trans. by H. Rackham. London: Heinemann, 1960.

Compton, A. H. *The Freedom of Man*. New Haven: Yale University Press, 1935.

Cranor, Carl. "Towards a Theory of Respect for Persons." *APQ* 12 (1975): 309-20.

Cummins, Robert. "Dispositional States and Causes." *A* 34 (1974):194-204.

D'Angelo, Edward. *The Problem of Freedom and Determinism*. Columbia: University of Missouri Press, 1968.

Dante Alighieri. *Paradiso*. Trans. by G. L. Bickersteth. Cambridge: Cambridge University Press, 1932.

Danto, Arthur. "Basic Actions." *APQ* 2 (1965):144-8.

_____. *Analytical Philosophy of Action*. Cambridge: Cambridge University Press, 1973.

Daveney, T. F. "Choosing." *M* 73 (1964):515-26.

Davidson, Donald. "Actions, Reasons and Causes." In Berofsky (66):221-39.

_____. "How is Weakness of Will Possible?" In Feinberg (69):93-113.

_____. "Mental Events." In L. Lester and J. Swanson, eds. *Experience and Theory*. Amherst: University of Massachusetts Press, 1970.

_____. "Freedom to Act." In Honderich (73).

Davis, Laurence. *Theory of Action*. Englewood Cliffs: Prentice Hall, 1979.

Davis, William H. *The Freewill Question*. The Hague: Martinus-Nijhoff, 1971.

Dennett, Daniel. *Content and Consciousness*. New York: Humanities Press, 1969.

_____. *Brainstorms*. Montgomery: Bradford Book Publishers, 1978.

Descartes, René. *The Philosophical Works of Descartes*. 2 vols. Ed. and trans. by Haldane and Ross. Cambridge: Cambridge University Press, 1931.

Donagan, Alan. *The Theory of Morality*. Chicago: University of Chicago Press, 1977.

Dore, Clement. "On the Meaning of 'Could Have'." *A* 23 (1962-63):179-81.

Downie, R. S. and Elizabeth Telfer. *Respect for Persons*. New York: Schocken Books, 1970.

Dworkin, Gerald, ed. *Determinism, Free Will and Moral Responsibility*. Englewood Cliffs, Prentice Hall, 1970.

———. "Acting Freely." *N* 4 (1970a):367-83.

Dworkin, Ronald. *Taking Rights Seriously*. Cambridge: Harvard University Press, 1977.

———. "Liberalism." In Stuart Hampshire, ed. *Public and Private Morality*. Cambridge: Cambridge University Press, 1978, pp. 113-43.

Eccles, J. C. *The Neurophysiological Basis of Mind*. Oxford: Oxford University Press, 1953.

———. *Facing Reality*. New York: Springer-Verlag, 1970.

Edwards, Jonathan. *The Freedom of the Will*. Indianapolis: Bobbs-Merrill, 1969.

Edwards, Paul. "Hard and Soft Determinism." In Hook (58):117-25.

Edwards, Rem B. "Is Choice Determined by the Strongest Motive?" *APQ* 4 (1967):72-8.

———. *Freedom, Responsibility and Obligation*. The Hague: Nijhoff, 1969.

Einstein, Albert. "On the Electrodynamics of Moving Bodies." In L. Williams (68).

Encyclopedia of Philosophy. Ed. by Paul Edwards. 8 vols. New York: Macmillan and Free Press, 1967.

Enteman, Willard F. (ed.) *The Problem of Free Will*. New York: Scribner's, 1967.

Erasmus-Luther. *Discourse on Free Will*. New York: Frederick Ungar Publishing, 1961.

Erwin, Edward. *Behavior Therapy*. Cambridge: Cambridge University Press, 1978.

Falk, Arthur E. "Some Modal Confusions in Compatibilism." *APQ* 18 (1981):141-8.

Farrer, Austin. *The Freedom of the Will*. New York: Scribner's, 1958.

Feinberg, Joel, ed. *Moral Notions*. Oxford: Oxford University Press, 1969.

———. "Action and Responsibility." in Max Black. ed. *Philosophy in America*. Ithaca: Cornell University Press, 1965.

———. Review of Glover (1970). *PR* 81 (1972):237-40.

Feldman, Fred. "The Principle of Moral Harmony." *JP* 77 (1980):166-79.

Ferré, Frederick. "Self Determinism." *APQ* 10 (1973):165-76.

Fischer, J. "Responsibility and Control." *JP* (1982):24-40.

Fingarette, Herbert. "Responsibility." *M* 75 (1966):58-74.

Fleming, Noel. "On Intention." *PR* 73 (1964):301-20.

Flew, A. "Divine Omnipotence and Human Freedom." In *New Essays in Philosophical Theology*. Ed. by Flew and A. MacIntyre. London: SCM Press Ltd., 1955: 144-69.

Foley, Richard. "Deliberate Action." *PR* 86 (1977):58-69.

———. "Compatibilism." *M* 87 (1978):421-8.

Foot, Philippa. "Free Will as Involving Determinism." In Berofsky (66):95-108.

Frankena, William. "Value and Valuation." *Encyclopedia of Philosophy*, Vol. 8: 229-32.

Frankfurt, Harry. "Alternative Possibilities and Moral Responsibility." *JP* 66 (1969):829-39.

_____. "Freedom of the Will and the Concept of a Person." *JP* 68(1971):5-20.

_____. "Coercion and Moral Responsibility." In Honderich (73):65-86.

_____. "Three Concepts of Free Action II." *Proceedings of the Aristotelian Society* Supplement. Vol. 44 (1975):113-25.

Franklin, R. L. *Free Will and Determinism*. London: Routledge & Kegan Paul, 1970.

French, Peter. *The Scope of Morality*. Minneapolis: University of Minnesota Press, 1980.

Gale, R. M. "Pure and Impure Descriptions." *AJP* 45 (1967):32-43.

Gallie, W. B. "Free Will and Determinism Once Again." Inaugural Lecture, The Queen's University of Belfast. Belfast: Marjory Boyd, 1957.

Gallois, Andre. "Van Inwagen on Free Will and Determinism." *PS* 32 (1977): 99-106.

Gauthier, David. *Practical Reasoning*. Oxford: Oxford University Press, 1963.

Gendron, Bernard. *Technology and Human Nature*. New York: St. Martin's Press, 1977.

Gert, Bernard. *The Moral Rules*. New York: Harper & Row, 1973.

_____ and Duggan, Timothy. "Free Will as the Ability to Will." *N* 13 (1979): 197-218.

Gewirth, Alan. *Reason and Morality*. Chicago: University of Chicago Press, 1978.

Ginet, Carl. "Can the Will be Caused?" *PR* 71 (1962):49-55.

_____. "Might We Have No Free Choice?" In Lehrer(66):87-104.

Glover, Jonathan. *Responsibility*. London: Routledge & Kegan Paul, 1970.

Goldman, Alvin. *A Theory of Human Action*. Englewood Cliffs: Prentice Hall, 1970.

Gomberg, Paul. "Free Will as Ultimate Responsibility." *APQ* 15 (1975):205-12.

Graham, K. "Ifs, Cans and Dispositions." *R* 14 (1972):195-7.

Greenspan, P.S. "Wiggins on Historical Inevitability and Incompatibilism." *PS* 29 (1976):235-48.

_____. "Behavior Control and Freedom of Action." *PR* 87 (1978):225-40.

Grice, G. R. *The Grounds of Moral Judgment*. Cambridge: Cambridge University Press, 1967.

Grünbaum, Adolf. "Free Will and the Laws of Human Behavior." *APQ* 8 (1971): 299-317.

Gustafson, D. F. "Momentary Intentions." *M* 77 (1968):1-13.

Haksar, Vinit. *Equality, Liberty and Perfectionism*. Oxford: Oxford University Press, 1979.

Hall, James W. "Deciding As a Way of Intending." *JP* 75 (1978):553-64.

Hamlyn, D. W. "Causality and Human Behavior." In Care and Landesmann (68): 48-67.

Hampshire, Stuart. *Thought and Action*. London: Chatto and Windus, 1959.

_____. *Freedom of the Individual*. New York: Harper & Row, 1965.

Hancock, R. "Choosing as Doing." *M* 77 (1958):575-6.

Hardie, W. F. R. "My Own Free Will." *P* 32 (1957):21-3.

Hare, R. M. *Freedom and Reason*. Oxford: Oxford University Press, 1977.

Harmon, Gilbert. *The Nature of Morality*. New York: Oxford University Press, 1977.

————. "Moral Relativism Defended." *PR* 74(1975): 3-22.

Harré, Rom. *The Principles of Scientific Thinking*. London: MacMillan, 1970.

————. *Social Being*. Littlefield, Adams, 1980.

Hart, H. L. A. *Punishment and Responsibility*. Oxford: Oxford University Press, 1973.

Hartshorne, Charles. *The Logic of Perfection and Other Essays*. Lasalle: Open Court, 1962.

Herskovits, Melville. *Cultural Anthropology*. New York: Alfred Knopf, 1947.

Hick, John. *Philosophy of Religion*. Englewood Cliffs: Prentice Hall, 1973.

Hintikka, Jaakko. "Time, Truth and Knowledge in Ancient Greek Philosophy." *APQ* 4 (1967):1-14.

Hobart, R. E. "Free Will as Involving Determinism and Inconceivable Without It." In Berofsky (66):63-94.

Hobbes, Thomas. *Leviathan*. Indianapolis: Bobbs-Merrill, 1958.

————. *The English Works of Thomas Hobbes*. Edited by W. Molesworth. Vol. 5. Scientia Aalen, 1962.

Hofstadter, Douglas. *Gödel, Escher and Bach*. New York: Vintage Books, 1980.

Honderich, Ted, ed. *Essays on Freedom of Action*. London: Routledge & Kegan Paul, 1973.

————. "One Determinism." In Honderich (73):183-215. Referred to as (73a).

Hook, Sidney, ed. *Determinism and Freedom in the Age of Modern Science*. New York: Collier-MacMillan, 1958.

Hospers, John. "What Means This Freedom?" In Hook (58): 126-42.

————. *Human Conduct*. New York: Harcourt, Brace and World, 1961.

Huby, Pamela. "The First Discovery of the Free Will Issue." *P* 42 (1967):353-62.

Hughes, G. E. "Motive and Duty." *M* 53 (1944):314-31.

———— and Cresswell, M. J. *An Introduction to Modal Logic*. London: Methuen & Co., 1968.

Hume, David. *An Inquiry Concerning Human Understanding*. Indianapolis: Bobbs-Merrill, 1955.

————. *A Treatise On Human Nature*. Ed. by L. A. Selby-Bigge. Oxford: Clarendon Press, 1960.

Hunter, J. F. M. "Aune and Others on Ifs and Cans." *A* 28 (1968):107-9.

James, William. *The Principles of Psychology*. Vol. 1. New York: Henry Holt, 1907.

————. "The Dilemma of Determinism." In James, *The Will to Believe and Other Essays*. New York: Dover, 1956:145-83.

Jones, Hardy. *Kant's Principle of Personality*. Madison: University of Wisconsin Press, 1971.

Kamp, Hans. "The Logic of Historical Necessity." Unpublished typescript, 1979.

Kant, Immanuel. *Critique of Practical Reason*. Trans. by L. W. Beck. Indianapolis: Bobbs-Merrill, 1956.

_____. *Critique of Pure Reason.* Trans. by N. K. Smith. London: Macmillan, 1958.

_____. *Foundations of the Metaphysics of Morals.* Trans. by L. W. Beck. Indianapolis: Bobbs-Merrill, 1959.

Katz, Bernard. "Kim on Events." *PR* 87 (1978):427-41.

Kaufman, Arnold. "Ability." *JP* 60 (1963):537-51.

_____. "Responsibility, Moral and Legal." *Encyclopedia of Philosophy*, Vol. 7: 183-8.

Keeney, R. L. and H. Raiffa, *Decisions and Multiple Objectives.* New York: Wiley, 1976.

Kenny, Anthony. *Action, Emotion and Will.* London: Routledge & Kegan Paul, 1963.

_____. *Will, Freedom and Power.* Oxford: Basil Blackwell, 1976.

_____. *Freewill and Responsibility.* London: Routledge & Kegan Paul, 1978.

Kierkegaard, Soren. *Either/Or* Vol. 1 and 2. Garden City: Doubleday & Co., 1959.

Kim, Jaegwon. Review of Berofsky (71). *JP* 68 (1971).

Kluckholm, Clyde. "Ethical Relativity." *JP* 52 (1955):663-77.

Korner, S. "Science and Moral Responsibility." *M* 73 (1964):161-72.

_____, ed. *Practical Reason.* New Haven: Yale University Press, 1974.

Kovesi, Julius. *Moral Notions.* London: Routledge & Kegan Paul, 1967.

Kretzmann, Norman. "Omniscience and Immutability." *JP* 63 (1966):409-42.

Kuhn, Thomas. *The Structure of Scientific Revolutions.* Chicago: University of Chicago Press, 1962.

Ladd, John, ed. *Ethical Relativism.* Belmont: Wadsworth Publishing Co., 1973.

Lakatos, Imre, ed. *Criticism and the Growth of Knowledge.* Cambridge: Cambridge University Press, 1970.

Lamb, James W. "On a Proof of Incompatibilism." *PR* 86 (1977):20-35.

Lamont, Corliss. *Freedom of Choice Affirmed.* Boston: Beacon Press, 1969.

Landé, Alfred. "The Case for Indeterminism." In Hook (58):83-9.

Langford, Glenn. *Human Action.* New York: Doubleday, 1971.

Laurence, Roy. *Motive and Intention.* Evanston: Northwestern University Press, 1972.

Lehrer, Keith. "Can We Know We Have Free Will by Introspection?" *JP* 57 (1960):145-57.

_____. "'Could' and Determinism." *A* 24 (1963-64):159-60.

_____, ed. *Freedom and Determinism.* New York: Random House, 1966.

_____. "Cans Without Ifs." *A* 28 (1968):29-32.

_____. "'Can' in Theory and Practice: A Possible Worlds Analysis." In Brand and Walton (76):241-70.

Leibniz, G. W. F. *Selections.* Ed. by P. Weiner. New York: Scribner's, 1951.

Lewis, David. *Counterfactuals.* Oxford: Basil Blackwell, 1973.

Lewis, C. S. *Perelandra.* New York: Collier Books, Inc., 1962.

Linssen, Robert. *Living Zen.* New York: Grove Press, 1958.

Locke, Don. "Ifs and Cans Revisited." *P* 37 (1962):245-56.

Locke, John. *An Essay Concerning Human Understanding.* Ed. by A. C. Fraser. Vol. 1. New York: Dover, 1959.

Lucas, J. R. *The Freedom of the Will*. Oxford: Oxford University Press, 1970.

Luce, R. D. and H. Raiffa. *Games and Decisions*. New York: John Wiley & Sons, 1957.

Luria, A. R. *The Working Brain*. Trans. by B. Haigh. Hammondsworth: Penguin Books, 1973.

MacIntyre, A. C. "Determinism." In Berofsky (66):240-55.

MacKay, D. M. "On the Logical Indeterminacy of a Free Choice." *M* 69 (1960): 31-40.

_____. "From Mechanism to Mind." In *Brain and Mind*. Ed. by J. R. Smythies. London: Routledge & Kegan Paul, 1965.

Mackie, J. L. *The Cement of the Universe*. Oxford: Clarenden Press, 1974.

_____. *Ethics: Inventing Right and Wrong*. Hammondsworth: Penguin. 1977.

Malcolm, Norman. "The Conceivability of Mechanism." *PR* 77 (1968):45-72.

Mansel, Henry. *Prolegomena Logica*. Oxford: William Graham, 1851.

Matson, W. I. "On the Irrelevance of Free Will to Moral Responsibility and the Vacuity of the Latter." *M* 65 (1956):489-97.

May, K. O. "A Set of Independent, Necessary and Sufficient Conditions for Simple Majority Decision." *Econometrica* 20 (1952):680.

Mayo, B. "On the Lehrer-Taylor Analysis of 'Can' Statements." *M* 77 (1968): 271-8.

McCann, Hugh. "Volition and Basic Action." *PR* 83 (1974):451-73.

_____. "Trying, Paralysis and Volitions." *RM* 28 (1975):423-42.

McInerney, Peter. "Self Determination and the Project." *JP* 76 (1979):663-77.

Meehl, Paul et al., *What Then Is Man?* St. Louis: Concordia, 1958.

_____. "Precognitive Telepathy II." *N* 12 (1978):371-96.

Meiland, Jack. *The Nature of Intention*. London: Methuen, 1970.

Melden, A. I. *Free Action*. London: Routledge & Kegan Paul, 1961.

Mellor, D. H. *The Matter of Chance*. Cambridge: Cambridge University Press, 1971.

Mill, J. S. *On Liberty*. New York: Liberal Arts Press, 1956.

_____. "From an Examination of Sir William Hamilton's Philosophy." In Morgenbesser and Walsh (62):57-69.

Miller, David. *Modern Science and Human Freedom*. Austin: The University of Texas Press, 1959.

Milton, John. *De Doctrina*. In *The Student's Milton*. Ed. by F. A. Patterson. New York: Crofts, 1936:919-1075.

Montague, R. "Deterministic Theories," In *Decisions, Values and Groups,2*. Oxford: Pergamon, 1962, 325-70.

Morgenbesser, Sidney and James Walsh, eds. *Free Will*. Englewood Cliffs: Prentice Hall, 1962.

Morowitz, H. J. "Rediscovering the Mind." *Psychology Today*. (August, 1980): 12-18.

Mortimore, G.W. ed. *Weakness of Will*. London: MacMillan, 1971.

Mourelatos, Alexander P. D. "Events, Processes and States." *Linguistics and Philosophy*. 2 (1978):415-34.

Munn, A. I. *Free Will and Determinism*. London: MacGibbon & Kee. 1962.

Nagel, Thomas. *The Possibility of Altruism*. Oxford: Oxford University Press, 1970.

_____. *Mortal Questions*. Cambridge: Cambridge University Press, 1978.

Narveson, Jan. "Compatibilism Defended." *PS* 32 (1977):83-8.

Nathan, Nicholas. "Freedom of Indifference." *R* 18 (1976):124-30.

Neely, Wright. "Freedom and Desire." *PR* 83 (1974):32-54.

Neville, Robert C. *The Cosmology of Freedom*. New Haven: Yale University Press, 1974.

_____. *Reconstruction in Thinking*. Albany: State University of New York Press, 1982.

Nielsen, Kai. *Reason and Practice*. New York: Harper and Row, 1971.

Nowell-Smith, P. *Ethics*. Baltimore: Pelican Books, 1954.

_____. "Ifs and Cans." In Berofsky (66):322-38.

Nozick, Robert. "Coercion." In Morgenbesser et. al. *Philosophy, Science and Method*. New York: St. Martin's Press, 1969.

_____. *Anarchy, State and Utopia*. New York: Basic Books, 1974.

_____. *Philosophical Explanations*. Cambridge: Harvard University Press, 1981.

Ockham, William. *Predestination, God's Foreknowledge and Future Contingents*. Trans. with an introduction by M. M. Adams and N. Kretzmann. New York: Appleton Century Crofts, 1969.

O'Connor, D.J. "Possibility and Choice" *Proceedings of the Aristotelian Society*. Supp. Vol. 34 (1960):1-24.

_____. *Free Will*. Garden City: Doubleday, 1971.

Ofstad, Harald. *An Inquiry Into the Freedom of Decision*. Oslo: Norwegian University Press, 1961.

_____. "Recent Work on the Free Will Problem." *APQ* 4 (1967):179-207.

Ogilvy, James. *Many Dimensional Man*. New York: Harper & Row, 1979.

Oldenquist, Andrew. "Causes, Predictions and Decisions." *A* 24 (63-64):55-6.

_____. "Choosing, Deciding and Doing." *Encyclopedia of Philosophy* 2:96-104.

O'Shaughnessy, Brian. "Observation and the Will." *JP* 60 (1963):367-92.

_____. *The Will*. Vols. I and II. Cambridge: Cambridge University Press, 1980.

Pears, D. F. ed. *Freedom and the Will*. New York: St. Martin's Press, 1963.

Peirce, C. S. "The Doctrine of Necessity Examined." In G. Dworkin (70):33-48.

Peters, R. S. *The Concept of Motivation*. London: Routledge & Kegan Paul, 1958.

Philo of Alexandria. *Philo*. Trans by F. Colson., Vol. 3. Cambridge: Harvard University Press, 1954.

Pico della Mirandola. *Oration on the Dignity of Man*. Trans. by A. R. Caponigri. Chicago: University of Chicago Press, 1956.

Pike, Nelson. "Divine Omniscience and Voluntary Action." *PR* 74 (1965):27-46.

_____. *God and Timelessness*. New York: Schocken Books, 1970.

Pitcher, George. "Necessitarianism." *The Philosophical Quarterly*. 11 (1961): 201-12.

Plantinga, Alvin. *The Nature of Necessity*. Oxford: Oxford University Press, 1974.

Plato. *The Dialogues of Plato*. Trans. B. Jowett. Vols. 1 and 2. New York: Random House, 1937.

_____. *Plato's Cosmology: The Timaeus of Plato*. Trans. with commentary by F. M. Cornford. London: Routledge & Kegan Paul, 1937a.

_____. *The Republic*. Trans. by Desmond Lee. Hammondsworth: Penguin Books, 1974.

Pollock, John L. *Subjunctive Reasoning*. Dordrecht: D. Reidel, 1976.

Popper, Karl. *Objective Knowledge*. Oxford: Oxford University Press, 1972. (Contains "Of Clouds and Clocks," pp. 206-55.)

_____. *The Open Society and Its Enemies*. London: Routledge & Kegan Paul, 1962.

Priestley, Joseph and Richard Price. *A Free Discussion of the Doctrine of Materialism and Philosophical Necessity*. London, 1778.

Quine, W. V. O. *Word and Object*. New York: Wiley, 1960.

_____. *Ontological Relativity and Other Essays*. New York: Columbia University Press, 1969.

_____. *The Web of Belief*. New York: Random House, 1970.

Raab, F. V. "Free Will and the Ambiguity of 'Could'." *PR* 64 (1955):60-77.

Radhakrishnan, S. *Eastern Religion and Western Thought*. London: Oxford University Press, 1974.

Rahula, Walpola. *What the Buddha Taught*. New York: Grove Press, 1959.

Ranken, Nani. "The 'Unmoved' Agent and the Ground of Responsibility." *JP* 13 (1967):403-8.

Rankin, K. W. .*Choice and Chance*. Oxford: Basil Blackwell, 1961.

Rawls, John. *A Theory of Justice*. Cambridge: Harvard University Press, 1971.

Raz, J. "Reasons for Action, Decisions and Norms." *M* 84 (1975):481-99.

_____, ed. *Practical Reasoning*. Oxford: Oxford University Press, 1979.

Reid, Thomas. *Essay on the Active Powers of the Human Mind*. Ed. by Baruch Brody. Cambridge: MIT Press, 1969.

_____. "Some Arguments for Free Will. In G. Dworkin (70):85-97.

Renouvier, Charles. *Traite de psychologie rationelle*. Vol. 1 Paris: Armand Colin, 1912.

Rescher, Nicholas and Robinson, John. "Temporally Conditioned Descriptions." *R* 8 (1966):46-54.

Rescher, Nicholas. *The Logic of Decision and Action*. Pittsburgh: University of Pittsburgh Press, 1966.

_____. *Introduction to Value Theory*. Englewood Cliffs: Prentice Hall, 1969.

Richards, David A. J. *A Theory of Reasons for Action*. Oxford: Clarendon Press, 1971.

Richman, R. J. "Responsibility and the Causation of Actions. *APQ* 6 (1969):186-97.

Roberts, Fred S. *Measurement Theory*. Reading: Addison-Wesley Publishing, 1979.

_____. "What If Utility Functions Do Not Exist?" *Theory and Decision*. 3 (1972): 126-39.

Roberts, M. *Responsibility and Practical Freedom*. Cambridge: Cambridge University Press, 1965.

Rorty, Amelie O. "Where Does the Akratic Break Take Place?" *AJP* 58 (1980): 333-46.

Rorty, Richard. *Philosophy and the Mirror of Nature*. Princeton: Princeton University Press, 1980.

Rosenthal, David M., ed. *Materialism and the Mind Body Problem*. Englewood Cliffs: Prentice Hall, 1971.

Rose, Steven. *The Conscious Brain*. New York: Vintage Books, 1976.

Ross, W. D. *Foundations of Ethics*. Oxford: Clarendon Press, 1939.

Rowe, William. *Philosophy of Religion*. Encino: Dickensen Publishing Company, 1978.

Ryan, A. "Freedom." *P* 40 (1965):93-112.

Ryle, Gilbert. *The Concept of Mind*. New York: Barnes & Noble, 1949.

Sankowski, Edward. "Some Problems About Determinism and Freedom." *APQ* 17 (1980):291-99.

Sartre, Jean Paul. "From *Being and Nothingness*." Trans. by Hazel Barnes. In Morgenbesser and Walsh (62):95-113.

Saunders, J. T. "Of God and Freedom." *PR* 75 (1966):219-25.

Schlick, Moritz. "When is a Man Responsible?" In Berofsky (66):54-62.

Schlesinger, George. "The Unpredictability of Free Choices." *British Journal of the Philosophy of Science*. 25 (1974):209-21.

Schick, F. "Toward a Logic of Liberalism." *JP* 77 (1980):80-98.

Schopenhauer, Arthur. *Essay on the Freedom of the Will*. New York: Bobbs-Merrill, 1960.

Schwartz, Adina. "Moral Neutrality and Primary Goods." *Ethics* 83 (1973):294-307.

Schwayder, D. S. *The Stratification of Behavior*. New York: Humanities Press, 1965.

Scotus, John Duns. "From The Oxford Commentary." In Morgenbesser and Walsh (62):35-39.

Scott, Stephen. "Practical Reason and the Concept of a Human Being." *JP* 73 (1976):497-511.

Sellars, Wilfrid. "Thought and Action." In Lehrer (66):105-40.

_____. "Fatalism and Determinism." In Lehrer (66a):41-176.

_____. "Meditations Leibnitziennes." In Sellars, *Philosophical Perspectives*. Springfield: Thomas, 1967.

_____. "Reply to Alan Donagan." *PS* 27 (1975):149-84.

_____. "Volitions Reaffirmed." In Brand and Walton (76):47-66.

_____. "On Reasoning About Values." *APQ* 17 (1980):81-102.

Sen, A. K. *Collective Choice and Social Welfare*. San Francisco:Holden-Day, 1970.

Shaffer, Jerome. *Philosophy of Mind*. Englewood Cliffs: Prentice Hall, 1968.

Shaw, Daniel J. "Compatibilism: A Reply to Richard Foley." *M* 88 (1979):584-5.

Singer, Peter. *Animal Liberation*. New York: Random House, 1975.

Slote, Michael A. "Understanding Free Will." *JP* 77 (1980):136-151.

_____. "Selective Necessity and Free Will." *JP* (1982):5-24.

Skinner, B. F. *Walden Two*. New York: Macmillan, 1962.

_____. *Beyond Freedom and Dignity*. New York: Vintage, 1971.

Skinner, R. C. "Freedom of Choice." *M* 72 (1963):463-80.

Smart, J. J. C. "Free Will, Praise and Blame." In G. Dworkin (70):196-213.

Smith, C. U. M. *The Brain: Towards an Understanding*. New York: Capricorn Books, 1972.

Smith, Huston. *The Religions of Man*. New York: Harper & Row, 1958.

Smith, John E. *The Spirit of American Philosophy*. New York: Oxford University Press, 1963.

Snyder, A. Aaron. "The Paradox of Determinism." *APQ* 9 (1972):353-6.

Sosa, Ernest, ed. *Causation and Conditionals*. Oxford: Oxford University Press, 1975.

Stace, W. T. *The Concept of Morals*. New York: MacMillan, 1937.

Stalnaker, Robert. "A Theory of Conditionals." In Sosa (75):165-179.

Strawson, Peter. *Freedom and Resentment and Other Essays*. London: Methuen, 1974.

Suarez, Francisco. *Disputationes Metaphysicae*. Vols. 25-26, Opera Omnia, 28 vols. Paris: Vives, 1856.

Suppes, Patrick. "Decision Theory." *Encyclopedia of Philosophy*, vol. 2:310-14.

Suzuki, D.T. *Zen Buddhism*. New York: Doubleday, 1956.

Taylor, Charles. *The Explanation of Behavior*. London: Routledge & Kegan Paul, 1964.

Taylor, A. E. "The Freedom of Man." In J. Muirhead, ed. *Contemporary British Philosophy*. Second Series. London: George Allen & Unwin, 1953.

Taylor, Paul. "Four Types of Ethical Relativism." *PR* 63 (1954):500-516.

Taylor, Richard. "I Can." In Morgenbesser and Walsh (62):81-90.

_____. *Action and Purpose*. Englewood Cliffs: Prentice Hall, 1966.

_____. "Determinism." *Encyclopedia of Philosophy*, vol. 2:359-73.

_____. *Metaphysics*. Englewood Cliffs: Prentice Hall, 1974.

Teitelman, Michael. "The Limits of Individualism." *JP* 69 (1972):545-56.

Thalberg, Irving. "Freedom of Action and Freedom of Will." *JP* 61 (1964):405-15.

_____. "How Does Agent Causality Work?" In Brand and Walton (1976):213-39.

Thomason, Richmond. "Indeterminist Time and Truth Value Gaps." *Theoria* 36 (1970):264-81.

Thomson, Judith Jarvis. *Acts and Other Events*. Ithaca: Cornell University Press, 1971.

Thorp, John. *Free Will: A Defense Against Neurophysiological Determinism*. London: Routledge & Kegan Paul, 1980.

Tuomela, Raimo. *Human Action and Its Explanation*. Dordrecht: D. Reidel, 1977.

van Inwagen, Peter. "The Incompatibility of Free Will and Determinism." *PS* 27 (1975):185-99.

_____. "Reply to Narveson." *PS* 32 (1977):89-98.

_____. "Reply to Gallois." *PS* 32 (1977):107-11.

_____. "Ability and Responsibility." *PR* 87 (1978):201-24.

Vendler, Zeno. *Linguistics and Philosophy*. Ithaca: Cornell University Press, 1967.

Vesey, G.N.A. "Volition." *P* 36 (1961):352-65.

Vivian, Frederick. *Human Freedom and Responsibility*. London: Chatto & Windus, 1964.

Warnock, G. J. *The Object of Morality*. London: Methuen, 1971.

Wartofsky, Marx. Review of Pears (63). *JP* 61 (1964):308-15.

Watson, Gary. "Free Agency." *JP* 72 (1975):205-20.

———. "Scepticism About Weakness of Will." *PR* 86 (1977):316-39.

Weiss, Paul. *Man's Freedom*. New Haven: Yale University Press, 1950.

White, A. R., ed. *The Philosophy of Action*. Oxford: Oxford University Press, 1968.

Whitely, C. H. "Can." *A* 23 (1962-63):91-3.

———. *Mind in Action*. Oxford: Oxford University Press, 1973.

Wiggins, David. "Towards a Reasonable Libertarianism." In Honderich (73).

Wilkins, Burleigh T. "Concerning 'Motive' and 'Intention'." *A* 31 (1971):139-42.

Will, F. L. "Intention, Error and Responsibility." *JP* 61 (1964):171-9.

Williams, Bernard. "The Idea of Equality." In Feinberg (69):153-71.

———. *Morality: An Introduction to Ethics*. New York: Harper & Row, 1972.

Williams, Clifford. *Free Will and Determinism*. Indianapolis: Hackett, 1980.

Williams, C. J. F. "Logical Indeterminacy and Free Will." *A* 21 (1960-61):12-13.

Williams, L. Pearce, ed. *Relativity Theory*. New York: Wiley, 1968.

Wilson, E. O. *On Human Nature*. New York: Bantam Books, 1979.

Wilson, J. "Freedom and Compulsion." *M* 67 (1958):60-9.

Winch, Peter. *The Idea of a Social Science*. London: Routledge & Kegan Paul, 1958.

Wisdom, John. *Problems of Mind and Matter*. Cambridge: Cambridge University Press, 1934.

Wolf, Susan. "Asymmetrical Freedom." *JP* 77 (1980):151-66.

Wolff, Robert Paul. *Understanding Rawls*. Princeton: Princeton University Press, 1977.

Young, J. Z. Review of *The Life Sciences*, by P. B. and J. S. Medawar. *New York Review of Books*, July, 1977.

Index of Names

Index of Topics

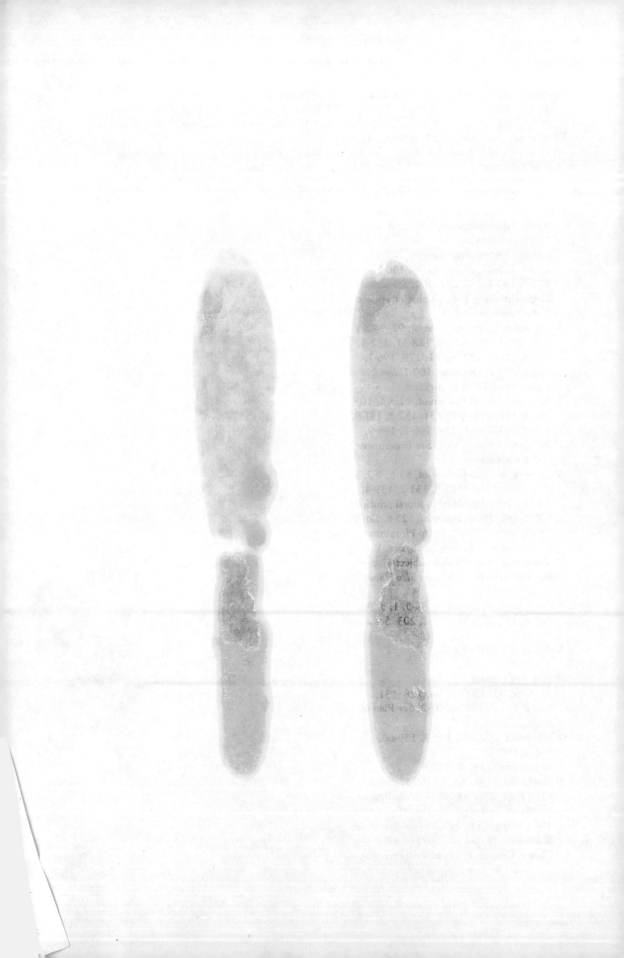